"Our Indian Princess"

School for Advanced Research
Global Indigenous Politics Series

James F. Brooks
General Editor

"Our Indian Princess"
Subverting the Stereotype

Nancy Marie Mithlo

School for Advanced Research
Global Indigenous Politics Book

School for Advanced Research Press
Post Office Box 2188
Santa Fe, New Mexico 87504-2188
www.sarpress.sarweb.org

Co-director and Executive Editor: Catherine Cocks
Manuscript Editor: Laurel Gladden
Designer and Production Manager: Cynthia Dyer
Proofreader: Kate Whelan
Indexer: Judith V. Anderson

Library of Congress Cataloging-in-Publication Data:
Mithlo, Nancy Marie.
  "Our Indian princess" : subverting the stereotype / by Nancy Marie Mithlo. — 1st ed.
    v. cm. — (Global indigenous politics series)
  Includes bibliographical references and index.
  Contents: Our little Indian woman : beyond the squaw/princess — Imagine trying to convince the world you exist — They never liked the dark ones : exclusion, conformity, and restrictions — Born an artist — Art stars and other honorary whites — They've got it all wrong : uses and abuses of Indian representations — I know what's going on.
  ISBN 978-1-930618-97-8
  1. Indian arts—North America. 2. Indian women in art. 3. Indians in art. 4. Indian women artists—North America. 5. Stereotypes (Social psychology) in art. I. Title.
  E98.A73M58 2009
  709.01'1—dc22
                    2008048480

Copyright © 2008 School for Advanced Research. All rights reserved.
Library of Congress Catalog Card Number: 2008048480
ISBN: 978-1-930618-97-8 (paper).
First edition 2009.

Portions of the text were previously published in Nancy Marie Mithlo, A Realist View of Image Politics: Reclamation of the "Every Indian." *In* [Re]inventing the Wheel: Advancing the Dialogue on Contemporary American Indian Art. Nancy J. Blomberg, ed. Pp. 104-125. Denver: Denver Art Museum, 2008.

Cover illustration: Roxanne Swentzell, *Waiting for Diego*, 1999; sharpie on paper, 14" x 17"; photograph by Eric Tadsen.

Contents

List of Plates	vi
Preface	vii
Introduction "Our Little Indian Woman": Beyond the Squaw/Princess	1
Chapter 1 "Imagine Trying to Convince the World You Exist"	15
Chapter 2 "They Never Liked the Dark Ones": Exclusion, Conformity, and Restrictions	43
Chapter 3 Born an Artist	75
Chapter 4 "Art Stars" and Other "Honorary Whites"	100
Chapter 5 "They've Got It All Wrong": Uses and Abuses of Indian Representations	121
Conclusion "I Know What's Going On"	145
Appendices	154
References	159
Index	173

Plates

Following Page 22

1. Nora Naranjo-Morse: *Our Symbols*, 2001
2. Tammy Rahr: *Wedding Moccasins*, 2005
3. Jimmy Goins, 2004
4. Emmi Whitehorse: *Nahasdzáán (Earth)*, 2005
5.a & b Jean LaMarr, with Jack Malotte and youth from the Susanville Indian Rancheria: *Our Ancestors, Our Future*, 1987
6. Emmi Whitehorse: *F.O.N.*, 2006
7. Gloria Emerson: *Rock Desert*, 2007
8. Gloria Emerson: Untitled, 1991–2007

Following Page 86

9. Roxanne Swentzell: *Woman in Stone*, 2000
10. Tammy Rahr: *Portrait with David*, c. 1986–1987
11. Roxanne Swentzell: *Remote Woman: "I'm Getting that Far Away Feeling Again,"* 1996
12.a & b Laura Fragua Cota: *Just Because You Put Feathers in Your Hair, Don't Make You an Indian*, 1990
13. Pat Courtney Gold: *Anti-Barbie Doll, Indian version*, 2000
14. Christopher A. Pardell: *Sacajawea*, 2001
15. Laura Fragua Cota: *Aboriginal Daughter with Great White Mom and Dad*, 1988
16. Shelley Niro: *The Shirt*, 2003

Preface: The Sting

As the mother of two daughters—one grown and one approaching adolescence—I have become increasingly weary of confronting the willful ignorance of contemporary Native American identities in popular culture and the schools. Recently, I was surprised to encounter the following math question in my daughter's homework: "Sarah is making an Indian war shield. If she paints three of the four quadrants red, how many are left to paint blue?" As I groaned out loud and dropped my head into my hands, my child demanded, "What's wrong, Mom? It's just my homework! Why do you always hate my school?"

My childhood was less complicated—at least, that's how I remember it. Growing up in the Deep South in the 1960s, the conflicts I witnessed were not about identity, but about race—black versus white. I recall running with my brother and sister to ask our father which side we were on—Union or Confederate. Dad gave an exasperated answer: "Neither! You kids are Indians!" We countered, "But D-a-a-d! We're not playing Cowboys and Indians, we're playing North and South!"

It amazes me that our family made it in a segregated South; even in our neighborhood, crosses were burned, the synagogue was bombed, and "whites only" drinking fountains still existed at the local zoo. We were part of the great federal influx into the South, where a fearful government infused employees into the capitol city of Jackson, Mississippi, in reaction to the racial tensions of the Civil Rights era. In the newly built subdivision we moved into when I was three, two FBI agents were among our neighbors. My father, an engineer, worked for Housing and Urban Development and often traveled. Under school desegregation policies of the 1970s, my mother, a home economics teacher, was transferred to an all-black junior high school across town. Fearing that the quality of educational instruction was suffering because of the bureaucratic chaos of desegregation, she chose to pull us out of public schools and send us to one of the newly formed private ones in Jackson. We were not raised with any formal religion, so it was a shock to find myself in a uniform attending Mass in a high school gym. Our mother was right, though—the classes were rigorous.

I imagine that for my parents, it was best not to assert any physical differences, although they certainly existed. My father was fond of saying, "When you are young and good-looking, everyone wants to own you. To my university professors, I was a smart young Jewish boy; at the Italian restaurant, I was a good-looking Sicilian." When *Hawaii Five-O* came out on television, all the neighbors were excited because Dad looked so much like Don Ho. Did people treat my Apache father badly in the race-conscious South? A large, handsome man who was quick-witted and charming, Dad didn't let on to us kids that he was the target of hateful speech or acts. Yet he spoke vividly about being in Memphis the day that Martin Luther King Jr. was shot. He heard the news on his car radio and drove the four hours straight back to our home in Jackson without stopping.

In my parents' generation, racism was overt and common; today, racism operates more subtly. It is often a private and painful affront, manifest in innocuous settings like Disney movies, museum exhibits, school curricula, advertisements, and tourism. You may not lose your life in these times, but you could lose your soul. As a fair-faced Indian, I "pass" in both Native and white communities. No one claims me; it is often up to me to assert my heritage—as a Native, as a Chiricahua Apache, as a Mithlo. I am not torn about how others perceive me; I'm too old for that now. But I am hurt and often enraged by how my children experience their Indianness in mainstream America.

I am an academic, and like my dad, I have traveled a lot. I have lived in the mountains of North Carolina, the Connecticut River valley of New England, the San Francisco Bay Area, and northern New Mexico. My children have been exposed to varying degrees of knowledge about Indians in their schools and in their social lives on the East Coast, on the West Coast, and in between. Yet the sting of ignorance is fresh and painful each time I encounter it. I wonder, how can I ignore this destructive thinking? How can I respond each and every time? Ignoring it means I will tolerate ignorance—even assist in its reproduction. Addressing each and every act of ignorance means I will always be led by the actions of others, always a servant to their lack of motivation to learn, always giving.

In early 2007 I visited a private elementary school described to me by other parents as alternative and experimental. I was considering sending my younger daughter there and was allowed to observe a typical classroom. On the low tables covered with newspaper were papier-mâché masks. I thought to myself, "Please do not let them be Indian masks." But as I slowly looked around the room, all the evidence was there—posters declaring that Indians had little body hair; books with awkwardly drawn depictions of Native dress; and lists of "typical Indian foods," such as corn, beans, and squash. I held in my anger and frustration while the director gave me a tour of the other classrooms. I held it in while she showed me the curriculum, with *Indians* placed between *beavers* and *bears* in their topics list, but I could hold it in no longer when she stated, "We encourage students to work in multimodalities because when they make something themselves, they understand it fully. When they depict it, they own it." Slowly, calmly, I told her that my daughter and I are Chiricahua Apache. I told her that no one could own us by making masks. I told her that I felt sick to my stomach, that I was hurt deeply by her callousness. "I am sure you have wonderful students and really skilled teachers, but this place is not for us." I couldn't drive away fast enough.

Alfred Young Man (1991:12) has written, "It would not be stretching credulity by much to say that graduates of most, if not all, universities in North America and Europe still harbor a child's awareness and feelings on North American Indians, their art, and metaphysics, if they have an awareness at all." As a college professor, I find Young Man's statement to be disappointingly true. Most of my students and many of my colleagues display a profound lack of understanding of contemporary or historic Native American realities. Upon arriving in New England to teach at an elite women's college, I would often introduce myself by explaining that I had transferred from a tribal college in New Mexico. While most politely asked what a tribal college was, some actually laughed out loud. Apparently, American Indians were such an anachronism that it was unimaginable that they should be capable of running a college!

Given the great sacrifices made by Native Americans to ensure that future generations survive, what can be done to address the sting of racism, the continued oppression of invisibility, and—worst of all—the misappropriation and distortion of Native American identity? While many outstanding scholars and educators have traced the path of Indian imagery in the white imagination and chartered hopeful directions for new educational mandates, I have chosen a different route. My story concerns the orientation, thoughts, and desires of Native American people, specifically, Native American women artists.

The Native arts world is a place I have occupied for more than twenty years—as a student, museum director, curator, professor, nonprofit chair, researcher, daughter-in-law, wife, friend, and mother. Like many other hardworking people in Native arts, I have tended the souls of students, friends, and family. I was fortunate in the mid-1980s to attend the tribal college where I later taught—the Institute of American Indian Arts (IAIA) in Santa Fe, New Mexico. This pantribal urban arts institution is the only tribal college in the United States devoted to the verbal, visual, and dramatic arts of Native North Americans. As a consultant, a friend, and an occasional critic, I have also been privileged to be a part of the conversation surrounding the establishment of the Smithsonian National Museum of the American Indian (NMAI). Key mentors, both Native and non-Native, have kindly aided me by providing internships and commenting on my work.[1]

These experiences in Native arts have impacted heavily the way in which I interpret the research I present here. The personal and political significance of the issues I debate in this book cannot be separated from the academic findings I engage, nor have I attempted to separate them. While I exercise the right to speak from where I stand, I also recognize the responsibility of such a position. Consequently, I have chosen not to expose individuals in ways that may endanger their integrity or privacy.

My work with seven pivotal artists over a twenty-year period provides the basic framework of my analysis. The interviews I present here have been reviewed by the artists, and when a conflict has arisen, either the components have been deleted or—in at least one case—the individual has chosen not to participate. Because of the public nature of the Native arts world, completely anonymous citations would only lead to speculation and possibly inappropriate attributions. Although the artists may not agree with all my conclusions, I hope that I have rendered their words accurately. Any mistakes in interpretation are my own.

A close colleague at the NMAI tells of how school groups regularly arrive at the entrance to the museum wearing paper-feathered war bonnets. The floor personnel at the museum (an all-Indian staff) explain to the teachers that the war bonnets are inappropriate and ask to have the children remove them. The teachers dutifully follow this request, and the class tours the museum. At the end of their visit, however, the children place the bonnets right back on their heads and run out the door yelling war chants. This uphill struggle for accurate representation of Native American realities cannot be addressed by only one institution or methodology. I hope the words and thoughts of the Native women artists featured in this book will help rectify the sting of racist behaviors, however innocently enacted.

Note

1. My scholarly mentors have included Michael M. Ames, Frédérique Apffel-Marglin, Clifford R. Barnett, Julie Cruikshank, Edith Colvard Crutcher, Charles Dailey, Harry Fonseca, Rayna Green, LaDonna Harris, Bea Medicine, N. Scott Momaday, Lloyd New, Nancy Parezo, Linda Poolaw, Neal Salisbury, Dave Warren, Gloria Cranmer Webster, and W. Richard West Jr.

Eternal thanks to the artists who have devoted their efforts to this project and especially to my family and friends, who have seen me through the long process of writing. This book is dedicated to my daughters.

INTRODUCTION
"Our Little Indian Woman"
Beyond the Squaw/Princess

ROXANNE SWENTZELL: I remember one Indian Market I got to my booth. It was still kind of dark, and there were all these people there, and I was still trying to wake up because it was still early. And I was preparing myself to open the door and get out and face all these people and…I had not put on my shoes yet because it was too early. So I decided I will just unload without my shoes so I don't trip. So I got out, and I started unloading, and then it became this thing that I was this barefoot sort of artist person. It fed into these people's ideas of who I am. In their mind…I was so earthy…and they really liked that. And maybe I am and I don't see that. But it wasn't done for an image. It was only practical reason. And if I showed up, like if I wanted to wear something fancy, for instance, and I showed up maybe in some heels or like that, I think people would be very upset that I'm not keeping to my image of what they have of me. And that's another box.

NANCY MITHLO: How does that differ for guys, do you think? Is there more pressure on you as a woman to be a certain thing as an artist?

ROXANNE SWENTZELL: I think there's different pressures. I really do. I think women are seen as much more as….It doesn't really matter so much for men what they look like. They can still be artists and make it. But sometimes I think it's harder for women. I think there's much more of a pressure on what you can [do].

NANCY MITHLO: Would that be true across the board, no matter what career you have?

ROXANNE SWENTZELL: Yeah.

NANCY MITHLO: What is it about the art—the Southwest art—that would make that even more different?

ROXANNE SWENTZELL: To add the Indian thing. The pretty Indian princess.

NANCY MITHLO: I remember you used to tell me people would pat you on the head because they thought you were so young.

ROXANNE SWENTZELL: Mmm. Hmm.

NANCY MITHLO: Do they still pat you on the head?

ROXANNE SWENTZELL: In a way. [*laughs*] Well, now I'm getting older, so I'm curious as to how that will change as I get older and older. Will they still go, "Ohh!"? I can see them doing that to an old lady too: "Our little Indian woman."[1]

My research, teaching, and activism stem from the premise that images are essential in constructing and conveying personhood. Native American artists, as image makers, struggle with the economic, cultural, and historical exploitation, erasure, and control of their cultural icons. Demeaning expressions—be they oral ("one little, two little, three little Indians" and other children's rhymes), visual (Land O'Lakes butter packages), or dramatic (sports mascot Chief Illiniwek)—are ingrained American symbols that actively "work" to degrade and diminish Native personhood. This colonial legacy is often gendered, with the Native women as "alter." As Michael Taussig (1993:129) states, "In the visual scheme of things, it is not the men but the Indian women who are alter, and here everything pivots on releasing the spirit powers of appearance." Roxanne Swentzell, a Santa Clara Pueblo artist from New Mexico, conveys a strong awareness of how her physical appearance as an Indian woman supports ideas of cultural authenticity even as she diffuses its power by satire. Her experience as a professional in the arts-saturated city of Santa Fe informs the major concerns of this study—representation, identity, and power.

The "power of appearance" in contemporary Native imagery relates both to Native women artists as people and to the work they produce. The Indian woman embodies national ideologies, popular culture, and tribal identity in her person and her products. This double expectation, that you be Indian in physical appearance and that your work conform to Indian art standards, could be argued to exist in equal strength for Native men and women, but in my work, it is the women who bear the responsibility as communal artists, thus positioning Native women as being closer to what may be considered a more accurate register of indigenous arts practices.

These ideas and generalities will be borne out further in subsequent chapters, but I wish to delineate first why I was led to focus my research on Native American women in particular. There are two compelling reasons—and both, I must admit, are fueled by my own personal orientations and motivations.

An Accidental Ethnography

As a graduate student in cultural anthropology at Stanford University in the late 1980s, I was instructed, for my dissertation on contemporary Native American arts, to attempt to find balance in my research methodology. Consequently, I chose to interview both male and female artists from a variety of regions and age groups. Returning to Santa Fe—where I had attended tribal college—to work and live after completing my doctorate, I continued to be in touch with most of the artists I had interviewed. Santa Fe is, in essence, a small town, and I faced life choices similar to those of my peers—both male and female—concerning the paucity of meaningful work and the constrictions of the Indian arts market. But I also found myself appreciating the same simple, communal enjoyments of raising children, sharing good food, and appreciating the beauty of the land and the culture of the city. Eventually, I turned to writing for local arts periodicals, serving on city arts boards, and curating exhibits, as well as teaching at regional colleges. Opportunities for interviews with artists presented themselves in these contexts—artists often required articles, résumés, or exhibit pamphlets to be authored for upcoming exhibits.

What I noted as time passed was how the women I worked with were curious to know more about one another's lives (and mine) whereas the men saw the interviews more as tasks to be completed. They were professional and polite, but the work did not bear the same type of poignancy that I sensed with the women. I also began to take note of the fact that fewer women were professionals in the arts field than had been the case some ten years before, and many were not being recognized publicly for their work in the same manner as their male peers. An urgency arose for me as I sensed that the women whose artistic lives I was chronicling were sharing in something passing or temporal.

Time has instructed me that my concerns over passing eras or lost opportunities likely have had more to do with my own sense of the precariousness of life than any real urgency, for as these women have turned away from the arts, they have seemed to adopt fluidly other, related professions, such as research, language retention, arts therapy, veterinary medicine, and school teaching. My own move to work in higher education out of state limited my ability to conduct informal interviews in New Mexico, but I soon had opportunities to speak with artists at openings in New York, in residencies in Vermont, in homes in California, or at meetings in Arizona. Their lives were just as complex and mobile as mine.

This initial sense of my own displaced "salvage ethnography" was complemented by a second development. As I started writing this text (arising from the necessity in a tenure-track academic system to produce monographs, something that had not presented itself as an urgent task in my life as an educator and writer in Santa Fe), I was able to think deeply over a period of time about why identity registers for women seemed to be so stubbornly fixed. In my interviews with artists, themes of comparison—with non-Natives and with men, both Native and non—had appeared. Again, my Stanford training rose to the fore: wasn't this comparative grouping a dated structuralist theory? Didn't an "us and them" philosophy indicate a cultural stability that denied change or complexity? Additionally, what about this professional rejection of the concept of pan-Indianism? Why was I getting such criticism of my few published articles for generalizing on the basis of multitribal referents, when in the social context of the art community I knew (my tribal college in Santa Fe), the label "Native American artist" was adopted so readily?

As I often tell my students, when something really irks you, this usually means that you have enough passion to dedicate time and energy to writing at length on the topic. I was disturbed that my Santa Fe colleagues continued to experience oppression in their chosen professional field and that my efforts to talk about this bias in print were somehow relegated to nonscholarship because their orientation did not fit existing, trendy poststructuralist theories. Hemmed in by an inability to generalize on the level of multitribal referents in anthropology, I sought out the literature on urban Indians, women artists, stereotypes, feminist theory—anything that might closely resemble the quandaries with which I had been presented in the interviews.

The result has been an exercise in what is currently termed "intervention." I have sought to survey multiple disciplines, including Native American studies, African American studies, art history, and American studies; to investigate varied theoretical perspectives, such as feminism, identity politics, and postpositivist realism; to apply several methods, such as narrative analysis, oral histories, and museum studies; and to cover topics as diverse as humor, racist memorabilia, censorship, and commerce. In many ways, this is not ethnography at all—it is an accidental ethnography that is rooted in the problem-solving exercise of how to make sense of continued oppression in the world of contemporary Native arts.

Authority in Testimony

The analytical process I have adopted (experiential and personally situated) has enabled a wide-reaching analysis in the form of testimonials from Native women in the arts presented as a platform for questioning academic literature. To return to the opening narrative from Swentzell, how do we understand her positioning as an artist who is subjected to pats on her head at art openings? While Native American men most certainly experience similar acts of racial oppression in their careers in the arts, the pressures for Native women are, according to Swentzell and theorist Taussig (1993), unique. My own conclusion is that if we are searching for a counternorm to overly stylized notions of Indianness, the women artists reflect that Native aesthetic register. Why? Because their testimonials embody the communal aspects of aesthetic expressions, and I take these communal aspects to be primary in the construction of what an indigenous art theory looks like. It is my own thesis that an indigenous aesthetic has yet to be articulated in a manner that may be mobilized to counter harmful negative stereotypes. I have no illusions that my work alone will solve this quandary, but I do believe that by surveying the fields of scholarly references available, interested readers might be able to begin to mend old, ineffective approaches and gradually move towards a sense of what avenues are most productive for doing this type of work.

For example, both Taussig and Swentzell have concerns about the fact that Native women are utilized as cultural icons in more salient ways than their male peers. Thus, the appearance of woman as iconic of community (as Taussig argues, more likely to be cast as the "cultural other") is similar to the life histories of Native women artists who also mirror this conception of the female as a register for community. Swentzell contributes to Taussig's theory by suggesting that there are concrete reasons why this might be the case, given her responsibility to ensure her family's stability. Swentzell's 2000 interview, taken at a key moment when her children were beginning to leave home, highlights these differences in comparison with males.

As the sole breadwinner for her two children, Swentzell had entered the arts field in response to a professional as much as a cultural calling. The arts are important because they enable her to provide a home for her children. This sense of domestic stability is a key consideration for her—so much so that when I interviewed her in 2000, she was struggling to decide whether she should continue at all in the arts, because her children were grown. Laughingly, she countered that she should just go to town and begin a new career scooping ice cream at Baskin-Robbins.

I thought for a long time that men are just more career oriented than women, just naturally. They are more, maybe not *career*—that's the wrong word—more like they're more caught up in having it made than women are. When I see women, they get more caught up in their kids and how their kids are doing and caught up in the things they love. And men are more heady people; they're caught up more in ideals...having a name is an ideal. And as my career keeps going and my kids are grown up, I feel kinda lost. I do, because I think if I were a man, I would be riding high and happy because I made it. But because I am a woman, I feel very lost because why I was doing this was for my family. And now my family are grown up and are leaving, and I really don't know why I'm doing it now. But I'm thinking, well, do I want to be doing this for myself? What is it for? Because I always did it for somebody else, for my children. And I think that's different. So I think I'm going through a little crisis of identity because it's like if you fed, made dinner all your life for your family. Your whole mindset was, "What will I feed them tonight?" And you are caught up with that. And suddenly they all leave, and it's like, "I'm supposed to make dinner for myself? And I'm supposed to...sit at this table by myself and eat it all alone?" Somehow it just doesn't feel the same satisfaction. And that's a difference between men and women. Men will be happy to have gotten to this point. I don't know if that's good or bad. But I really do think that's a difference.

So I don't know if—oh, boy—I've got this thing, I got money, I got these little things that I haven't had so much of before. And it's empty. I could seriously think maybe I should just go work at 31 Flavors, and at least I'll be around people and watch them be happy eating ice cream. [*laughs*]

Swentzell's professional challenges as a woman and as a Native person are intricately intertwined. She is restricted—but perhaps also, in other ways, positively enabled—by her positioning as a Native woman, and her motivations as a cultural carrier are not translatable to the economic values of western capitalism.

Although I will focus primarily on Native women artists to define an indigenous sensibility in the arts, in this book I have chosen not to foreground the aspect of gender as a primary theoretical concern. In other words, the variable of gender will not lead my analysis as an isolated variable. The topic of how Native women's lives intersect with women's studies, art history, and feminism is rich and complex. Given the unique readings of what constitutes gender, power, and prestige in Native American contexts (with examples of the third gender, complementarity, and gender equality), the field is fertile for this type of intellectual inquiry. My aim in this particular work is to address the variables of stereotypes, creativity, pan-Indianism, alterity, and realism in an attempt to understand the resiliency of persistent demeaning icons and to chart a direction towards their demise by embracing indigenous knowledge. Native women as image producers and as primary subjects of the colonial gaze are experts on the meanings of these images. Their narratives will provide valid theoretical contributions to the discussion, much as any other academic theorist's might. Thus, although my interviews are restricted to Native women artists, I have refrained from fully describing the women's lives and their positioning (age, tribe, training, appearance, residence), just as any academic writer would not describe the personal attributes of scholars being quoted. I realize that this is a risk, given the popular genre of Native American arts publications that in "coffee-table-book" style provide striking color portraits of the artists and glossy reproductions of beautiful artistic works. While this is an approach not often taken in the field of Native arts in particular, it is a necessary step towards reaching intellectual parity in this field of scholarship.

The Problem

Clearly, the Indian squaw/princess, as demeaning and disturbing as this image often is, serves a deep-seated need in the American consciousness. C. Richard King (2003:3) describes the use of *squaw* as a "keyword of conquest" and "a trope of extraordinary power and influence in American culture." Rayna Green (1983:587–606) attributes the prevalence of Indian stereotypes to the "xenophobic sociocultural framework into which they were channeled" in American culture, noting that the Indian woman "finds herself burdened with an image that can only be understood as dysfunctional" ([1975]1990:17). Numerous texts (Bataille 2001; Berkhofer 1979; Bird 1996; Deloria 1998, Huhndorf 2001; Jolivétte 2006; Mihesuah 1996) have analyzed the negative impact of Indian stereotypes and cultural appropriations, frequently attributing the consumption of these ready-made images to the desires of the white imagination rather than to contemporary or historic reality. This lack of accurate information about Native American women in educational institutions and popular culture led Wilma Mankiller, past principal chief of the Cherokee Nation, to charge that "even the most committed feminist scholars [know] little about contemporary Native American women or our history" (1998:xvii).

Why do these complexes of ideas and images (the exotic other, the alluring and sexually available squaw, the pretty traditional princess) continue to exist? Most scholars and activists would answer that historically accurate data is not readily available for the American public to consume. It would follow, then, that if only there were more sensitive images and role models of Native women available and in circulation, a shift in policy might occur and Native women would be less scrutinized for their adherence to, or deviation from, these conventional representations. Although ignorance and racism may account for the persistence of the princess/squaw complex, I question the premise that more accurate data will necessarily lead to its demise. If stereotypes persist because of a lack of accurate information, then why is this data so hard to come by?

Patricia Albers argues (1983:6–7) that "the moribund state of the literature on American Indian women" was not the result of a lack of interest on the part of scholars but a reflection of the "general pessimism" about the possibility of doing significant research on the conditions of American Indian women, because of sparse or biased primary source materials and tribal restrictions on conducting new research. She concludes that "generalized studies on the role and status of modern women...would not be considered a research priority when poverty, unemployment, and resource development are issues requiring immediate attention" (6–7).

Although tribal restrictions on original research indicate a proactive control over intellectual resources, this rationale can also suggest that Native women's issues are not important enough to be tracked. This proposition is disrupted by the twenty years of studies on Native women's issues conducted since Albers's conclusion (Hernández-Avila 2005; Mihesuah 2003; A. Smith 2005; Trask 1993) and is negated by Green's (1983) expansive listing of sources published the same year as Albers's text. Green's argument critiques not the amount of data available but the content of the publications. She states, "Native women have been neither neglected nor forgotten... but...the level and substance of most passion for them has been selective, stereotyped and damaging" (1983:1). If the prevalence of more publications about (and, one can infer, more images of) Native women does not automatically eradicate the existence of stereotypical norms, then what strategy is called for?

Sociologists Sarah Fenstermaker and Candace West (2002) propose an approach to sex and gender studies that they term "doing gender," in which gender is not so much an attribute as an accomplishment arising from social situations. Gender is thus "the activity of managing situated conduct in light of normative conceptions" (West and Zimmerman 2002:5). This strategy for understanding social behavior and norms can be applied to an effort to articulate an indigenous women's perspective of what constitutes an indigenous aesthetic. What happens in the "doing" of producing and distributing images as an alternative to those commonly circulated as the squaw/princess? A central premise of tracking these specific identity and role performances is referencing the historical register of colonialism as a backdrop.

The Role of Colonialism

Anthropologist Julie Cruikshank (1990) notes that Athapaskan women in the Yukon experience greater consistency than men between traditional narrative models of behavior (proscriptions of certain deeds and actions) and normative expectations regarding their roles in contemporary Western society. Women's implementation of learned, shared, and practical knowledge, for example, is interpreted by social agencies as their greater adaptability in coping with change than men's. This distinction is directly tied to the disruption of traditional land-based economies: "Athapaskan/Tlingit women are more likely to be rewarded by Western institutions for behavior consistent with their traditional roles, whereas the decline in land-based activities has forced men to make more dramatic adjustments" (Cruikshank 1990: 345). This gendered variable of communal identification is demonstrated by Cruikshank's findings that Athapaskan men tend to pursue solitary arts productions whereas women engage more in expressive social art forms, such as storytelling. Women appear to cope with social crises "within a framework of familial and social responsibilities," yet tragically "the majority of alcohol-related deaths and suicides involve men, often men recognized as having particular creative talent" (346).

This Athapaskan phenomenon mirrors the dimensions of forced acculturation for other North American tribes. Native men, as carriers of patriarchy via capitalism and warfare, inhabited singular, individualistic roles under colonialism, while women often maintained identification as culture bearers and mediators, both symbolically and physically (Kidwell 1992). A productive inquiry into this gendered divide in the arts would be a consideration of how the arts profession reflects larger genocidal tendencies that have targeted men and women to play different assimilated roles in America. This inquiry, which, fully drawn, is outside the scope of the present work, could examine how complementary gender norms in Native North America were impacted by such federal legislation as the Indian Reorganization Act of 1934, which secularized traditional religious leadership roles, dividing church and state while simultaneously installing patriarchal leadership as the norm. Santa Clara Pueblo artist Nora Naranjo-Morse surmises that these strategic choices had everything to do with state practices of control and confinement:

> The bottom line was, and still is, to get Indians to be a part of mainstream thinking. Whatever it took—manipulation, violence—to get these savages clean and dependent on the social structure that was then being put into place. When people are farming, building their own homes, there is an independence of will and thought. You have to be an aware, thinking person to live a creative, independent lifestyle. What was and still is threatening and potentially dangerous to dominant culture is for people to think independently. And to have women think? Oh no, not good! To role-model and teach children how to build their own home, how to establish their specific relationship to the environment and in the process cultivate their internal space is an empowerment but, again, is a threat.
>
> This holistic worldview embraced religion, economy, and self. Historically, there was an equal distribution of work and power among men and women in our communities. After contact with the Europeans, all of this changed. Spanish friars came into the kivas and destroyed sacred altars, called us heathens, and began to introduce a new worldview. Men were put in charge, and women became subservient as a part of the new world order.
>
> Now we get into our cars and work as secretaries typing someone else's letters. I'm not putting that form of employment down—that's what has happened, that's where we're at now. This is our reality. It's easier to be told what to do than to think, "Wait a minute. Why did they do that?" or "I want to know why." Because the second we start thinking, then we start questioning and reconnecting to our sense of self. We start building again—building ourselves up. Building our homes. Typing our own letters. If only a few people do it, then that's permissible, but it becomes troublesome when it becomes a movement.[2]

Naranjo-Morse's philosophical orientation as an artist may be read as an exercise in indigenous knowledge (see plate 1). Her decision to, in her words, "think," to not be a consumer dependent upon the structure of a capitalistic wage economy but to engage in traditional behaviors of making structures (homes, installation art), enacts indigenous knowledge systems. Making art is Naranjo-Morse's personal strategy for pursuing an anticolonial project. Problematically, this strategy of resistance is encompassed by the US capitalistic economy, confined within a web of economic constraints and opportunities (see chapter 2). Naranjo-Morse constructs her own histories, but, not always as she pleases and not always under conditions of her own choosing. Anthropologist Purnima Mankekar adopts this conceptual approach in her ethnography of television, womanhood, and nation in postcolonial India as she seeks to problematize women's agency as they respond to, and participate in, the hegemonic discourses of national television dramas. She argues that resistance and compliance are not mutually exclusive categories but a means by which identity is conceived. The narratives she presents are about women "who construct their own [hi]stories, but not as they please and not in conditions of their own choosing" (Mankekar 1991:29).

To claim identity beyond the squaw/princess, Native women artists create sites of knowledge production; they enact a cultural identity that embraces the communal, even as that act alienates them from trendy dialogues of fine arts cultural hybridity and feminist transnational projects. This pro-cultural act ensures that Native women and their communities receive continued acknowledgment as sovereign entities, eligible for recognition as indigenous nations, whereas individualistic or hybrid identity claims actually jeopardize this standing. This female affiliation with the communal is why an indigenous knowledge systems approach is an appropriate interpretative tool for Native women's arts production, in addition to political mobilization.

Navajo artist and educator Gloria Emerson speaks to the way in which assimilation has impacted more communal norms in the arts:

> Navajo society—well, it used to be—was matriarchal, and there is a lot of ownership of our own property, of our this and that, and the men's roles were almost secondary. And it's changed—flip-flopped, it seems—with the return…the men returning from the wars, with their attitudes about gender roles and such, with Westernization processes, education, and so on. And maybe there are a lot of conflicts yet. I don't know. I think a lot of kitchen art is created that way—art around the kitchen table. Clear the table to cook, to feed, and then when everybody is sleeping, that's the time they can take the table back for their own work. And it's just not…there's very little give and take, I think.[3]

In a standard feminist critique, these accounts of women's marginalization would surely be followed by calls for change based on a social justice agenda, including organized resistance and direct confrontation with oppressive gender practices. If we consider the multiple readings of this imaginative feminist intervention for a moment, it becomes clear that separate value systems are at play. The variables of racism, ways of belonging, and concepts of time and tradition find differing relevance in classic feminist ideology and indigenous ideology.

Indigenous Readings

Native American women and men continue to respond to the legacy of colonialism based primarily on their race, not their gender. Native men and women were systematically killed, tortured, enslaved, and imprisoned by foreign nations upon contact; these histories continue in struggles for present-day sovereignty, rendering race and ethnicity primary. Gender, however, cannot be dismissed as irrelevant, for the ways in which Native American men and women have experienced the genocide of the past five hundred years have been, and continue to be, unique. In many ways, Native communities became gendered communities as a result of colonialism, disrupting other intellectual traditions of leadership and uses of power. A balanced relationship between the sexes—complementarity—may represent just one of these indigenous intellectual traditions.

Maori researcher Linda Tuhiwai Smith's *Decolonizing Methodologies* (1999) outlines how people's collective rights to intellectual and cultural property are manifest in recognized "moral messages" that define indigenous research protocols. These include respecting people; presenting the seen face; looking, listening, and then speaking; sharing with and hosting people; being generous; being cautious; not trampling over the mana of people; and not flaunting your knowledge (120). Guidelines for "the way we behave" are enacted similarly in the arts, as Native women follow certain protocols of belonging as communal people. These tribal standards are often defined in terms of female roles, reinforcing the iconic status of women as symbols of Native nations.

Similarly, Hawaiian activist and scholar Haunani-Kay Trask, in a chapter in her book *From a Native Daughter* (1993), argues that although under colonialism Hawaiian men have often been rewarded with government jobs, "they internalized the values of that system: politics is a man's world, family life is a woman's world" (120). Significantly, as native land rights were championed under self-determination, it was not the political leadership of men that was effective but "a new form of power based on a traditional Hawaiian belief: women asserting their leadership for the sake of the nation" (94). Trask describes how "on the front lines, in the glare of public disapproval, are our women—articulate, fierce, and culturally grounded" (121). This "great coming together of women's mana" is attributed to the belief that "caring for the nation is, in Hawaiian belief, an extension of caring for the family, the large family that includes both our lands and our people" (121).

Emerson elaborates on the ways in which the "large family" concept extends to this arts analysis:

> NANCY MITHLO: What is an issue that you have to address in your work because you're a woman? Are there things that come up that are unique for you, that you have to negotiate?
>
> GLORIA EMERSON: Time. I think, time...I think, time on women. Women's time is owned by others. You're not—you don't belong to yourself. You belong to your family, your clan, your mother, your parents, your relations. In Navajo, it's even stronger, that sensibility of belonging to a community of relations, clan, family. They all have demands on you, and you have to respond if you want to maintain your place in that social fabric. If you want to be honored and respected, you have to respect others too. And part of respecting others is giving up your time. Right?

In a fashion similar to the narratives of Swentzell, Naranjo-Morse, and Emerson, Cayuga bead worker Tammy Rahr describes the responsibility she feels to share her knowledge with others as a gendered expectation:

> NANCY MITHLO: How would you describe your role as a woman artist? Do you run into certain obstacles, or do you feel like it is an asset? Or is it something that you have to negotiate?
>
> TAMMY RAHR: From the other side of that, from what we talked about before, is the education. I think that because I have recognized finally that the beadwork...the techniques, are my gift, that I have to give back. That's the way it works. So I feel that through my work comes the role of the educator.... And I feel that is the women's role—regardless of the fact that I am Indian, that I am a woman, period. That's part of it, certainly. But I think that just the fact that something was given to me, I now sort of give back.[4]

"The way it works" for Rahr and other Native women artists closely reflects related scholarship in Native studies that asserts, "American Indian studies...must serve the values and institutions of American Indian communities" (Champagne and Stauss 2002:8). The strong similarities in the definitions of *community* and *femaleness* in Native American contexts suggest that acts of "doing gender" as a situated knowledge may serve equally well as indicators of "doing tribal nationhood"—one exercises perceived inherent rights and responsibilities, and in the doing, identity is structured, legitimated, and rationalized. A nuanced account of these gendered responses in the arts is essential in the struggle to reclaim socially relevant Native American representations.

Notes

1. Quotations from Roxanne Swentzell in this chapter are from the author's interview with her on September 12, 2000.

2. Nora Naranjo-Morse, interview by author, August 11, 1997.

3. Quotations from Gloria Emerson in this chapter are from the author's interview with her on December 7, 2002.

4. Tammy Rahr, interview by author, June 5, 1991.

1 "Imagine Trying to Convince the World You Exist"

TAMMY RAHR: Oh yeah, you get frustrated. There's no doubt. I get asked the dumbest questions. I was told there was no such thing as a dumb question, but these people need to be educated. You know, if someone has a misconception about Indian squaws, well, you need to set them right. You need to let them know where it's at. You know, "Hey, I can speak English. I can speak very good English. As a matter of fact, I can even write it. I went to school. I'm not ignorant. I'm a very caring, loving person." I've had people thank me. They've sent me gifts for taking the time to talk to them.

NANCY MITHLO: Is part of that presenting yourself as an Indian artist instead of as just an artist?

TAMMY RAHR: When I am out there, I am a woman, I am an artist, I am a mother, I am Indian. I am all of those things. If I can reach someone …we are all related somehow. If I can utilize that, I will.[1]

Are images and representations central to understanding Native Americans? How do Native artists, as producers of visual culture, respond to what art critic Lucy Lippard (1990a:13) calls "the overwhelming burdens" of Indian art? Cayuga artist Tammy Rahr expresses a felt responsibility to address the misconceptions of non-Indians she encounters in her work as a bead worker and an arts educator. This impulse to "set them right" is articulated as a humanist reaction, not simply an economically motivated response. Further, she clarifies her self-identity not simply as an artist or an Indian artist but as a totality of gender, ethnicity, and professional and communal standing. Rahr's narrative highlights the topics I will examine in this inquiry: the power of stereotypes, the utility of pan-Indianism, the significance of realist ideologies, and the employment of alterity in Native American arts. My interest is how visual referents communicate across cultural divides—how images "work" in the pursuit of certain social aims.

Although this inquiry is centrally about stereotypes, I aim to deconstruct that term's common usage. The word *stereotype* has such negative connotations that its use is inherently burdened with only one interpretation, that of insensitive, demeaning, and even racist depictions. Instead, I will be talking about a more open, nonjudgmental reference to conveying otherness. I will employ phrases such as "strategic essentialism" and "conventional representations" to describe the ways in which disparate groups tend to employ damaged knowledge in trying to communicate self values and the values of contrast groups. I am generous in my analysis, attributing the uses of such "clusters of meanings" less to malice than to a lack of other conceptual tools. I do this because I want to examine how Natives and non-Natives employ conventions of representations for similar ends.

In seeking to understand those who are unlike ourselves, do we enact symbolic injustices? Often, yes. Should we then eliminate the use of these images in order to avoid potential negative consequences, such as a lack of self-esteem or the perpetuation of racism? At times, absolutely yes. The censure of clearly malicious and hurtful images should certainly be pursued when these typecasts intend to and do inflict harm. My aim is to reorient the conversations around race and representations from victimizers and victims, to the innovative subversion of hateful images by creative image producers. Why do we tend to regard the subjects of the gaze (those minority cultures so often depicted in one-dimensional typecasts) as solely passive recipients of negative naming rather than as active constructors of symbolic icons? While I agree with critical theorists who argue that mass media advertisements of generic Indian products may result in continued colonization, including denial of political claims, I additionally seek to demonstrate that other outcomes are also available, including political mobilization in concert with these images. Image producers have the most to gain and to lose in these fraught processes of racial representations because the stock in trade under consideration is their livelihood.

Rahr's articulation of the inseparable nature of her roles in life—"I am a woman, I am an artist, I am a mother, I am Indian. I am all of those things"

—reminds us that multiple perspectives are required to understand fully the complex ways in which image politics are currently employed. Gender and race as variables, then, must be treated "intersectionally," to use law professor Kimberle Crenshaw's (1991) term. Intersectionality as a concept denotes the ways race and gender interact, especially for oppressed groups who experience racism and sexism equally.

The dismissal of common female attributions, including fertility, softness, and domesticity (relegation to craft), does not erase these qualities from the public's imagination, nor does it necessarily empower women who may choose to distance themselves from overt expressions of tribal sensibilities. The cultural values of gender and economics in the arts are both constitutive of and reactive to established paradigms of knowledge. These multiple sites of knowledge have the opportunity to be contested in the social arena of arts production and consumption, thereby allowing for highly charged articulations of identity claims. Qualities such as femaleness, maleness, isolation, belonging, and community find voice in the moments when conflicting ideologies meet.

These variables and how they interact are illustrated in the following passage from my interview with Santa Clara Pueblo sociologist Tessie Naranjo in 2000. In the ten years since I had previously interviewed her, Naranjo had completed a PhD in sociology at the University of New Mexico. Our relationship was, in part, defined by our shared experience of working on graduate degrees concurrently, and I was curious as to how her academic achievements had informed her ideas of self-identity.

> NANCY MITHLO: I was wondering, do you now call yourself something different, like, if you're giving a paper at a conference and they want you to put something in parentheses, do you now choose to say sociologist, artist, tribal person, woman—how do you handle that?
>
> TESSIE NARANJO: How do I define myself?
>
> NANCY MITHLO: Yeah.
>
> TESSIE NARANJO: Um...[*pauses*] It's neat that you ask that question. And people have asked me—every time there's a presentation to be made, they say, "How do I introduce you?" And I say, I have a passion for community, I have a passion for family. Please tell in your introduction that I am from the community and I am very much a part of my extended family. So that's what they'll do. In terms of the labeling, the PhD thing, I almost never use it to define myself. I just say that I'm Tessie Naranjo, and as far as a sociologist is concerned, almost never do I say that, but I do know that privately they have

impacted my life so, so significantly, but that's my private experience. For the public world, I...don't need to, I don't need to define myself in that way. In fact, I almost...well, for sure, I prefer not to. I prefer not to because it is almost as if you are [*sighs*] depending on those labels to define you and I don't need to have those labels define me. But I do need to let the rest of the world know I am from Santa Clara Pueblo and I am a woman who treasures the wisdom of our past and who treasures the wisdom of what we still have and those are the ways that I work.[2]

Naranjo's narratives explore the meaningful ways in which the multiple identities of tribal person, artist, and woman intersect. These connections appear to contradict prevailing intellectual trends in feminist theory, art criticism, and cultural studies. For example, although hybridity is heralded as a normative reference for contemporary arts dialogues, tribal communities claim segmented spaces. Lippard's *Mixed Blessings* claims, "Faced with the facts of nomadism and displacement, many artists are trying to form a new hybrid cultural identity and to locate themselves therein," and she adds that tribalism in its exclusive sense "is a perverted, embattled form of community" (Lippard 1990b:153). By comparison, Naranjo writes of tribalism as an organic philosophy of life:

> The notion of the container is crucial to the worldview of the pueblo. The lower half of our cosmos is a pot that contains life, the womb of the mother. The notion of containment also is evident in the pueblo plaza, which contains outdoor community activities and is bounded by the house forms and the hills and the mountains. As the house forms are made of the mud of the earth, so are the pots. [Naranjo 2000:8]

Despite the prevailing acceptance of homogenized global sensibilities in media productions, many Native American and other indigenous artists continue to articulate a sovereign, bounded, and discrete identity based on land, family, and memory. A continued sense of separateness, fully positioned in the unique status of tribal nations and their special relationship to the federal government, prevails. This boundedness, however, cannot be interpreted as static; belonging is not enforced but rather employed according to political, technical, economic, and educational developments and changes in the world at large. Both material and ideological constructs enable communal paradigms to exist simultaneously with gendered identities.

Native Identity at the Crossroads—
The New Stereotype

This text follows my interest in the ways Native American women in the arts describe and define their lives as professionals, family members, tribal members, and activists. The narratives I discuss testify to the dynamic, fluid character of self-definition as Native women resolve conflicting mandates in economic, political, and personal spheres. They also expose the problematic nature of conceptualizing self-identity as static—or even as an object—instead of an active, continual process.

The active interplay of self-definitions and societal definitions of self that I document here resists standard linear structures of assimilation, accommodation, or resistance. What I hope to show is that although contemporary Native women artists are at times limited by market values, media norms, and race and gender bias, these constraints are not all-encompassing. In fact, active self-narration is often structured in reference to how external stereotyping is flawed. In other words, self-definition may stem from negating the false images others project. Utilized as one productive resource among many tools of self-expression, these counternarratives provide rich insights into how contemporary indigenous realities are conceptualized and conveyed in visual registers.

While previous academic works have often collapsed Native identity formation and Native identity expression, I seek in this text to pursue a more nuanced approach. I argue that assertions of identity formation (and here one may productively substitute ethnicity, community, or even racial identities) are too ambitious and prone to overgeneralization. A more accurate reading, I believe, may be drawn from inquiring as to how individuals express identity through cultural productions in the arts. This line of reasoning privileges the communication of self via image politics as one means of understanding self-inscription. In all, the goal is to untangle the already overly complex and sometimes circular lines of reasoning that dialogues of race and representation typically take.

The approach of privileging counternarratives as a genre draws from similar theoretical approaches of symbolic inversion, alterity, othering, or binary tensions. I find this definition of differencing to be related to stereotyping in multiple ways that I will explore here. It is important to note that the societal use of popular icons in Native communities has a certain weight and importance that illuminates, but also challenges, the type of inquiry I pursue. Stereotypes of Natives by non-Natives—such as demeaning sports mascots, cartoons, films, and other visual forms—are known to have a negative effect on the mental health of Native peoples. Opponents of stereotypes call for the eradication of negative images of Native Americans by erasure, such as changing place-names like Squaw Peak or retiring racist sports mascots like Chief Illiniwek. In 2005 the American Psychological Association (APA) called for the immediate retirement of all American Indian mascots, symbols, images, and personalities by schools, colleges, universities, athletic teams, and organizations (American Psychological Association 2005). Proponents of Native stereotypes argue that the images are not racist, claiming either that they are harmless or that they honor Native communities.

Stereotype as a term thus generally references solely negative images by whites that exploit Native American communities. I reference the use of patterned images in less judgmental terms. What I attempt to draw from my interviews is how Native women deal with essentialized images pragmatically—as well as how their own projections of white behavior may also be viewed as a form of stereotyping or essentializing. This type of othering by those commonly perceived to be the others has largely been unexamined. My discussion draws directly from Robert F. Berkhofer's work (1979), which asserts that white images of Natives tell us more about whites' attitudes and beliefs than about Native realities. Because my interest is not in whiteness studies but in Native American studies, I will explore whether Native views of whites serve a similar purpose of defining expressions of Native identity. I hope to demonstrate the utility of these iconic constructs as a means of communicating self-definition and maneuvering in hostile environments. Shorthand knowledge evident in stereotypes is then seen as a type of currency that exists and is employed in various social worlds.

This work is largely an intervention in theory, but it also aims to solve very basic social problems of alienation, dominance, and control. Readers will find that my analysis tends less toward victimizing Native American artists as powerless pawns in an alien market and more toward capturing perspectives that demonstrate an active defiance of limiting norms and an open challenge to oppressive economic and social parameters. My study has benefited from the recent scholarship of postpositivist realism in reference to the necessity of strategic essentialism (using image categories pragmatically) for advancing political claims in the public domain. Importantly, however, as Linda Martin Alcoff (2000:323) demonstrates, the "raw" use of strategic essentialism often serves to alienate the "knowing" theorists who use identity strategically from the "unknowing" activists who still believe in unmediated, essentialist identity constructs. Theory intervention in itself can be a somewhat elitist goal, so I have endeavored to embrace an interdisciplinary approach to the literature.

I am opportunistic about the breadth of the academic works I cite, gathering together theorists and artists in unlikely pairings to find where their interests intersect and diverge. While this survey approach method may be challenging to readers who desire a more straightforward analysis, I counter that the field of contemporary Native American art has yet to be defined and it cannot be defined by one individual or in one generation. The wealth of indigenous knowledge is vast and largely incomprehensible to those viewers and listeners trained to expect entertaining and easily comprehensible messages. The arts are particularly prone to these expectations, being associated with commerce and pleasure alone. Yet it is the artists of our communities who serve as our intellectual guardians and who, in these recent generations, have been treated largely as entertainers instead.

The Context

Context, as something more than ethnographic evidence, is central in the presentation of this material. My challenge is to create a sense of the "art worlds" contemporary American Indian artists inhabit, without falling into older patterns of exoticism or timelessness. Again, I issue a word of caution. Readers will not find alluring descriptions of the sights, sounds, and smells of native homes, pueblos, and landscapes. Disappointment may reign, but I also will not convey the beauty, presence, and allure of Native women for consumption under the rubric of intellectual knowledge. Not only do I wish to bring consumers of contemporary Native American arts to a level of maturity that has been starkly absent under the sway of consumerism, but I also have an obligation to construct a conversation between myself and the reader that is ethical to the communities with which I work. I am a polite conversationalist who will not betray secrets, yet I will also address topics so unused to seeing the light of day that I am confident readers will be engaged.

I foreground Native artists as knowing participants in the employment of essentialized identities, instead of naïve subjects of such theorizing. In order to do so, I mobilize Native women's narratives as authoritative texts, much as published works might be cited. A reviewer who read early drafts of this book criticized my use of Native women's narratives as "disembodied." The suggestion was made that I "flesh out" and make "alive" their personalities. I refuse to do so. Given the decades of analysis by mainly non-Native writers who treat Native American artists as specimens, a personalized appraisal (what the artist looks like, where she was born) is, at this time, inappropriate. Just as I will not describe, for example, how a scholarly theorist looks, his age, or his residence, I refuse to dissect Native women's lives for personal examination. Their words, their narratives will be assessed as intellectual data in a manner similar to the published works of academics.

Native American arts scholarship has traditionally been pursued according to discipline-related or commercial criteria, such as anthropological descriptions of material culture; celebratory coffee-table books geared toward the consumer; museum catalogues; and the formal, stylistic examinations of Native works as art objects. More recent scholarship seeks to understand the total life of the object by exploring the history of collectors, tourism, and curatorial practices (Duncan 2001; Steiner 1994). In this work, I have chosen to focus on the ways in which a segment of a contemporary, urban, self-inscribed Indian community challenges, changes, and adapts to social influences that it defines as barriers or boundaries to its self-expression in the arts. This manuscript finds an affinity within literature on the urban Native experience, as well as Native women's life histories and cultural ethnographies (Cruikshank 1990; Lobo 2001). Unlike standard ethnographies, this research will not present a comprehensive analysis of "a people" in reference to categories such as social organization, politics, economics, or ecology. Standard regional assessments of traditional Native arts scholarship will not be pursued—but rather internationalism, cosmopolitanism, and political mobilization (Fixico 2000; Lobo 2001).

My methodology cannot accommodate the traditional sense of ethnography in which one maintains healthy objectivity or alternatively claims to have been adopted into regional communities. In my early twenties, I searched out opportunities to learn more about my tribe by pursuing internships in museums and attending the Institute of American Indian Arts (IAIA) in Santa Fe, New Mexico, under a Bureau of Indian Affairs Higher Education Grant. I was fortunate to have as mentors key thinkers in the cultural revitalization movement of the 1980s and 1990s. Important teachers, intellectuals, artists, and activists informed my thinking and gave me opportunities to learn by doing, whether that meant making coffee and cleaning the toilet or forming an archive and curating exhibits. Larger-than-life figures in the Southwest who wrote the history of contemporary Native arts are as much a part of this story as the artists profiled. People such as Chuck Dailey, Manuelito Lovato, Lloyd Kiva New, Ed Ladd, Rick Hill, Jonathan Batkin, Anna Marie Houser, and Allan Houser have been friends, relatives, and teachers throughout the years. While these individuals have been influential in how I approach my subject, because of my strong-willed nature, it is likely that I have not taken their advice as seriously as I should have; therefore, any mistakes are my own.

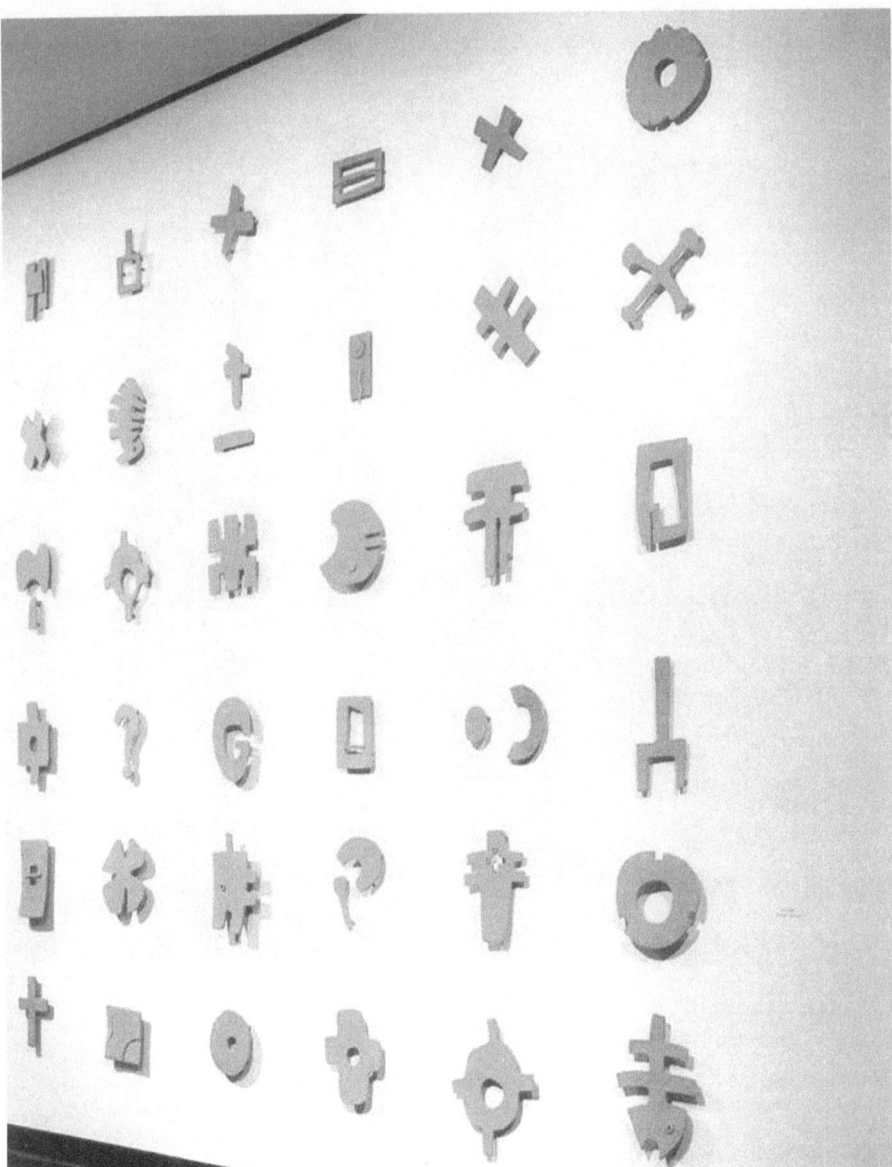

Plate 1.
Nora Naranjo-Morse: *Our Symbols*, 2001. Clay, 204 x 264 x 4 inches. Courtesy of the Eiteljorg Museum of American Indians and Western Art, Indianapolis. Photograph by Dirk Bakker

Naranjo-Morse's intervention in a traditional ceramics-based Southwestern arts practice has strong political saliencies. Her 2001 installation *Our Symbols* creates a unique iconography of fifty-four symbols presented in a gridlike fashion across a vertical surface. The varied shapes produce no recognizable pattern; we cannot "read" the meaning, although the visual presentation appears familiar. We intuit that the symbols are to be read from left to right, top to bottom, but how do we know that this is correct? The viewer is thus denied the security of instruction, with no obvious orientation, template, or translation made available. Naranjo-Morse creates the very instability experienced in the process of colonization. The oppressiveness, confusion, and attendant fear of the unknown disorient the viewer while asserting the power of an indigenous landscape.

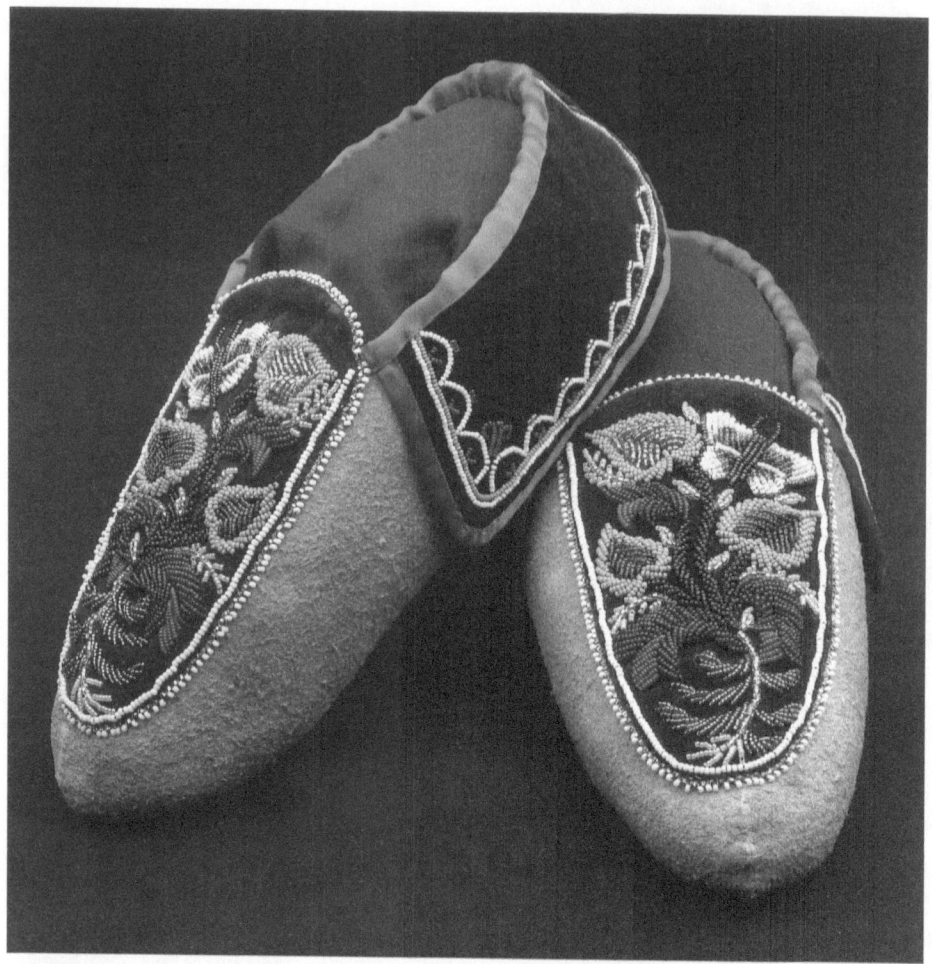

Plate 2.
Tammy Rahr: *Wedding Moccasins*, 2005. Brain-tanned and smoked deer hide, velvet, and glass beads, 8 x 4 inches each. Photograph by Stephanie Johnson

Rahr's perfection of craft in the realm of beadwork is renowned. Her participation in the "art worlds" of regional, national, and international art production evidences a complexity that belies conventional notions of "traditional arts" as stagnant. While her skill in producing Iroquoian-designed wearable arts may, on a surface level, seem to indicate replication of established craft norms, her participation in the arena is less about commerce and more akin to performance art. Rahr's exactitude of line, color, and design, and her attention to detail enact specific, coded visual signifiers while also speaking to communal concerns and responsibilities. In this piece, Rahr gifted a friend with footwear for a traditional wedding. The making, gifting, and wearing thus enact a holistic process, substituting in an informed sense for the commission, purchase, and exhibition model of traditional Indian arts consumption.

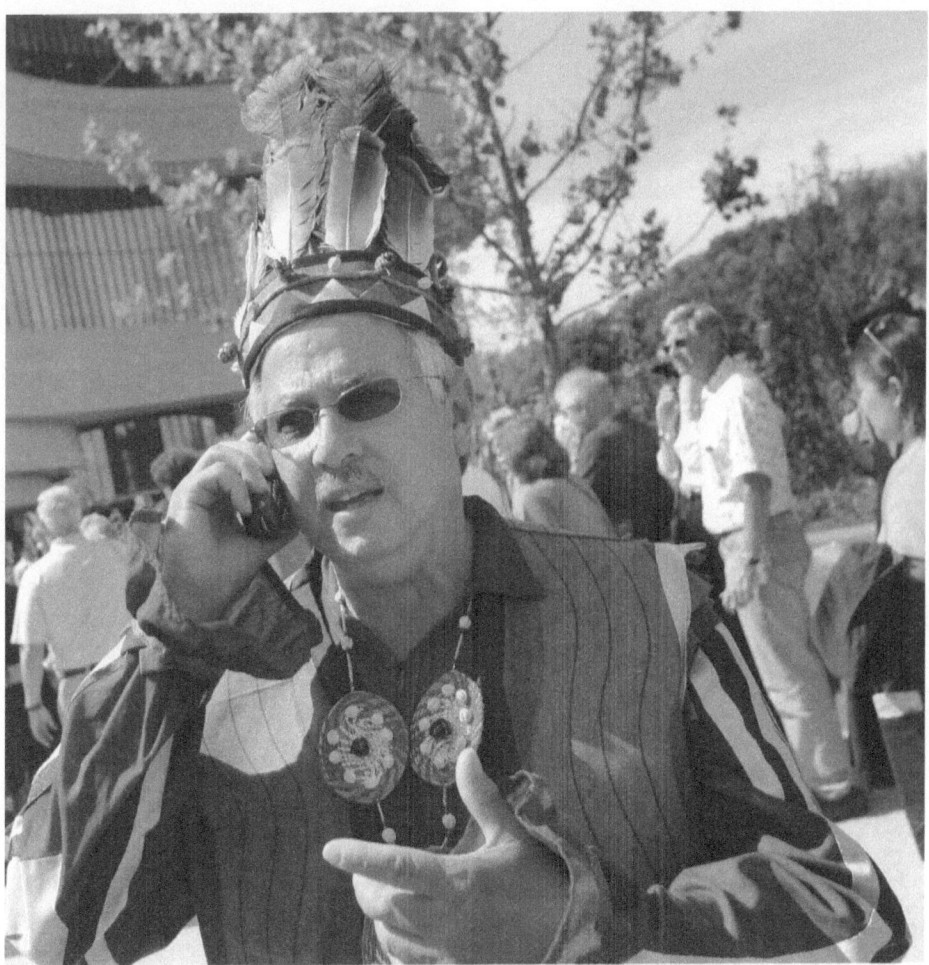

Plate 3.
Jimmy Goins, 2004. Photograph by Susan Biddle, *The Washington Post*

"Everyone came to see Indians, and everyone got to see some," columnist Hank Stuever observed of the 2004 First Americans Festival on the National Mall in Washington, D.C. Held in conjunction with the opening of the Smithsonian National Museum of the American Indian, the festival boasted an estimated 25,000 registered Native American participants.

The original caption for this photo read, "Talking on his cell phone as he waits to enter the new museum, Jimmy Goins from North Carolina seems almost an anachronism." Stuever observes that "the modern, living Indian of 2004 is the best thing yet seen in connection with the Indian Museum. Imagine trying to convince the world you exist" (Stuever 2004:C1).

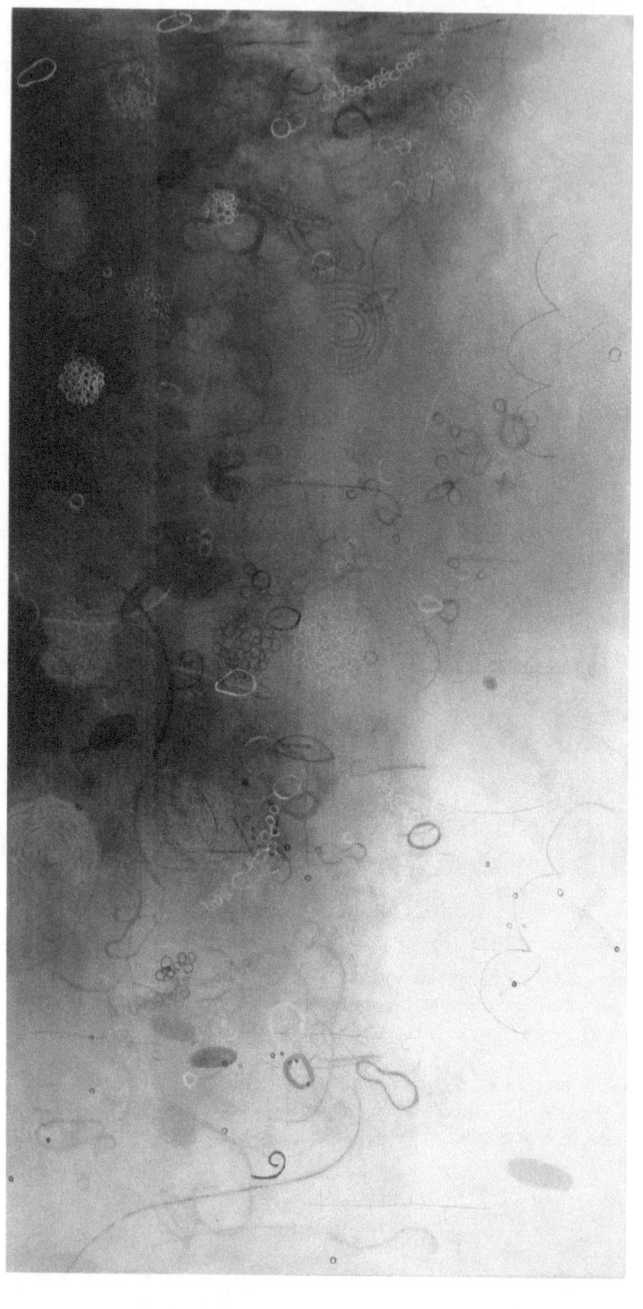

Plate 4.
Emmi Whitehorse: *Nahasdzáán (Earth)*, 2005. Oil on wood panel, 49 × 97 inches. Photograph by Neil Ambrose/Black Brothers Photography
Nahasdzáán (Earth) vividly creates a sense of movement using the aesthetic principles of light, space, and color yet remains ethically in tune with indigenous (specifically Navajo) cultural norms regarding balance, process, and intent. Reading the work requires a contextual knowledge of artistic process in concert with strictly visual principles of style.

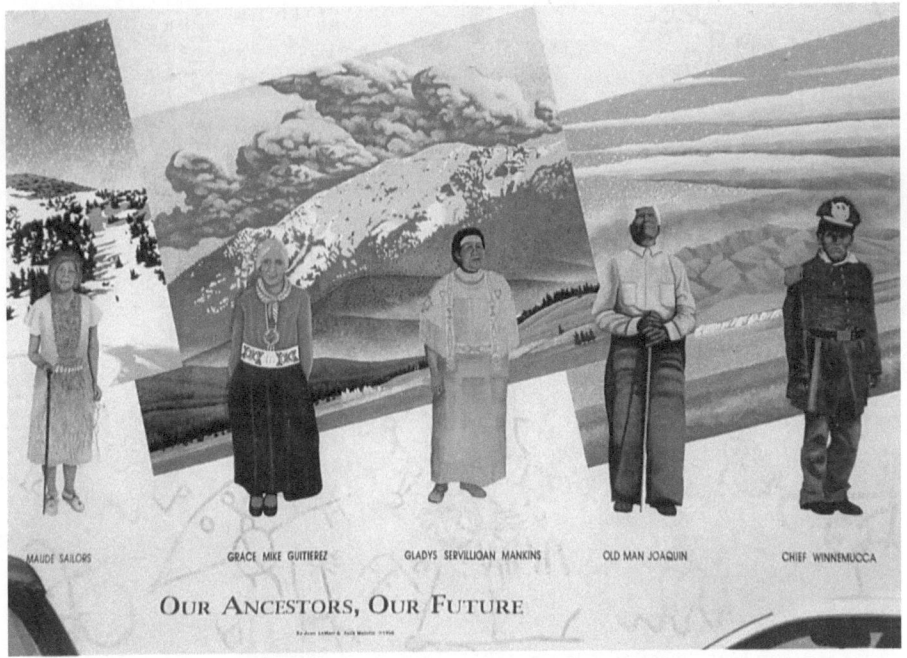

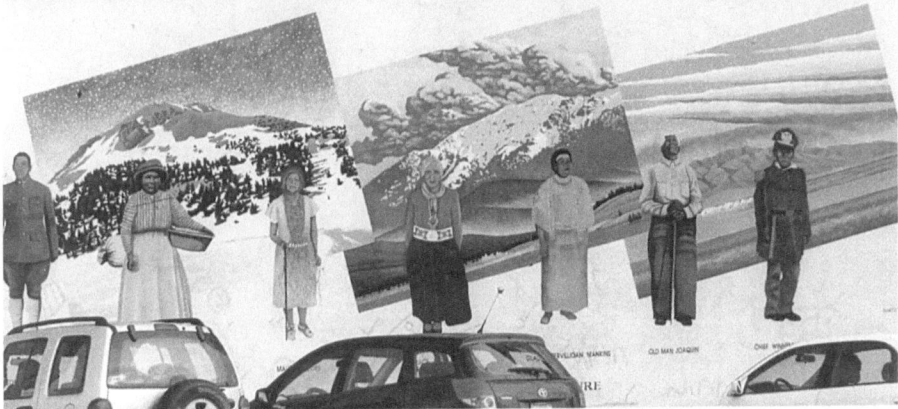

Plates 5a, 5b.
Jean LaMarr, with Jack Malotte and youth from the Susanville Indian Rancheria: *Our Ancestors, Our Future*, 1987. Acrylic graffiti paint and varnish, 20 x 60 feet. Photograph by Nancy Marie Mithlo.
Individuals depicted in mural, *from left*: Tommy Tucker (Maidu Indian, first soldier from Larsen County killed in World War I), Susie Evans (matriarch of the Maidu, storyteller, and medicine woman), Maude Sailors (traditional Maidu storyteller with many descendants in Susanville), Grace Mike Guitierez (representative for the Susanville centennial commemoration), Gladys Servillioan Mankins (carried on the Bear Dance tradition), Old Man Joaquin (chief of the Wada-Vatuka–Paiute), and Chief Winnemucca (chief of the Numa Nation).

Jean LaMarr situates her work (printmaking, installation art, collage, and murals) primarily in political contexts. Believing strongly in the empowerment of making art for the masses (which she attributes to her long association with Chicano artists in the Bay Area), LaMarr stated, "I want people to learn from my work. I think it is valuable information they should learn—about Indians, about the earth, about the environment. Young people, non-Indian people, all races should know how life was for us" (LaMarr, interview with author, May 16, 1991). *Our Ancestors, Our Future* conveys the centrality of art as a communal response. The frontal poses of seven key historical figures indicate a spatial ownership. Their size and bearing combined with their number establish an undeniable presence over the local landscape. Confronting these images, we are forced into a space of remembrance.

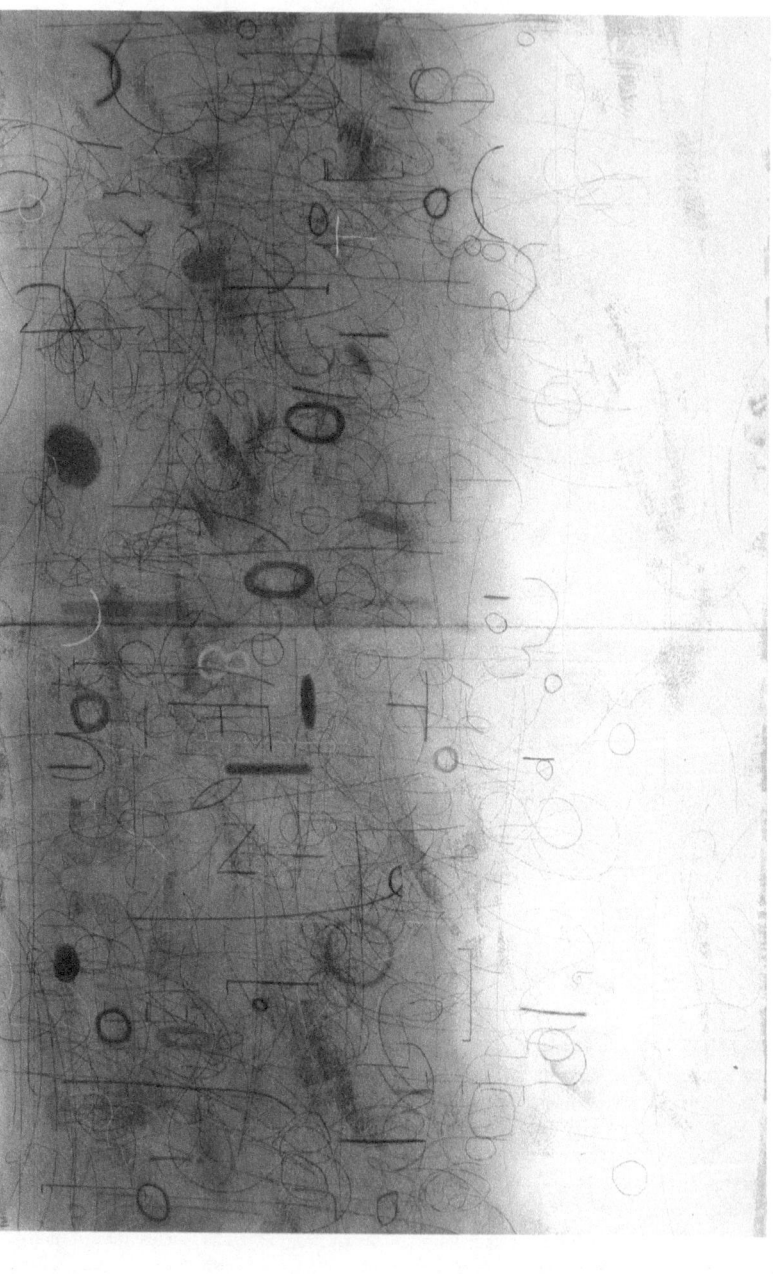

Plate 6.
Emmi Whitehorse: *F.O.N.*, 2006. Oil and chalk on paper on canvas, 51 x 78.5 inches. Photography by Dan Morse/Firefly Studios

"I've always been very stubborn. I've always done what I wanted to do. I know I have one problem...I had a problem with one dealer who always liked the light, froufrou-looking things. They never liked the dark ones, the really dramatic ones, the moody ones. They never liked it. So every time I did stuff like that, they would send it back and say, 'This is too dark. We don't want this.' I'd say, 'Fine. I like the stuff. I'll keep it.' And I'd say, 'Well, you'll just have to wait until I do some work. I'm very busy now'" (Whitehorse, interview with the author, May 8, 1991).

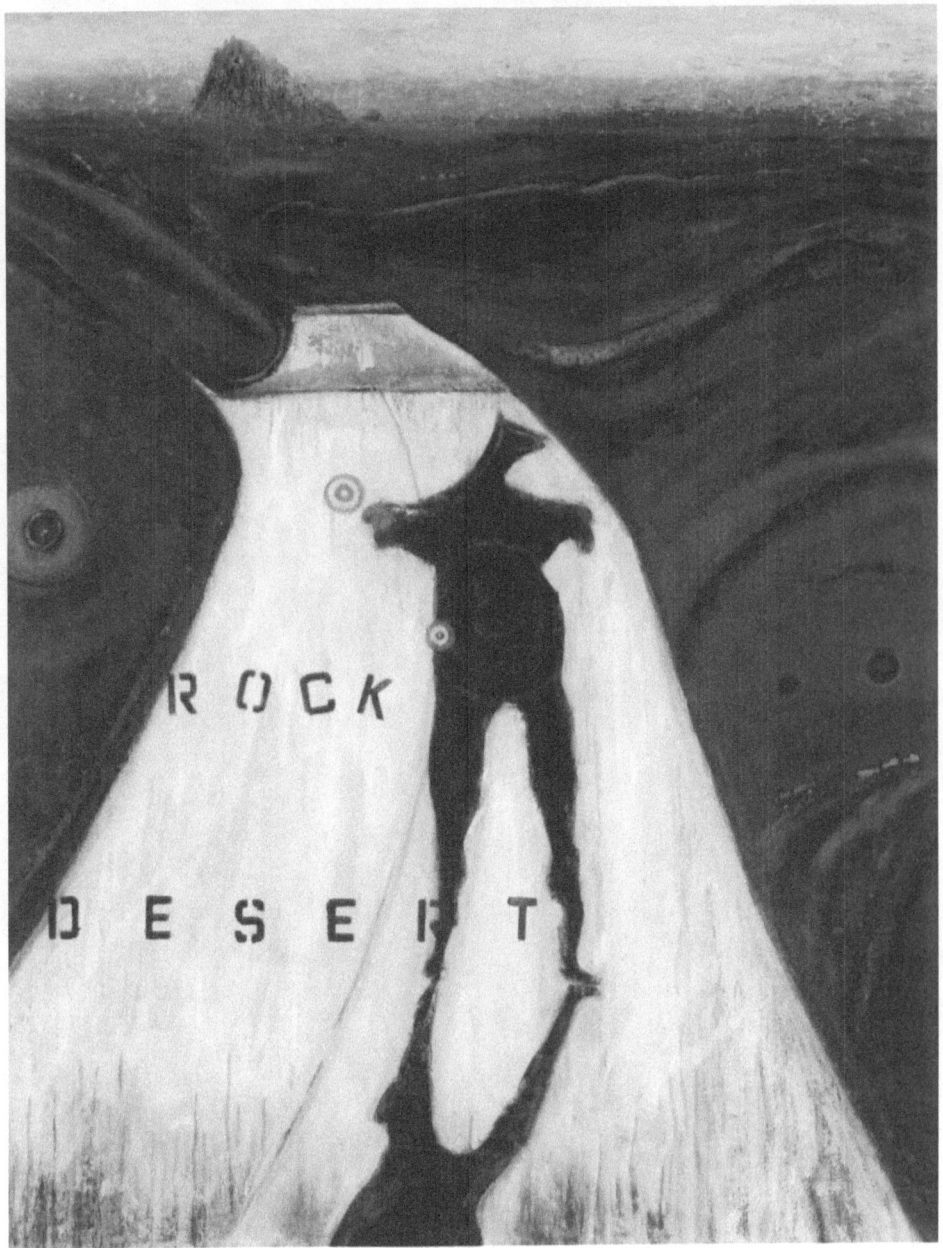

Plate 7.
Gloria Emerson: *Rock Desert*, 2007. Acrylic and oil sticks on canvas, 36 x 48 inches. Photograph by Walter BigBee, The Big Picture

"This painting is my response to a company wanting to build a gasification (coal) company, Desert Rock, in Navajo country. There are already two non-Indian coal companies emitting toxins and pollution in the area. Desert Rock will be Navajo owned, with backing from Blackstone, Inc." (Emerson, interview with the author, May 1, 2008).

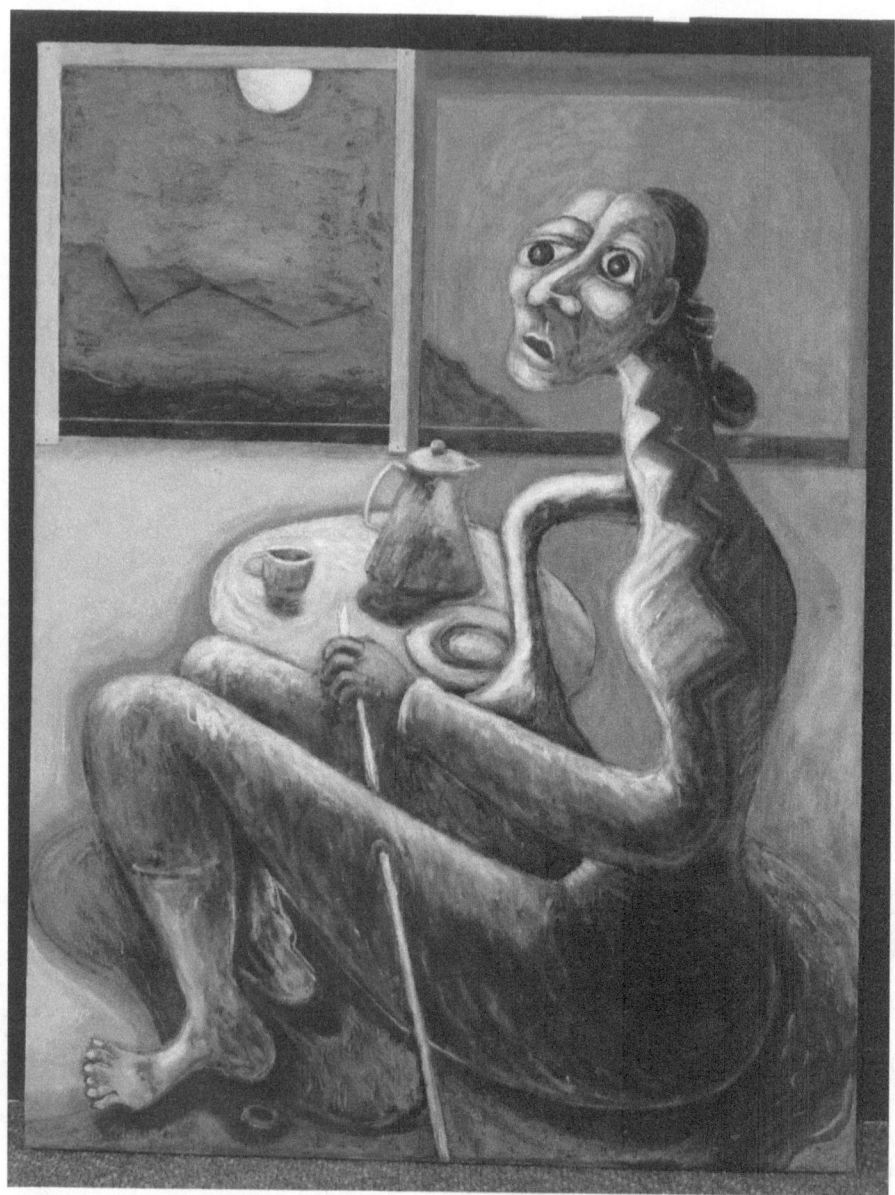

Plate 8.
Gloria Emerson: Untitled, 1991–2007. Acrylic on canvas, 56 x 60 inches. Photograph by Walter BigBee, The Big Picture

This piece was pursued over the span of sixteen years. Emerson describes it as "highly intuitive, long in the development" (Emerson, interview with the author, May 1, 2008). A single female form is projected in an interior space defined by the domesticity of a table, saucer, cup, and coffee-pot. She looks beyond the viewers, her painful gaze averting ours, her mouth askew. A sense of extreme dislocation is emphasized by the bisected torso—a patterned, jagged edge of light and dark runs up her neck. She is at once clothed and not clothed, vulnerable and protected.

This divide is carried further by the window she turns away from—outside, a high moon outlines the mountainous landscape—in a classic reference to nature versus culture. The serene and balanced interior/exterior, illumination/darkness dichotomy is offset violently by an apparent spear severing the woman's thigh. She holds the spear gently. This painful disjuncture of the composition provides a telling example of Emerson's transgression into what she describes as the "elitist" exercise of painting.

I have not pursued research as much as I have sought answers to social problems in the arts that often present as exercises in racism. When artists are denied entry to a mainstream gallery, exhibit, catalogue, or competition on the basis of their Native American ethnicity, the problem is not so much a debate about aesthetics as a violation of civil rights. In one of my early case studies, a male Native American artist tested his suspicions of bias by first approaching a contemporary arts gallery in person to ask whether it was accepting new artists. After he was turned down, he immediately mailed slides of his work and a résumé (carefully omitting references to his Navajo background) to the same individual and was immediately called back. Other related identity constrictions in the arts market simultaneously exist—such as the pressure to produce only nonpolitical or decorative Native-themed arts. The arts serve as objects of manifold importance, but in the Southwest, where arts production is the engine that runs the household economy, as well as many aspects of state government and tourism, these debates hold more than aesthetic importance alone.

Returning to the IAIA over the years as a graduate student, I sought ways in which to make sense of the alienation of contemporary Native arts from consideration as fine arts. As an outgrowth of my work developing the Artist Resource Files at the IAIA Museum under Chuck Dailey, I began to tape interviews with artists and formulate a dissertation topic that addressed marginalization. Some of the work presented in this text draws directly from those early interviews (1989–1991). Other transcripts were made at the request of the museum director, Richard W. Hill, for the IAIA Museum opening in 1992. I began taping conversations with Native women artists again only in 1997, when I served as a professor of museum studies at the IAIA. Since then, I have continued periodic interviews with artists in Santa Fe and elsewhere.

The Native women profiled here generally like the idea of seeing their words from a decade ago and are very curious about what the other women have said and thought over the years. In fact, we are curious about one another—about our children, our relatives, our tribes, our homes, and our careers. At one point, I remember Tessie Naranjo asking how I felt in the morning. I didn't understand her question at first, but then she clarified, "Do you wake up and jump out of bed full of energy, or are you a bit stiff and tired?" When I replied that I was more likely stiff and tired, she seemed genuinely pleased that I, too, was aging along with the women I had spoken with over the years.

The conversations with artists have occurred on reservations in New Mexico and California; in New York City; Washington, DC; Albuquerque,

New Mexico; Venice, Italy; and Atlanta, Georgia. One artist interviewed is an Alaskan native who attended school and had children in New Mexico, moved to Hawaii, and spoke to me during her gallery opening in Vermont, testifying to the global realities of contemporary Native American life. Now that the Internet is so prevalent, I often speak with the women in cyberspace. How did I go about choosing artists to partner with? The Native women with whom I have spoken shift and change over the years according to their availability, interest, and accessibility. Since completing my graduate work, I have not actively sought out a representative "sample" of people to interview but have worked organically by following opportunities as they arise and listening to what I am told is important. Critical readers will likely find the epicenter of Santa Fe influencing the flow of ideas and data and will notice a concentration on urban Indians. In terms of a relative time frame, my interest is contemporary Native American arts—meaning, roughly, the work that has been produced since 1962, the year the IAIA was established.

Readers will note that I actively embrace the idea of the "every Indian" as a pantribal construct, as well as the reference "non-Indian." As problematic as a generic Indian construct has been in reference to negative stereotyping, I suggest that the essentialism inherent in pantribal causes is also inevitable, given centuries of active colonial practices via various legislative acts (the General Allotment Act of 1887, the Indian Reorganization Act of 1934, the Bureau of Indian Affairs Relocation Program, 1948–1979). Since contact with Native North American groups, the US government has enacted specific policies that have resulted in common legacies. I have worked in American Indian contexts for decades, and I can readily anticipate the challenges facing Native American communities (poverty, substance abuse, inadequate health care) as well as the strength of their core social values (allegiance to family, attachment to land, a holistic perspective). Like other identity constructs, the category of pan-Indianism exists and is employed variously as a means of locating self, a communicative device, and a political tool.

Finally, I have not sought to cross-reference the artists' statements against historical records or other published accounts of their work but have incorporated their stories into a wider range of cultural studies discourses, highlighting areas of congruence and exploring issues of difference. In many ways, this work reflects a contemporary employment of subjective analysis, and as such, it may be seen to fall into the category of autoethnography (Reed-Danahay 1997) or narrative analysis. My study is qualitative, in-depth, and rich with a temporal complexity, reflecting twenty-three years of work with Native American communities and the arts.

Arts, Women, and Essentialism

I have chosen to concentrate on three variables for this discussion: the world of contemporary Native American arts, the experience of Native American women working professionally in this field, and the dynamics of essentializing and other forms of referencing ethnic and racial differences. Each of these fields of inquiry carries with it inherent tensions and assumptions that I hope to expose in providing key narratives from women's lives. A brief review of these apparent binaries and their histories may be helpful as an introduction.

The Native arts scholarship I encountered as an anthropology graduate student in the late 1980s was defined in terms such as *tribal arts* or *ethnographic arts*. Studies concerned the dilemma of the individual artist within a tribal community whose creativity was inhibited by communal norms or whose creativity forced him to disrupt collective behavior. Works such as Robert Layton's *The Anthropology of Art* (1991) sought to move beyond this functionalist and static interpretation of the arts by considering the factor of social change. Layton states, "Anthropologists have come to realize how false is the assumption that societies which lack a written history of change must necessarily be unchanging, and this must apply as much to art as to other aspects of culture" (198–199). Layton argues that sociocultural relationships emerge from interaction rather than constraint by the "disembodied realities" suggested in the model of cultural constraint. He emphasizes that culture acquires meaning through the ways in which social relationships are constructed, declaring, "The dichotomy between cultural tradition and individual innovation is a false one" (199).

Certainly, the constructs of individualism and communalism are constantly at play in so-called "tribal arts" discourse, but contemporary Native arts cannot today be productively defined under the category of "ethnographic." Assumptions about the primacy of communal norms are more likely to be expressed using terms such as *identity* or *culture*—descriptives that not only are specific to "small-scale" societies but could also be applied to any social unit. The movement of Native artists in mainstream fine arts and rural reservation communities defies the dated analysis that strictly sees the tribal as separate in time and space from the modern.

Several years ago, I attended an opening for American Indian artists at the American Craft Museum (now the Museum of Arts & Design) in New York City. I was pleased to see several of the exhibiting artists attending, as we had last met in Italy on the occasion of the Venice Biennale. It was a typical formal affair with wine and cheese. In the midst of the opening, the curator took to the microphone to welcome all the Native artists who, in her words, "had traveled so far from their homes on the reservation!" This perspective sadly exposes prevailing notions of timelessness, authenticity, and bounded geography. However, by the same token, my cosmopolitan orientation also exposes the specific class and power location from which I speak and that informs the content of this inquiry. Alison Wylie (2003) calls this a "standpoint," and for better and for worse, it does matter.

I fully recognize the type of prestige at play in the actions and values of educated, globally aware, and mobile professional Native spokespeople. An engagement in Native arts or culture commerce from a base in Santa Fe (as most of the artists interviewed had at one point or another in their career) requires several things: political standing as a Native person; some institutional recognition as a student, teacher, worker, or gallery artist; and enough wealth to travel between cities, mount publicity, make long-distance telephone calls, and perform any of the other myriad tasks involved in running a business. I recognize that this class standing, in particular, is a limiting factor for the universal application of my analysis, and I cannot claim that my work can be applied equally to all Native American artists.

The application of key terminology is an important consideration as well. Artist Jaune Quick-to-See Smith (Enrolled Flathead Salish, member of the Confederated Salish and Kootenai Nation of Montana) observes, "There tends to be considerable confusion about Native art and how it should be defined and what do terms mean such as *contemporary* and *traditional*.... The problem is that colonists have muddled meanings to suit their pur-pose" (Quick-to-See Smith, personal communication, February 14–15, 2007). Quick-to-See Smith cites the 1981 exhibit and text *Magic Images: Contemporary Native American Art*, by Edwin L. Wade of the Philbrook Art Center (produced with Rennard Strickland). The stylistic descriptions in this text are historically oriented, traditional, modern, and individualistic. Quick-to-See Smith notes that the label "modernist" is misleading, because it is "out of sync with Modernism in the mainstream, which happened in the 1930s" (2007). Other labels are viewed as equally problematic, including "the label Tribal Art, which is used by French ethnographers, as well as Sotheby's, and means all people's art everywhere who are not white. So then it has scarcely any meaning at all" (2007). Quick-to-See Smith concludes, "Because there is so little interpretative writing about Contemporary Native Art in the form of books, monographs, catalogs or good critical reviews, there is little understanding yet in the mainstream museums or with art historians" (2007). She suggests that, "like mainstream art, with its myriad categories, we could add some descriptive terminology to delineate more precise meaning in our long history of Native art" (2007). I hope to follow Quick-to-See Smith's analysis in reviewing commonly employed categories and terminology for their utility: often rejecting, reappropriating, or substituting more relevant understandings.

The concept of Native Americans as simultaneously mobile, contemporary, and tribal has not yet been recognized by the non-Indian public. Although most Native artists in this study would not inherently see themselves as insurmountably grappling with two foreign cultures—one traditional, one modern—their lives are still patterned and restricted by the ethnic qualifier "Indian" and the inherent misconceptions of those unfamiliar with contemporary Native cultures. Do these perceptions of others lead to self-inscription? More specifically, does the act of addressing these misconceptions fuel identity? If so, can even negative referents advance positive self-representation? On the most general level of inquiry, do images and the labels that accompany them matter?

Given that American society is challenged daily to recognize and combat racism and that bias and oppression are lived realities for many ethnic groups, it is clear that the relevance of visual culture cannot be easily dismissed as unsubstantial. This study tracks how agency is exercised by Native women via the compromises, challenges, and appropriations of both external Western societal norms and manifestations of those Western norms incorporated as internal and indigenous. Purnima Mankekar describes how resistance and compliance cannot be viewed as mutually exclusive categories because "women's subjectivities cannot be conceptualized in terms of one or the other" (1999:29). Her analysis, like this one, seeks to demonstrate "the complexity of resistance." Importantly, Mankekar establishes the focus of inquiry as one directly addressing popular culture as a *"site of struggle* between dominant discourses and forces of resistance" (29).

For example, the debate of "individual versus tribal" finds expression most poignantly in the economic exchanges of the arts market but is also manifested in expressions of self-identity as an artist who is Indian. At a recent conference in Albuquerque, New Mexico ("Unlimited Boundaries," at the Albuquerque Museum of Art and History, 2007), Navajo artist Emmi Whitehorse, whose narratives are featured in this text, was questioned about her ethnicity as a label. In other words, was she an Indian artist? Whitehorse replied that, no, she preferred not to be referred to as an American Indian artist (even if the premise of the exhibit was to display works only by Native American artists). She preferred, if at all, to be known as a woman artist. While many in the audience may have assumed that the debate was centered between tribalism and individualism, Whitehorse reminded the viewers that she was a member of another, equally important community of artists—women artists. This resistance by Native women artists to be subjected to a limited analysis is an essential component of the narratives I document here.

The variable of gender in the arts calls forth parallel patterns of inclusion and exclusion, individual and communal. For women, these tensions are often based on the perceived dichotomy of public (male) and domestic (female) spheres of interaction. Patricia Albers and Beatrice Medicine argue against what they term "the widely held view in the anthropological literature on sex role and art...that women confine their artistry to domestic use and appreciation" (1983:123). Referencing the case of Sioux women and the production of star quilts, they maintain that for the Sioux, "unlike Western societies, there has never been a clear-cut separation between public and domestic spheres. In the Sioux scheme of things, family and community are one and the same thing. By extension, then, domestic art is ipso facto public and vice versa" (137).

The addition of gender to discussions of race necessarily complicates public perceptions of Native American women—and consequently the perceptions Native American women have of themselves. The conception of domestic and public spheres of interaction as separate and distinct carries over to my discussion of contemporary Native women artists' responses to societal notions of their role as bearers of tradition (the squaw) or exotic others (the Indian princess). These disparate stereotypes leave little room for Native women to position themselves concurrently as art professionals and committed family and tribal members.

Like the individual/collective binary, the scholarly literature and the lived realities of the "subjects" of such inquiries may well have moved beyond these conceptual divides—if the debates impacted them at all. (For instance, I doubt that the term *domestic* resonates with indigenous women.) It is important to note, though, that societal actors still struggle under the weight of these assumptions of identity, which are perceived to be all too alive in public discourse. For example, Cherokee leader Wilma Mankiller observes that the "appalling lack of accurate information about indigenous women fuels negative stereotypes. Television, film, and print media often portray indigenous women as asexual drudges or innocent children of nature," concluding that in the larger society, "the power, strength, and complexity of indigenous women are rarely acknowledged or recognized" (2004:8).

The narratives I have collected testify to an overriding concern with family and community. Naranjo, from Santa Clara Pueblo, articulated this clearly in my interview with her when I asked, "What is the appropriate role of an artist in society?" She replied,

> My role within the boundaries of this community is...as an individual...is to be responsible—or being in support of what the community defines as its personality. And if I'm a product of that, what are my responsibilities for helping to support the community role? And by that I mean things like language, things like ceremonialism,

things like art. Santa Clara is very big on art. We're one of the few communities, probably in the whole country, that is so art focused that we live, breathe art—even when we are not making art.

The public and communal spheres of interaction within this tribal community then intersect with the private and individual in ways that do not find congruence with standard Western norms. The artist is not at odds with society but rather a component of it. Art is not separate from community but rather an integral and philosophical aspect of community.

For other Native women artists, the economic necessity of making a living in order to support themselves and their families defines their rejection of the "individual artist at odds with society" paradigm. This "Van Gogh syndrome," as I have termed it (Mitchell 1993:58), may not inform the artist's orientation on a personal level, yet on a pragmatic level, the starving artist myth does have consequences. Jemez artist Laura Fragua Cota muses:

> Sometimes, I guess, when things are going rough and selling isn't going well and it's like, "Well, I think I'll go do the old Indian in a headdress on a horse, you know, and go try and sell that." You know, because people are stuck on that image, Indian on a horse, or the Indian in a teepee, 'cause that's what sells. And yet, it's kinda a vicious cycle 'cause you don't want to be drawn into that. You know, this is what sells, so you have to paint an Indian on a horse. If you want to make money, that's what you have to do. A lot of times…I say, "No, I don't want to paint that 'cause that's not what I feel and that's not what I want to say." And then when you are hungry and you're out of wood and you need money to buy something…you think, "Hmm, how long will it take me to do that horse?" [laughs]³

A compelling aspect of this economic tension is the perceived difference Native women express about their male counterparts. Women often challenge male Native artists for their unreflective acceptance of the separate spheres of interaction in the arts, their seeming acceptance, without critique, of the market's mandates to be a rugged individual. For example, a gendered response to individual artist–versus–communal artist expectations and standards is evidenced in the following comments by Charlene Teters, a Spokane artist, educator, and activist:

> NANCY MITHLO: I wonder if you could comment on how your role as a woman informs your work. And is that different, do you suspect, than what maybe other artists, male artists, are doing and how their work is informed?

CHARLENE TETERS: Well, I think it can't help but be a part of it, but I'm not really conscious of it.... I think, as women, we always think about the next generation or how it impacts future generations. Where... I think it's pretty apparent to me that our colleagues who are male, you know, think more about how this is going to impact me. You know, right now, how is this going to help me or whatever.[4]

This embrace of the societal responsibility by indigenous artists indicates alternative knowledge systems at play. The legacy of colonialism thus finds continued manifestation in the choices artists make in alignment with or rejection of market pressures.

Lastly, my discussion of image and stereotypes deals with another enduring ideological tension—that of insider and outsider as perceived by idealized identities, often referenced in the literature as essentialism. Berkhofer's *The White Man's Indian* (1979) demonstrates that white images of Indians tell about white attitudes and perceptions more than they elucidate any realities of Indian life. In this "paradigm of polarity," whites assume uniqueness as classifiers and Native Americans as classified only through the content of specific imagery that persists over time: "Since Whites primarily understood the Indian as antithesis to themselves, then civilization and Indianness as they defined them would forever be opposites" (29).

Berkhofer is concerned by how this false binary results in a generalization of Indianness rather than a recognition of specific tribes and histories. He decries the essentialized image of the Indian, stating that it poses "major dilemmas for modern Whites as well as for Native Americans" (Berkhofer 1979:195). Although the use of a pan-Indian identity for Native political expediency is recognized, Berkhofer primarily advocates for cultural pluralism in the form of recognizing individual tribal identities over generic pan-Indian typecasting.

I critique Berkhofer's stance on this issue for not recognizing the important historical impact of pan-Indian organizations nationally (Hertzberg 1971) and the concomitant sense that only individual tribal entities deserve recognition as authentic purveyors of Native identity. This divide of pan-tribal versus individual tribal recognition is a complex argument for both Native and non-Native communities to grapple with, and I hope my attention to this issue will clarify relevant points of departure.

It is important to note that in my documentation of topics defined by tension and negotiation, I do not claim to resolve the binaries in any definitive way. I also hope that my discussion of perceived oppositions does not reify these categories. My work aims to demonstrate the multiple ways in which subjectivity is exercised, despite the contradictory predicaments of modernity, including notions of authenticity, the feminine, commercialization, and individuality. This study finds familiarity with the approach taken by Fred Myers in his analysis of indigenous ownership of copyright in the Aboriginal arts of Australia (2004). His interest in the local understandings of what he terms "object-ideologies" reveals indigenous value systems that emerge from contestation and dispute. These "social dramas" and contested evaluations allow and make more real the values, strategies, and resources that indigenous artists exercise.

Because the economic necessity of marketing Indian arts does throw these dichotomous categories (individual/communal, public/private, insider/outsider) into high relief, I do attend to the ways community and family concerns are negotiated within economic constraints. However, because racism and sexism continue despite economic success, other modes of inquiry than economic determinism are needed for examining the experiences of Native women artists. I hope to take readers into my confidence concerning my own dilemmas in conveying the play between agency and victimhood in this cultural arena. Thus, defining moments of conflict are often highlighted in the narratives as vignettes illustrating the broader issues of what constitutes the feminine and how individual actors creatively play with restrictive categories of perception.

Tammy Rahr's 1991 interview, for example, contains a painful story of how a beaded moccasin commission was contested after the buyers refused to pay for her work (see plate 2). Her intent had been to engage in an economic exchange characterized by traditional notions of respect, but she ultimately relied upon the Western legal system to obtain her wages.

> I do my artwork the same for all people…because of the techniques, the traditional techniques. I don't have any kind of patent on these things. I can't hold a patent. It's not right for me to say, "They're mine." They are not mine—[they are], you know, for everyone. Whether that person be Indian or non-Indian, if they have a certain amount of respect, they can have the piece. And whether they give me cash money, whether they give me a load of wood, whether they will do a trade for materials, it doesn't matter, because I am getting some sort of service, some sort of goods.
>
> Even if I don't sometimes necessarily like the person that I am working for, sometimes you have to say, "Okay, this is strictly a money thing." But the work does not change. I don't sit there and say, "Grr! I don't like this person" while I'm beading. I love my beadwork. That's the way I do it. I even had an instance where I didn't like the people—I really, I really didn't like the people, and afterwards I sort

of wished that I hadn't done the work.... The people got fully beaded moccasins from me for a price that I felt was a little bit low. But I needed the money...I couldn't turn it down. I had to work for these people. Which, you know, was like—you have to do things you don't like sometimes for the good of your family. You got to put food on the table. They burned me bad. They ripped me off. They didn't want to pay me when it was done. They actually accused me of doing shoddy work. They said the designs were nothing close to what they had commissioned, and they were exact! I used real good beads. I felt...I didn't know what to feel! You know, I was mad. I wanted to spray-paint their cars! They refused to pay me. I said, "Well, okay, I guess—I don't want to argue with you, so I'm going to have to look into this from a legal standpoint." They harassed me. They gave me a hard time. I finally went to court and figured out how I had to do what I had to do. I took them to court. I got my money. In fact, I got three times my money...I look at it in this way—these people have some of the best work I ever did. The medicine in those moccasins is very good. She's going to be—she is the one who wears them. And I know that people will stop her when she is wearing those shoes, and they are going to say, "Beautiful moccasins. Who did them?" Eventually, it will turn around. And she will learn, too, you know, that you can't take advantage of people, because it's not right.

Apparently, the operative ideology of the buyers was a consumer relationship in which they might strike a bargain with a Native woman craftsperson, perhaps utilizing their status to gain the greatest advantage for themselves. Rahr was engaging in an exchange that was also ostensibly defined as a monetary transaction yet was equally informed by notions of reciprocity and respect. When this traditional frame of reference broke for her, she translated the exchange into a Western legal context to gain her earnings. Tellingly, this move was not an absolute, for she additionally applied a model of respect in which the transgressor would ultimately "pay" in being forced to acknowledge Rahr's talents publicly. These multiple, and at times contradictory, contexts of Native arts production and reception compellingly expose competing paradigms of knowledge.

Debating the Power of Images: "Everyone Came to See Indians, and Everyone Got to See Some"

"Everyone came to see Indians, and everyone got to see some," columnist Hank Stuever observed of the 2004 First Americans Festival at the National

Mall in Washington, DC. Held in association with the opening of the Smithsonian National Museum of the American Indian (NMAI), the festival boasted an estimated twenty-five thousand registered Native American participants. Confessing that a "non-Indian couldn't be blamed for delighting in the banal details that make today's Indians seem less mythological and quite real," Stuever recites a multitude of observations that "Brings Tradition to the Light of Today," the subtitle of his piece "A Family Reunion."

> Wizened grandmas scooted around in late-model motorized wheelchairs. Traditional music came out of the sound system, with occasional modern backbeats mixed in behind it. Indian families pushed high-end strollers, drank Diet Pepsi, and wore fanny packs under their shawls. Indians in full ceremonial garb waited for the morning procession to start, and everyone seemed to be using flip phones [Stuever 2004:C1].

A large accompanying photo is captioned "Talking on his cell phone as he waits to enter the new museum, Jimmy Goins from North Carolina seems almost an anachronism" (see plate 3). Stuever concludes, "The modern, living Indian of 2004 is the best thing yet seen in connection with the Indian Museum. Imagine trying to convince the world you exist" (C1).

Images of Indians appear to be consumed by the American public in even greater frequency than in decades past, thanks to the rapid reproduction of mass-produced images, the mobility of tribal people, and increased opportunities for tribes to communicate and congregate. Whereas an analysis such as Berkhofer's *White Man's Indian* could claim in 1979 that the "description, interpretation, explanation, and manipulation of the image of Indian as image *and person* were and are inextricably combined in White minds" (xvi, emphasis added), can the same hold true in an age when most tribes boast their own Web pages and casinos have reintroduced Indians in the public's imagination? Stuever's article seems to indicate a willingness to challenge, even with a slight glee, his own formulaic notions of imagery of Natives. Does this indicate a shift in public perception of Nativeness in the new millennium? The juxtaposition of perceived modern and traditional signifiers suggests that the image clusters for Native Americans are so tightly related that they are inseparable. It is this inseparable quality that can productively be mobilized in an understanding of how contemporary Native American arts continue to be restricted in their circulation. Conventional representations dictate that "real" Indian arts are infused with traditional, communal, and crafts-oriented connotations. Contemporary Native American fine arts violate this clean division by collapsing categories of the individual and the communal, the traditional and the modern. The impenetrability of this categorization is demonstrated when either the artist is delegitimized ("Real Indians do not make that kind of art") or the artist's work is ("This fine art is crap. Real Indian art—craft—evidences skill").

Although some developments seem to indicate that Native Americans are no longer prisoners of another's imagination of them, other problems persist and are a cause of heated internal dialogues in marginalized communities. Image production politics demand consideration of material constraints. Native North Americans in general do not have access to the mainstream media outlets that would allow for proactive self-representation. Inhibited by economic constraints and external power structures, communities are torn between addressing others' inaccurate images of them or ignoring these in order to direct scarce resources to tribally defined concerns such as land and water rights, health care delivery, or access to decent housing. The emerging literature on indigenous media representations (Ginsburg, Abu-Lughod, and Larkin 2002) and notable exceptions to this generalization—including such important media venues as the Sundance Institute's Native American and Indigenous Initiative, Aboriginal Peoples Television Network (APTN), Igloolik Isuma Productions, and newspapers such as *Indian Country Today*—provide insights into the manner in which these restrictions might be addressed, given adequate infrastructure.

At an Indian arts conference in New York City, I was pushed toward a reporter collecting information on the "buckskin ceiling." This concept draws from the feminist "glass ceiling" theory and maintains that qualified contemporary Native American artists are kept out of fine arts because of racist stereotyping. Arguing the counter position—that stereotypes should not be interpreted as a defining factor—my opinion found its way into that week's Sunday *New York Times* Arts and Leisure section:

> If you look at native tribes today, there is an office for children's services, an office for senior nutrition, an office for housing, education, for land issues. We don't have an office for stereotypes. It's not on the landscape. Of course stereotypes affect us. But native people have ways to deal with that, to take control of our own destiny. If we are still complaining about stereotypes, that means we are a disempowered people. And I just don't buy that. [Shulman 2000]

I wouldn't change that quote today, even if its lack of nuance appears to align me against many of my professional peers. I respect and support committed efforts to overcome negative stereotypes. What I wish to do, however, is move the locus of discussion away from the actions and motivations of the oppressors and toward the experience of the oppressed. Those who perpetuate degrading images such as sports mascots deny Native people's basic human rights. Their actions do have power and consequences. Yet this struggle to educate others about the realities of contemporary Native life necessarily takes precious resources (time, expertise, and money) away from Native communities and into (comparatively) affluent non-Native communities. It is this expenditure of resources that is rarely brought to the fore of identity debates.

In an age of global communication, clear restraints on what images are given public play do exist and are a cause for concern. A 2004 editorial in *Indian Country Today* titled "Natives Must Educate America, or Perish" indicates the depth of this concern. Citing the growth of anti-Indian propagandist efforts led by groups such as One Nation, the author threatens, "Indian country leadership dismisses it at its own peril" and continues:

> In America circa 2004 public metaphor is everything. One Nation and other groups that need someone to attack, joined to the politicians of various states, are now onto something: The power of the Indian image in the American mind can perhaps be damaged and reversed: From legitimate governments comprised of the first people and rightful property owners of this land, to greedy, special-interest casino kingpins.
>
> The campaign to dislocate the Indian image in the public mind and relegate it to the outer edges of American consciousness—along with other "troublemakers" or anti-Indian elements—puts in peril the Indian generations. Indians must do one better. We need to cover the same ground much, much, better; much more consistently, with better quality and, most importantly, with the truth.
>
> There are positive, negative, confusing, and simply neutral media stereotypes. American Indians have suffered them all, and of all of them the one most closely tied to reality, even when romanticized and overused, is the American Indian as "caretaker" of these lands. [*Indian Country Today* 2004]

Calls for eradication of stereotypical images that are viewed as damaging are often coupled with a demand for the use of images that are accurate and more appropriate culturally. The power of images is thus recognized, and the mobilization of that power is championed. This opinion piece champions the use of a positive stereotype, that of the "Indian environmentalist," as an acceptable icon, given the manipulation of negative images elsewhere. The commentator is likely referencing the popular "crying Indian" 1971 ad campaign for Keep America Beautiful—"People start pollution. People can stop it." This very positive image of an Indian man as the natural caretaker of the environment was a welcome departure from earlier depictions of Native men as inherently warlike and fearless. Readers forty and older will remember how the actor (thereafter known only as "Iron Eyes Cody") was depicted in full buckskin, paddling through polluted waters and encountering a littered freeway. As a passing motorist tosses his discarded fast food at Cody's beautifully beaded moccasins, the actor turns to the camera and sheds a single tear. Ironically, "Iron Eyes Cody" was later exposed as an ethnic fraud; he was said to be of Italian descent and not Native American. Apparently, even a false image, if effective enough, justifies the perpetuation of positive image icons.

Contrasting debates characterize images in the arts and media as meaningless, calling for the rejection of a concern with stereotypes altogether. One recent editorial argued, "While the issue of appropriating Indian names and identities—the mascot controversy—is important, it...is a minor focus in the fundamental issue of tribal sovereignty survival and the preservation of tribal cultural integrity" (*Indian Country Today* 2006). Ironically, these dismissals of popular culture are often simultaneously paired with a longing for access to media as a potential source of political power in the form of self-representation. Certainly, one cannot deny the power of images (stereotypes) and simultaneously assert the power of images (self-representation).

A problematic dimension of the stereotyping phenomenon is the targeting of popular media (film, television, ads) as the racist culprit paired with the mandate to increase opportunities for Indian people to produce in these same industries (Mihesuah 1996). The Smithsonian National Museum of Natural History issued a report in 1996 titled "Erasing Native American Stereotypes," which cited a symposium on contemporary American Indian art at which "several Native American artists asked why their paintings and sculpture are rarely shown at fine arts museums, but are more likely to be exhibited at anthropology and natural history museums. Native American artists also question why their work is not combined with other American artists' work in shows on American art" (Smithsonian Institution National Museum of Natural History Anthropology Outreach Office 1996).

This sort of analysis seems intuitively to link image circulation with institutional resources—but without directly addressing the manufacturers of the images they see as redemptive. Native American image production is not a simple cause-and-effect phenomenon but entails the complexities of professional arts training; access to resources, supplies, and outlets; and the matching of perceived political aims and methods. Native American artists as image makers are experts on the meanings of stereotypes and are adept at reappropriating these images for generative ends, including critiques of white culture. Their ability to mount these critiques, however, depends upon the accessibility of an institutional framework that will enable their statement.

Mentalist and Realist

One way to conceptualize the relative import of imagery in Native North America is to consider the material and psychological consequences of visual productions and reception. In other words, why would a study like this be of importance to contemporary Native American communities? Aren't uninformed non-Indians just naïvely trying to make sense of Native others? Isn't the field of art secondary in importance to the more pressing concerns of health and economics?

In "Anthropology and History of the American Indian" (1981), Robert Bieder describes what he terms a mentalist orientation to Native American imagery. Rather than view Indian images as the product of "social, economic and political conditions," such as judicial history or Manifest Destiny, mental constructs of savagism argue that ideology influences public action and government policies; thus, "the image of the Indian as savage provided the rationale for his extinction" (Bieder 1981:320).

Drawing from these central premises, Berkhofer constructed a related argument, wherein he proposed that one group of scholars sees imagery "as the primary explanation of White behavior vis-à-vis Native Americans" and the other understands imagery to be "dependent upon the political and economic relationships prevailing in White societies" (Berkhofer 1979:31). Whereas the mentalists concentrate on imagery and ideas, the realists emphasize "policy and actual behavior toward Native Americans" (31). Thus, mentalists and realists argue opposing orientations in terms of cause and effect. Mentalists position imagery as primary, while realists privilege political and social acts. According to these frames of reference, my *New York Times* "I just don't buy that" stance would likely place me in the realist category.

I find the mentalist/realist theory to be a powerful mechanism for a deeper understanding of the debates over what Mary Louise Pratt (1982) has termed "conventions of representation." Mentalist and realist orientations, when they privilege causality, are often mobilized in ways that distract from, rather than clarify, key theoretical positions, for ascertaining causality does not substantially alter the manner in which one can make sense of the potency of image making and consumption. Pratt's textual analysis of literary devices in eighteenth-century fiction and travel accounts similarly addresses this question of causality. She asks, Does fiction follow autobiography, or does autobiography follow fiction? Her answer is that neither form suffices independently but that representational codes should be studied "across categories" (141). Her analysis decenters the questions of truth (travel writing) versus falsehood (fiction) and instead focuses on generalized strategies of representation that share similar core traits of employing systems of dominance (in this case, the "monarch-of-all-I-survey" scene).

The search for causality itself must be critically examined for its usefulness in understanding identity constructs and their employment. Political action for the elimination of Native American mascots premises causality as primary—racist acts follow racist images in a cause-and-effect argument. Eradication of racist images should result in greater tolerance and acceptance of pluralism, yet often racist acts continue despite these proactive measures. For example, the University of Illinois recently "retired" the problematic Chief Illiniwek mascot after decades of political mobilization by social justice groups (Des Garennes 2007). This act followed sanctions by the National Collegiate Athletic Association, which ruled that mascots like Chief Illiniwek were "hostile and abusive" (Zeller 2007). The sanctions would appear to signal a new awareness of the implications and harms perpetuated by race-coded icons that mock Native American spirituality and culture and thereby create an atmosphere of intolerance for Native students. Yet other universities that have eliminated Native mascots, such as Stanford University, find that alumni organizations continue to insist on resurrecting the Indian mascot, claiming their right to the symbol (Woodward 2001). Although the most egregious acts of bias and hate are likely diminished with eradication, the production and circulation of loaded images continue. David Pilgrim, curator of the Jim Crow Museum of Racist Memorabilia, similarly reports on the "mammy," "Sambo," and "coon" collectibles recently reproduced and available on eBay (Papadopoulos 2005).

Of the many problems inherent in the Chief Illiniwek figure, one prominent issue is his configuration as a generic pan-Indian in Plains regalia, which is not congruent with Illini tribal dress or religiosity.[5] Pan-Indian configurations are often collapsed into a critique of stereotypical imagery (including mascots) and therefore become a part of the total complex of relationships that privilege mentalist arguments. My research has identified what I term "clusters of analysis" that surround mentalist and realist arguments (see appendix two). The manner in which these clusters "work" demonstrates how a theoretical basis of Native arts inquiry is challenged. In sum, mentalist codes privilege tribally specific, historically accurate imagery. Pantribal referents are critiqued as the central element aiding the construction of negative stereotypes. Berkhofer states, "Most Whites who use the word *Indian* have little idea of specific tribal peoples or individual Native Americans to render their usage much more than an abstraction, if not a stereotype" (Berkhofer 1979:26). The understanding is that a sensitive

America will relinquish legacies of hate and discrimination once it becomes fully informed of tribal diversity. Realist concerns tend to accept modern engagement in hybrid and urban pan-Indian environments, arguing that access to material resources will hold more sway over public policy than solely mentalist ideas about Indians.

Although images are essential to communicating values and norms, what we don't know (and what is beyond my capacity to prove here) is whether images actually form identity or impact policy substantially. I argue that instead of debating the primacy of cause, a more productive route is to consider how people think of images—how these are constructed, produced, and used and with what intentions. As image producers, artists have a major role to play in this process, yet even their construction of new images may be appropriated into other prevailing norms. John Hutnyk reminds us in *Critique of Exotica* that

> visibility does matter in a context where exclusion from resources and opportunities is much more than an absent-minded and myopic blindness of the dominant cultural groups, to be repaired by policy. But it is also my argument that visibility here is only one part of a struggle, as state-sponsored celebration of increased visibilities for hitherto "marginal" groups can readily be turned into market opportunism. [Hutnyk 2000:115]

Thus, it is important to consider not only the character of images, the availability of images in the public sphere, and the authors of those images but also the use to which such imagery is applied. Source communities may find that a lack of recognition could be preferable to a manipulation of visual culture that fails to advance basic socioeconomic agendas. Control and purposeful manipulation of visual imagery become key variables in examining the impact of stereotypes. Should oppressed communities reappropriate derogatory imagery for their own political ends? Does this appropriation invalidate objections to stereotypes? Self-representation may be curtailed at many junctures—the production, consumption, and employment of images and ideas depend on a careful reading of context.

Testimonials and Alternative Knowledges

> I think for a long time…that I had to make clowns—that was what I was supposed to make, I guess…and I was like "No, I don't want to do that. That's like putting me in a little box and throwing away the key." And so I really pushed for that to not be the case. Also, for a long time I didn't want to be just labeled as "Indian artist." I just

wanted to be an artist that wasn't—again, it seemed like a box, because there was too many judgments on what it meant to be an Indian artist. Now...I was really into that for a while, where there was like "I'm not going to be an Indian artist. I'm not going to be labeled that. I'm a person first." But now I'm more "It doesn't matter. They can call me that if they want." I don't really care at this point because I am an Indian. I do have... It has affected me very deeply. And so what I make does come from how I was brought up. Which is partly Indian. And so it's okay, but I don't want to be then told what to make because of it.[6]

The introduction of a sense of history to the understanding of agency is an essential consideration, for not only do individual actors themselves mature and adjust in their negotiations with dominant ideologies, as Santa Clara Pueblo artist Roxanne Swentzell illustrates above, but disenfranchised peoples as a collective can also be said to exercise various strategies through time.

Norman L. Kleeblatt (1998:30) characterizes the cultural critique of minority artists (Latino, African American, Asian American, Native American) at the end of the millennium as "resistant," "defiant," and "radical." These "strident" discourses are programmed to "break barriers to educational opportunity and cultural authority" and to "crack systems of dominance from without" (30). This resistance is positioned opposite of models of assimilation (his example addresses Jewish artists after World War II) that were creative but generally operated within dominant paradigms. Offering an alternative model, Kleeblatt considers how minority artists may historically have spoken strategically through dominant power structures, operating somewhere between assimilation and defiant resistance.

The contemporary Native American experience that I am addressing mirrors Kleeblatt's middle space, as actors strategically position themselves both inside and outside dominant modes of artistic reception while maintaining the right to move freely between competing ideologies. While assimilation connotes victimhood and resistance signals unencumbered agency, the ability to speak through master narrative entails an active critical engagement with existing structures of reception. Swentzell's narrative illustrates how one actor may challenge societal restraints ("I'm not going to be an Indian artist") in the mode of resistance or, alternatively, allow the play of essentialist ideologies ("They can call me that if they want") in the sense of assimilation. The master narrative here is the act of labeling—"putting me in a little box and throwing away the key"—a destiny that is avoided as Swentzell refuses to be "told what to make because of it." Her statement is a testimony to the ability to speak through restrictive categorization.

Personal testimonies of oppression are thus a potential means of understanding multiple identifications enacted in certain contexts. Kay Warren (1997:23) describes the *testimonio* genre, widely used in Latin America as a means of "giving authority to subaltern voices." Testimonies are conceived as collective representations that draw power from the act of witnessing: "On the one hand, they represent eye-witness experiences, however mediated, of injustice and violence; on the other hand, they involve the act of witnesses presenting evidence for judgment in the court of public opinion" (22).

The embodiment of collective truths in the testimonial genre expands the field of theoretical considerations for ethnographic writing. The legitimization of collective truths entails multiple concepts of authority and, as such, is a crucial component of scholarly approaches reflective of indigenous realities. In this sense, testimonials reference a unique analytical stance that stands outside prevailing academic discourses that problematize individual and group identifications. A refusal to parse individuation from collective membership or even a privileging of collective identity can be seen, then, as a radical (in reference to the academy) departure from the way in which personhood is conceptualized. This consideration of indigenous knowledge systems represents an alternative interpretation of visual analysis.

An alternative knowledge base can also be manifest in the aesthetic decisions of artists. While abstract modernist work may appear to be visually free of obvious cultural indicators and definitely not adherent to Native American aesthetic icons, the impulse of the artist may closely adhere to Native American value systems. For example, Whitehorse describes her canvas as one in which "I intentionally paint beauty" (see plate 4), but her sense of beauty is a cognitive, as well as visual, attribute:

> The inequalities for Indian nations are frustratingly numerous, rarely fully understood, often outrageous, and even heartbreaking, yet I paint serene landscapes: worlds that are nonviolent, nonpolitical—whose social commentary is beauty. My works are purposely meditative and meant to be seen slowly. Light, space, and color are the axis around which my work revolves, applying principles of aesthetics and ethics to create balance or harmony in accordance with Navajo philosophy. I intentionally paint beauty, to protect and insulate myself—to keep sane. [Whitehorse 2007:70]

While Whitehorse's statement explicitly rejects the use of political registers in the content of her work, her philosophical approach to the process of making art is nevertheless unquestionably a political stance. This declaration of an indigenous approach to art making—communal, meditative, in accordance with Navajo philosophy—is at stark odds with notions of the artist as genius, the individual artist, the commercial artist, or even the easily readable ethnic artist creating works in the vein of a celebration of cultural diversity. This register of thought offers the viewer a glimpse into what might be available in the intellectual legitimization of contemporary Native American arts as a philosophical area of inquiry.

The following chapters will apply the critical issues of identity constructs to a specific group study. Chapter 2 explores the ways in which economic constraints and established fine arts paradigms foreground various ethnic affiliations, including the formation of pan-Indian identities. Chapter 3 considers indigenous conceptions of art practices, including political orientations and place-based aesthetics. Chapter 4 critically examines the aims and consequences of appropriated identities, asking, Is it true that when we engage in another's otherness (even in opposition), we become them by matching their criteria? I question how certain representations are privileged in Chapter 5. What do actors/image makers do with monopolized images? How do privileged "clusters of meanings" configure pantribal affiliation and activism?

I hope these forays into identity dialogues as they relate to the Native American experience in the arts may serve to expand the existing conceptualizations of Nativeness as constricted in time and space. While images are certainly essential to communicating values and norms, these same signals are also worked in unexpected ways: questioning, critiquing, and appropriating—yet never simply succumbing.

Notes

1. Quotations from Tammy Rahr in this chapter are from the author's interview with her on June 5, 1991.

2. Quotations from Tessie Naranjo in this chapter are from the author's interview with her on September 18, 2000.

3. Laura Fragua Cota, interview by the author, January 5, 1991.

4. Charlene Teeters, interview by the author, October 24, 1996.

5. See "A Challenge to the Chief," http://www.uillinois.edu/trustees/dialogue/report_files/V.html and www.retirethechief.org/, accessed January 24, 2007.

6. Charlene Teeters, interview by the author, October 24, 1996.

2 "They Never Liked the Dark Ones"
Exclusion, Conformity, and Restrictions

We had Native American Studies...I hung out with them, but as far as the art department...I was the only Indian in school. I hung out with the Asian students. And then I got to know the Chicano students—you know, we had to support each other. That was our support group.

My work was political, and I was never allowed...never invited to participate in any Indian art shows because my work was political. And so I would show with other political artists in the Bay Area or multicultured Chicano artists—mostly, Chicano artists would invite me to their shows. I was their token Indian.

I think what really got me when I went to Berkeley...[was] how they just...this certain little clique of white boys got to know all the secrets, and it just made me angry that I was paying tuition there, that I had a right to this education. And so they'd go off in a corner or go off in a dark room and then hear this strange woman's voice in there. I'd be in there. I'd follow them in there, and I'd get called crazy lady. They just thought I was a pushy, crazy lady...they just ignored me. You know, when people think you're crazy, they won't bother you? That's how it was with me.[1]

Pit River/Paiute artist Jean LaMarr's description of the art program at Berkeley in the mid-1970s could reflect the alienation of any marginalized group—women, gays, or blacks. Some would argue that all artists, even those from rather privileged backgrounds, struggle to have their work accepted. What makes Native arts any different? LaMarr's isolation stems from the unique experience of a Native California woman participating in a Bureau of Indian Affairs (BIA) urban relocation program designed to assimilate Native Americans into a wage-based, individualist economy.

Although the act of practicing the arts as a profession may appear to signal a straightforward career trajectory for most, within Native communities, two very contradictory agendas are enacted simultaneously, evoking ramifications for both the artists themselves and their audience, the consumer. Native American arts often signal the embracement of cultural traditions in a religious sense, yet that tradition may also be a mechanism to enter a cash-based wage economy. It is in this second sense that fine arts as crafts may also function as a means of reform—as manual training. Leah Dilworth describes the crafts movement impulse as a historic and a redemptive one concerned with "the 'Americanization' of immigrants, freed slaves, and Native Americans, and the rehabilitation of delinquents and the mentally ill" (1996:158).

LaMarr's trajectory as an artist illustrates some of the basic tensions inherent in understanding how contemporary Indian art carries multiple complex meanings. For example, the practice of art can be interpreted as an extension of indigenous healing traditions. Yet art training is also perceived as a means of acculturation for Native Americans to produce goods for consumer demand and assimilation to Western norms. After graduating from high school, LaMarr moved from Susanville, California, to Oakland under the BIA Relocation Program. Although Indian migration to urban areas was common in the postwar era, relocation as a government program was designed to encourage this move, providing transportation, subsistence funds, job placement, and vocational training. The relocation program is still considered "controversial," for, as Martha Briggs states, "some believed that industrial jobs freed Indians from BIA control, exposed them to improved education, and provided a means to end Indian poverty. Others believed that the program forced Indians to leave reservations without improving living conditions or the quality of job training"(2002). LaMarr's presence in college was then an anomaly for someone of her cultural background, a Native from the small northern California town of Susanville:

> I had no idea of going to college. I had no support whatsoever. My father was very strict about our high school education, so all of us girls [LaMarr and her sisters] were the only Indians that got our high school diplomas. In spite of the racism there, we were the only ones graduating —the only Indian students graduating. So it was easier to tough out the racism than to have the wrath of our father.

Given the lack of opportunity to pursue alternative means of garnering an income and the global push of development efforts to move indigenous populations into modernity, the arts provide a fertile forum for discussions of the appropriation, misuse, and contradictory meanings of materiality. Fred Myers (2004) references the manifold intercultural productions of art in Aboriginal Australia as "revelatory regimes of value." In this analysis, materiality is viewed as a revelation of knowledge in a broader, holistic system of meaning termed The Dreaming—a philosophical understanding of the nature of reality. Instead of simply being an inert object, art functions as a "distinctive mode of cultural production capable of generating and transmitting specific forms of value. The production of images within this framework, especially in ritual, is a fundamental medium in which a person's—or a group's—autonomy can be expressed and drawn into relationship with others" (Myers 2004:10).

Similar relational values can be ascribed to the arts in the context of Native North America, where the relational import of art is constantly foregrounded. LaMarr's instruction in this more holistic, indigenous philosophy is apparent in the following passage:

> I look at some of my grandmothers…the artwork that they did…and my great-grandmothers…their baskets. They were just exquisite—beautiful, perfectionist. They're medicine people. And I always felt like they were the artists. They created baskets for healing purposes, and some of the best work was done by medicine people. I always think, "Gee, if I had been born fifty years earlier, I probably would have been a great basket weaver," but I didn't have the opportunity to learn. By then nobody wanted it. You were not…you were totally discouraged from doing anything that dealt with Indian arts, and of course the materials weren't available any longer. They have been destroyed so fast. But I really appreciated them. I look at them all the time. I hung around my grandmothers all the time because they did such beautiful work…beadwork, everything. So I really encourage [students] to do that.

The tradition of art serving as a complex societal phenomenon is extended into contemporary practice by Native practitioners who subscribe to community service and indigenous values over commercial success as individual artists. For LaMarr, the greater responsibility to a Native American audience finds relevance both in her efforts to found a workshop for Native printmakers and in her pursuit of mural paintings, a result of her long association with Chicano artists of the Bay Area. When I last visited with LaMarr, in 2005, she was busily anticipating overseeing a mural project with children in her reservation community—the Pit River Tribe on the Susanville Indian Rancheria. We viewed her mural projects both inside the tribal offices and in the town of Susanville. The mural *Our Ancestors, Our Future*, featuring seven historic figures from her tribe, was created by LaMarr and Jack Malotte for downtown Susanville in an effort to educate the youth and the community about the Native history of the region (see plates 5a and 5b).

The significance of the arts as a mechanism for making political statements is a central factor for LaMarr, whose commitment to teaching has continued since her Berkeley days: "I want people to learn from my work. I think it is valuable information they should learn—about Indians, about the earth, about the environment. Young people, non-Indian people, all races should know how life was for us." Healing, economic gain, and political statement all occupy the same space of creative endeavor simultaneously, sending discrepant messages to art producers and their audiences.

The various readings of the purpose and function of art can situate Native artists in compromising and challenging positions. LaMarr's resolution of the economic aspect of art is to pursue less directly commercial mediums, such as public murals (see plates 5a and 5b). Her political aims are also served in the medium of printmaking, which she sees as a more publicly accessible and reproducible art form than painting or sculpture:

> Mural work is so important to me. I like to do large paintings, but I didn't like the European mentality of having one painting for one patron or just one person. I like the community art aspect. I was affected by the Chicano art movement. They did murals around town for the community. Also, I began in printmaking. I just loved to print because it was multiples—many prints for many people. I liked what Jules Heller had to say about the print medium: it is for so many thousands of people, while one painting is for one person for many thousands of dollars. [Lobo 1992]

The educational work LaMarr sponsors in her community, such as oral history projects, also addresses aspects of traditional healing. These strategies for maintaining her own cultural orientation as an artist (printmaking, arts instruction, community murals) work counter to the existent arts environments she occupies. In her words, she manages "in spite of the racism." The white reception of her work does not constrain her ability to move fluidly as a participant between art worlds in a knowing, active sense. She purposely situates her work within what she terms "the international language of arts":

> Because I recognize that there are certain audiences, and I try to keep my work in museums and institutions of higher learning...galleries, nonprofit galleries...people who are sensitive and understand...because I feel like my work needs some kind of artistic intelligence, as well as intelligence...recognizing what has happened to the Indian people... aware of what's happening in current events.

Western scholars have long grappled with the apparently incongruent orientations in the concept of an artist—in the "fine arts" sense and in the "cultural artist" sense of the word (Becker 1982; Dissanayake 1988; Dubin 2001; Layton 1991; McEvilley 1992; Otten 1971; Silver 1979). Writing in the late 1990s, media scholar Steven Leuthold outlines the major characteristics of an indigenous aesthetic in comparison with Western aesthetics:

> For contemporary Westerners art has several attributes; it remains relatively autonomous (not tied to physical, religious, political, legal, or other social goals), special, unique, nonutilitarian, ego-identified, self-validating, innovative, "without rules," and so on. In contemporary Western culture we associate art with its commodity status and exhibition value (its value as established through sale or exhibition); art is usually made by an "artist" (someone with special training and/or talent or psychological properties who has been recognized as an artist); art is relatively permanent (it and the values that it expresses last over time); and art is not dependent on collectively held religious beliefs for meaning. [Leuthold 1998:48]

According to these Western attributes, Leuthold argues, *art* is an inappropriate term for describing indigenous aesthetics. He summarizes as follows:

> Natives often believe there are social rules for art that they should follow and guard, including rules of content, context, form and personnel; that art should be community-oriented; that art is an expression of the sacred; and that art is useful, beautiful, and functional. The artist is not above or separate from society (not different, eccentric, or professional); there is little pressure for innovation for its own sake; and art is understood in the context of religious, communal, and personal narratives and through its utilitarian functions. [Leuthold 1998:49]

Leuthold is careful to qualify both Western and Native art attributes as common assumptions, arguing that while exceptions do exist (in his words, "especially as indigenous peoples become more assimilated into Western social and economic systems" [49]), the categories remain largely in place. Although Leuthold's binary descriptive does provide a useful starting point for discussion, I find his qualification especially troubling, as he seems to dismantle the very paradigms he structures by excluding the variable of change and contact, thus reinforcing, in an unhelpful manner, the tendency for Native peoples to be viewed as ahistorical and somehow precious in their perceived inability to withstand global and capitalist forces without abandoning cultural frames of reference. This type of unilateral appraisal of Native arts seems to position the artist as a passive victim who is unduly challenged by contact with Western influences rather than actively engaged in incorporation, exclusion, or transformation of new technologies, materials, values, and beliefs.

The Passive and the Active Artist

The variables of passivity and agency provide a useful platform for evaluating contrasting scholarship over time. The passivity reading is congruent with scholarship of twenty years past in regard to contact and change: "There are an increasing number of instances where the conquered minority artists have taken up the established art forms of the conquerors, following and competing with the artists of the dominant society. These are characteristic of extreme cultural domination and hence a desire to assimilate" (Graburn 1976:7). This quote is from the much cited text *Ethnic and Tourist Arts: Cultural Expressions from the Fourth World*, edited by Nelson Graburn. The unilateral interpretative stance evidenced in the language of assimilation denies the ability of contemporary artists to occupy a contemporaneous space—to, as historian Philip Deloria (2004:232) terms it, "create modernity in dialogue with others."

Graburn's assimilated artists are drawn directly from the equally much referenced text by J. J. Brody, *Indian Painters and White Patrons* (1971). Brody's work argues that early (1885–1916) paintings by American Indians —"ethnically Indian, but trained in a European manner"—had no effect on the development of modern Indian painting (82). Both self-taught and institutional painters of the succeeding decades were perceived to work only in response to white preconceptions and desires, producing "sterile," "meaningless," and "decorative" arts. Indian painters who did attempt to achieve works "beyond the decorative" were described as having failed in their efforts: "Victimized by incomplete understanding of the impossibility of being both a tribal Indian and an idiosyncratic painter, these few were defeated by acculturation as were so many other tribal Indians who attempted to make their way in urban White settings" (157). This analysis disallows contemporary Native American artists from being both tribal people and artists—the two are separate and impermeable. Any attempts to otherwise cross these established barriers are evidence of an "incomplete understanding" of how things work in the status quo. Acculturation is a punishing force that defeats these resistance efforts.

According to Brody, this scenario, in which "the role of the Indian artist has been primarily that of a performer, working from a script written by Whites" (Brody 1971:189), shifted in the 1960s with the establishment of the Institute of American Indian Arts (IAIA), a BIA school, and the concurrent advent of the "New Indian Painting." Previously, the form, vision, and purpose of Indian painting had been seen as purely acculturated. This new development (illustrated with examples only from male painters) was interpreted as "personal, expressive, and socially meaningful pictures by Indians" (204). These "separatist," "emotional," and "angry" works resulted in the equation that Brody advocates: "Indian artists…wish to be treated as painters rather than as 'just' Indian painters" (204). Clearly, the formula for success in Indian art, according to Brody, is to minimize or entirely reject Native American ethnicity, for to do otherwise is to succumb to paternalistic and stagnant ideologies.

Although Brody states in his introduction that he will analyze both formal and functional aspects of Indian painting, his analysis relies heavily on the formal investigation of Native American painting. A reader does not get a sense of how Brody conducts or interprets the interviews and conversations with Native artists from either the early institutional period of the 1920s and 1930s or the new modern phase he champions. It is therefore difficult to understand his celebration of a new individualism, given this lack of context. Why were institutional and economic constraints no longer seen as barriers to self-expression in the 1960s? What continuities exist with the artist's situational constraints and subsequent choices over time?

The passiveness of Native artists as performers in Brody's scholarship ("The role of the Indian artist has been primarily that of a performer, working from a script written by Whites" [Brody 1971:189]) has apparently defined the interpretation of contemporary Indian arts for the past three decades. Not only is there is no evidence in Brody's analysis of a Native voice—no quotes or citations to contradict this conclusion—but also his brief allusions to the conversations he engages in with the "New Indians" (see his appendix) are not in any way formalized. Researchers do not know when, where, or how these perspectives were acquired or where evidence of these conversations in print or tape may now reside. This academic style— exclusionary, male, and concealed—corresponds well with LaMarr's analysis of her reception in art school: the "boys in the back room" syndrome. Living voices, female perspectives, and a nuanced description of constraints and solutions are nowhere evident in this seminal, highly influential appraisal of Native arts.

The incorporation of the artist's perspectives in the interpretation of what has been termed "tribal arts" has not typically been pursued, even in anthropological works that privilege cultural factors. Robert Layton's *The Anthropology of Art* (1991) sets up a common quandary by stating that the artist's viewpoint is important while dismissing the possibility of actually incorporating the artist's perspectives. Like Brody's, Layton's analysis depends primarily on an interpretation of the art object. Layton states that "the investigation of the artist's intent (as far as he can express it), and the response of fellow members of his community, are of primary importance" (Layton 1991:11), yet he counters this by asserting a "philosophical objection." Arguing that one can never know another's thoughts directly but that thoughts are conveyed only by means of communication, Layton surmises that "in the artist's case, his work of art *is* the primary means by which he expresses himself" (12).

Given that many artists may object to the added responsibility of not only producing but also interpreting and critiquing their own works (a common response might be "My work speaks for itself"), in what ways are conversations with artists meaningful to interpretation? Howard Becker presents a sociological analysis of "art worlds" that uses as criteria "when, where and how participants draw the lines that distinguish what they want to be taken as characteristic from what is not to be so taken," including "what is and isn't art, what is and isn't their kind of art, and who is and isn't an artist" (1982:36). This perspective can be said to engage active notions of the artist. It does not present itself as a burden to interpretation of artistic works but as a legitimization of alternative artistic discourse. Becker's premise is one of relativity: "By observing how an art world makes those distinctions rather than trying to make them ourselves, we can understand much of what goes on in that world" (36).

Becker's analysis is important to this study, for not only are members of any given art community allowed to set the terms of definition, but material constraints are also taken into account: "Before people can organize themselves as a world explicitly justified by making objects or events defined as art, they need sufficient political and economic freedom to do that, and not all societies provide it" (Becker 1982:39). I would add, for the sake of this study, that societies provide differing levels of support for art worlds and colonized populations must contend with layered power differentials, constricted movements, and incorporation of existing but foreign value systems of production and exchange.

Becker's argument engages mainly Western art conventions—rock-and-roll musicians, quilt makers, and recognized fine arts painters and sculptors. In these art worlds, artistic freedom is assumed; the economic, political, and organizational constraints are pushed forward and made evident in a redemptive model. In assessments of tribal arts, economic, political, and organizational constraints are always evident, even exaggerated, and made not only real but also punishing. Native artists are made victims under the weight of white receptions of their work (the Brody model) and also by internal constraints (the Layton model). This analysis will strive to move between these seemingly inescapable interpretative paradigms (artistic freedom, cultural baggage), relying on first-person narratives as a guide.

"They Never Liked the Dark Ones"

EMMI WHITEHORSE: I've always been very stubborn. I've always done what I wanted to do. I know I have one problem…I had a problem with one dealer who always liked the light, froufrou-looking things. They never liked the dark ones, the really dramatic ones, the moody ones. [See plate 6] They never liked it. So every time I did stuff like that, they would send it back and say, "This is too dark. We don't want this." I'd say, "Fine. I like the stuff. I'll keep it." And I'd say, "Well, you'll just have to wait until I do some work. I'm very busy now." Or sometimes they have threatened to cancel my shows because I didn't do any painting…canvas pieces. I did works that were on paper, and they would get all upset. "We're going to cancel the show. You're not having a show unless you have canvas."

NANCY MITHLO: No!

EMMI WHITEHORSE: Yes! I've had stuff like that, and I've always just said, "Well, if you don't want the canvas pieces, I'll just sell them on the Plaza just like everyone else does and make my own way. The hell with you." I've never given in…I'm a terribly stubborn person—and to a point where I can really hurt myself. My own stubbornness can ruin me and hurt me.

NANCY MITHLO: Do you mean economically?

EMMI WHITEHORSE: Yes. My career—I could ruin my career because of my stubbornness. When I make up my mind to do something, or if somebody disagrees, like in this case, where the person wanted canvases instead of paper pieces, I just said, "What's the difference? The work is very strong...I just don't want to do the canvases...and I don't want to do the canvases because I know they would be terrible, and I don't want to sell terrible work.

NANCY MITHLO: You don't want to compromise your integrity.

EMMI WHITEHORSE: I wasn't going to do that. But anyway, she apologized, and it worked out fine in the end. I've always tried to do what I'm best at...what I'm capable of...putting out work that I felt was...I've never rushed myself. I've always tried to take my own pace, and that has people bullying me around. I don't know if I have a terrible reputation, but I do it my way...or do the canvas myself because if I give it to somebody to stretch, I hate it the way they do it and I redo it myself. It takes forever. I lose a lot of time doing that, but I'm stuck. I'm very picky. I want it done this way, just so. So I do spend a lot of time in the studio doing everything myself, whereas I should just get somebody to do it.

NANCY MITHLO: Do you have a role model that you learned from, or do you attribute it—that attitude—to someone in your life that's influenced you?

EMMI WHITEHORSE: I think maybe my grandmother. My grandmother could be very picky. So I think I picked that up from her. [2]

Artist Emmi Whitehorse has largely based her career in the market-saturated environment of Santa Fe, New Mexico. She has been showing and selling her work professionally since 1982, when she had her first one-person exhibition at the age of twenty-six. Of the artists featured in this book with whom I've worked since my earliest research efforts in 1991, only Whitehorse and Roxanne Swentzell have continued to engage full-time in Native American fine arts. This continuity is telling of Whitehorse's orientation as an artist—an extension perhaps of her "stubbornness."

My identification in this study of two artists out of seven who maintain commercial viability over time should not be read as an elevation of economic success alone. I would interpret this economic determinism analysis to be the same shortsighted appraisal that Brody pursues. Native women often express a commitment to cultural expression and continuity in the arts rather than solely economic gain. This value informs their movement in and out of commercial contexts as other economic opportunities arise or as family or community demands shift. For example, LaMarr has productively moved in and out of commercial spheres, working in Santa Fe at the IAIA as an instructor in printmaking for several years before moving back to Susanville. It is important to note how the noncommercial trait conforms to the Western archetype of the artist—the autonomy and ego that Leuthold describes. Can Western art traits be argued to exist in this Native context? How, then, is a Native art world unique?

Whitehorse's refusal to submit canvases had a practical aspect—she was particular about the stretching and preparation of the painting surface and did not wish to hire someone else to complete this stage of the work. This attunement to process, however invisible in her final product, is an essential consideration in Native American art contexts. When questioned about influences in her approach to the arts—her "stubbornness" and pickiness—Whitehorse cited her grandmother, a traditional Navajo woman, as a major influence. Elsewhere, Whitehorse has elaborated on this influence:

> Even in old age, I think the women still retain a grace that is unequaled. My grandmother is like that. She's very giving, and she instilled a lot of traditional values in us without having to preach. She was a weaver. She learned how to weave from her mother. Her work is elegant. She is very finicky, very concerned with what she wears in public. She won't go out on a short trip to the store without putting on her best clothes: a traditional Navajo velveteen top and three-tiered cotton skirt down to her ankles. She used to make her clothes, but now she has trouble seeing, so she has someone make them to her specifications. [Katz 1995:56]

Whitehorse's description of her grandmother as "finicky" finds congruence with the artist's self-described "stubbornness." It is important to note how occurrences of both these attributes take place in encounters that can be characterized as Western or non-Native: the trading post and the gallery. In many ways, one could argue that the art gallery is a modern-day trading post and that instead of a concern with personal appearance, Whitehorse has substituted a concern with the appearance of the painting. These meeting spaces—these "social dramas," as Myers would term them—are essential to considering how indigenous ideologies are often mobilized when cross-cultural communication is challenged and the possibility for conflict is high. Surface considerations (such as the exercise of free will in a market economy) can conflate the appearance of autonomy with a desire for participation in Western values rather than a consideration of cultural values. The articulation of indigenous aesthetics is challenged by these tropes, these mismatched pairings and assumptions of assimilation rather than creative application of what are considered traditional values.

Not Freedom Alone—Process

The anthropological literature on Navajo aesthetics is well established. Gary Witherspoon's *Language and Art in the Navajo Universe* (1977) articulates the Navajo belief in *hózhó*, a holistic concept of beauty experienced "most poignantly in creating it and in expressing it, not in observing it or preserving it" (1977:178). Similarly, Sol Worth and John Adair's 1966 research "The Navajo Film Themselves Project" concluded that a Navajo narrative style in film displays an unusual visual concentration on walking. They argue that this "extreme awareness of motion" (Worth and Adair 1977:204) favors a depiction of a journey as a "motion describing an event," not "a suspenseful story leading to an ending which will present a solution or satisfy in some way" (207). Their analysis suggests that this dynamism and movement correspond to the theme of the "long journey" in Navajo myths and tales.

I reference these historic studies not as a means of justifying contemporary parallels in a traditionalist manner but as a comment on the tendency to view behaviors and outcomes as being derived from the same sensibility. In this sense, then, the "symptoms" of individualistic, or "stubborn," behaviors do not indicate identical causes. Noncooperation with sales mandates may appear to be congruent with Western ideologies and may even be informed by Western ideologies but should not in an extreme approach be interpreted, in the same manner as Brody or Graburn, as "assimilation." This rather willful assignment of Western ideologies overlooks and assigns to obscurity an alternative reading of indigenous worldviews. By "willful" I mean collapsing outcomes and causes, process and product, in a predetermined and shallow manner.

Formalism plays a major role in how these conflations of assimilation are enacted. Economic determinism and an emphasis on the art product support and feed each other in a hierarchy of materialistic values. This diminishing of the art process not only alienates other possible interpretations but also victimizes artists as passive players in the foreign and perceived alien game of arts commerce. The inescapable nature of this equation becomes clear if one considers the way that economically successful Indian artists are then—sometimes willingly—stripped of their ethnicity. They are artists first, Indians second.

This rather negative reading is not intended to indicate a predetermined conspiracy but to recognize how related concepts cluster together so tightly that it becomes difficult to discern cause from effect. All manner of descriptions can follow this deterministic line of inquiry. Assimilationist art theories (in the style of *Indian Painters and White Patrons*) are evident in key "conventions of representations," including the desire to place Native people in bounded contexts of time and place, the investment in authenticity of person and product, the lure of the exotic, the vanished Native who needs protection, the innocent Native who is taken advantage of, the Native who sells out and is stripped of his or her culture. These narratives—speculative, imaginary, fictional—do exist in the expectations of Native arts consumers and therefore in the Native artists themselves as they navigate consumer desires. Thus tradition itself (the Navajos value process and movement over product and stagnancy) can be seen as a mode of response, a claiming of home territory that lies outside the assimilationist camp of pure accommodation and conformity.

Art historian Lucy Lippard incorporates Witherspoon's cultural premises in her description of a 1991 retrospective exhibition of Whitehorse's work, describing the "metaphysical views from the Navajo world" as "an untranslatable and eternal quality of human and environmental harmony and blessedness…combined with vivid motion, movement, change" (Lippard 1991:1). Lippard's concern with both formal qualities and the cultural context of art is representative of current critiques in multicultural arts. Her central work, *Mixed Blessings: New Art in a Multicultural America*, with its emphasis on "the ways in which cultures see themselves and others" (Lippard 1990b:4), is exemplary of this move away from an emphasis on the art object—or, in Leuthold's terms, specifically "its commodity status and exhibition value" (Leuthold 1998:48). Lippard's text highlights this concern with process: "In art by modernist Native American artists, the cross-cultural *process* is visible not so much in style as in attitude" (Lippard 1990b:109, emphasis added).

Claiming for a moment the premise that indigenous art is unique in certain key features, how do Native artists articulate their appropriation of Western mandates such as competition, individual merit, and economic returns of the market? In what ways is the dichotomy of Western art as autonomous and ego driven and tribal art as community oriented resolved? I will briefly examine three common arguments made in the literature to rectify this discrepancy: separatism, inclusion (pluralism), and reappropriation.

Separatism: "No Word for *Art* in My Language"

It has become common to claim, as many artists and critics do, that there is no corresponding word for *art* in non-Western contexts and therefore no equal basis of comparison from which to bridge conceptual gaps: "There's no word for *art* in my language" (Berlo and Phillips 1998:9; Carpenter 1969: 203; and Fauntleroy 1992:7). Fine arts theory and indigenous aesthetics thus remain separate and dichotomous. Related terminology and conceptual schema include notions of ethnic separatism, nationalism, the so-called ghettoizing of Indians arts, and extreme forms of sovereignty. While separatism is useful for articulating opposing values and actions, this position ultimately fails as a redemptive strategy for cross-cultural communication. Native American arts do find currency within the field of arts manufacture and reception. Native artists certainly participate in activities involving the label "art"—art exhibits and classes at art schools—so the suggestion that the term cannot be fairly applied is a rhetorical one. Separatism does function positively as a call for recognition of difference, as a platform for articulating alternative ideologies to be legitimized.

Navajo artist Leatrice Mikkelsen states,

> In the language of the Dineh there is no word for art. When I learned this, I laughed. I was so relieved. This word, and all that it drags with it, was not necessary.... What is art? People made beauty in objects, songs, movements. This was done day and night, moment to moment. They never created the issue of 'ART.' That is a whole life. [Mikkelson 1992:31]

The conceptual baggage Mikkelsen notes references the use of the word in a Western sensibility, signaling primacy of form and aesthetic judgment, uselessness of object, and notions of upper-class consumption and individuality. Rejection of the term *art* signals an assertion of an artist's alignment with a perceived oppositional "Native" sensibility—primacy of process, object functionality, noncommercial and communal. This Native identification may be primarily fictional in nature as the artist's behavior (if he or she participates in the market) closely matches the underlying correlations of art with aesthetics, beauty, and commerce.

The absence of a specialized language for art does not necessarily indicate that Native peoples did not or do not engage in arts activities. Writing in the volume *The Traditional Artist in African Societies*, K. Peter Etzkorn (1973:366) presents evidence that even contemporary American painters do not have a strong artistic vocabulary but rather use ordinary work terms to describe the process of their creations. Working from this premise alone, one might similarly summarize that these American painters could not be called artists because they do not have an artistic vocabulary. Is bias at play in overassertion of ethnic identifications?

Anthropologist Evelyn Payne Hatcher dismisses the "no word for *art*" stance altogether as nothing but semantics: "Confusion here lies in the fact that art is not a phenomenon but a concept. Being a concept it has no objective referent, and so one cannot say what it is or is not, but only what the user means by the term.... Many peoples do not have words for 'economics' or 'chromosomes' or 'religion,' but this does not invalidate these categories" (Hatcher 1985:8). She calls for an engagement with varied art theories, stating, "We need to compare not only the products, but the theories of artists—comparative esthetics or 'ethnoaesthetics'" (2). This contextual basis appears to offer more opportunities for sustained analysis.

Separatism has affinities with sovereign arts descriptives. In this sense, Native American arts stand apart from consideration of aesthetic evaluations alone, making appraisals in mainstream art reviews more challenging to accomplish. Organizations with explicit Indian markers, such as the National Museum of the American Indian (NMAI) or the IAIA, serve as reminders that the conceptual basis for inclusion is unique ethnicity.

Inclusion: "Artist First, Indian Second"

Etzkorn's and Hatcher's rejection of separatist arguments positions them as advocates of employing inclusive strategies for addressing conflicting art ideologies. The inclusive paradigm claims that both Western and indigenous artists enact similar conceptual behaviors in the pursuit of modern and postmodern aims. This assertion presents a mirror opposite to the separatist argument, which dismisses the category of art as a mutual reference. Instead of "no word for *art*" as a platform, inclusionists claim that there is only one word for art, often raising tribal or indigenous arts to an equal standing with fine arts—"as good as" fine arts.

This inclusive arts interpretation is described by Native arts scholar Gerhard Hoffman as pluralistic:

> It is obvious that the postmodern world, with its breakdown of ideologies and social utopias, of dogmatic nationalism and aestheticism, is again on the path to the irrational and the imaginative, and that Indian art and postmodern art go hand and hand in trying to remain open to this potential...the artistic striving of the minority coincides with the majority culture's entrance into the late phase of decentralization and pluralization. [Hoffman 1986:281–282]

This inclusionary approach effectively dismisses the premises of Leuthold, Witherspoon, Mikkelsen, and others who advocate for a unique indigenous aesthetic sensibility based on religion, myth, and culture. Although appearing politically progressive, a pluralist reading can also be read as essentially assimilationist and ahistorical. Native American artists who adopt this pluralist, postmodern premise may claim, "I'm an artist first, an Indian second" as a means of asserting their central positioning in a mainstream fine arts forum. In an extremist fashion, the phrase "Artist first, Indian second" connotes an antiethnic, assimilationist cannon (Himmelman 1989). A more generous reading of this ideology suggests a rejection of restrictive cultural connotations such as anonymity, commodification, and ethnic ghettoization.

Noted Luiseño artist Fritz Scholder came to epitomize this divide in the emerging contemporary Indian arts movement of the 1980s:

> In a way, I am a paradox. I have changed the direction of so-called Indian painting, but I don't consider myself an Indian painter. I am often called an "Indian artist" and I am on the official Government rolls, but still I am not simply an Indian painter.... An Indian artist must have the freedom to do anything he wants...like every other artist. To be strong, the work must come from a strong individual identity and then transcend all boundaries. If the artist is a full-blood Indian the work will be full-blood Indian and no one needs to worry about whether "Indian art" is coming to an end. [Highwater 1980:177]

The commercially successful artists from this study tend to employ the inclusion standpoint, especially when directly questioned whether they prefer to be called an Indian artist or simply an artist. I suggest that this direct line of questioning presents the interviewee with a limited repertoire of responses. If Indian artists answer in the positive—yes, primarily an Indian artist—the implication is that they produce crafts, their work is ahistorical, they are not interested in showing in exhibits and galleries that are not specific to Indian arts, and they are not current in fine arts dialogues. In these circumstances, the alignment as an artist in general may appear to be preferable. In a negative sense, a rejection of ethnicity is also politically problematic, for it may appear that the individual artists have garnered their success from association in ethnic contexts, only to turn around and toss away their heritage. This opportunistic reading is something that Native American artists and their peers are acutely tuned in to. Charges of appropriation, disloyalty, and selfishness are often levied at artists who alter their primary classification according to audience.

Reappropriation

The interpretative stance of reappropriation recognizes continuities between both indigenous and mainstream ideologies without elevating one or the other. This relativistic stance does not adhere to the comparative approach Hatcher advocates, nor does it seek to elevate Native arts to fine arts standards. Reappropriation calls for an active use of patterned modes of reception, taking as its point of reference the vast incongruities of Native arts interpretation. This attendance to the preconceptions and misconceptions of a largely unversed public could be argued to divert energies away from an engagement with indigenous norms—the "beauty way" of the Navajo, for example. The enactment of reappropriation makes the premises of Native arts misreadings (Native art is craft, Native artists are anonymous, they cannot be successful artists and Indian) real and available for debate, engagement, and even dispute.

Curator Joe Traugott (1992) uses the term *salvage* to describe the strategy of reappropriation. In his view, Native American artists are simply adopting the same ideology of Euro-Americans in salvaging material culture from native communities believed to be vanishing: "Just as the Cubists could tear tribal images from their cultural contexts, contemporary Native American artists can appropriate, totally out of the context of modernism, the cultural forms and aesthetic values of Euro-American consumer culture" (37). Using Whitehorse as an illustration, Traugott is careful to remind his readers of the clear distinction between Native appropriation of form (abstract expressionism) and the intended aim of the original work appropriated, stating that "similarity of mark does not indicate an analogy of content" (38).

In my own work with Whitehorse, she has indicated this difference not only in terms of form but also in terms of artistic process:

> NANCY MITHLO: Are there ways that you approach your work that are different because of your background?
>
> EMMI WHITEHORSE: I interact with a lot of…European artists, and their approach is always very different.… Their approach to their work is very cerebral. Everything is talked out. Everything is thought out, talked to death, over and over, written out precisely. And this is all before they even get started. They are very verbal in the sense that they really paint the angst, the anger, and all that emotion expressed so vividly, very visceral.… They project that emotion directly into the work as they're working. I can't work that way. I think that's something that comes from my background. It's always about seeking health, beauty, and harmony—everything has to be harmonious, well balanced. You seek that out in every aspect of your

life and your artwork. It's something I grew up with. When my grandmother worked, she would not impart her anger, her emotional pain. If she was upset with emotion, she would not work, because she was afraid that the work would become littered, filled up with those themes that were not balanced, not harmonious. And I find myself painting in the same manner. And I think that's one of the reasons why...I don't do works that are politically oriented or that show pain and angst. You don't see that because I have watched and learned how my grandmother approached her work. So you try in every aspect to be very mainstream, and sometimes you feel like you're pretty much integrated into the rest of the system of Western society, but there's always something to look at that makes you still feel like you are a foreigner. I find myself still even somehow always being very foreign.[3]

A key feature of reappropriation strategies is the existence of a "third eye" perspective. Film theorist Fatimah Tobing Rony (1996:4) describes this process as one in which a person of color living in the United States experiences "viewing oneself as an object." Rony cites W. E. B. DuBois's double consciousness as a similar enactment of recognition, seeing oneself as other—or, in Whitehorse's words, as "a foreigner." Rony extends this analysis to include recognition of the conditions that allow the differences to exist. A consciousness of the act of appropriating defines this strategy of addressing conceptual divides. Reappropriation will serve as this book's primary focus of investigation and alignment.

The documentation of these various art strategies—separatism, pluralism, and reappropriation—indicates that exclusive categories of analysis based on ethnic and racial differences do exist. Each of these approaches recognizes to varying degrees differential power: the separatist approach denies the power of a global economy; the inclusive analysis denies the power of racism and exclusion; and reappropriation assumes the ability of marginalized populations to enact a countercritique of established artistic paradigms, thus denying the reality of oppression.

Whitehorse's narrative illustrates the manner in which each of these strategies may interact. Although her positioning in the Western mainstream appears unproblematic and she has gained entry to the fine arts world on economic, educational, and formalistic grounds, her ability to reappropriate is limited by cultural values—she will not "litter" her work with negative feelings or features. This adherence to traditional standards, like her adherence to the process of preparing her canvases in the right manner and not being rushed, is identified as a Navajo trait learned by observing her grandmother. Both examples also have potential economic consequences: she risks exclusion by not conforming to select Western standards of form and content (canvas, political works, bright colors). Attending for a moment to the beauty of these alignments, Whitehorse demonstrates continuity and a holistic engagement in life and art that is unique to Native sensibilities. Are Whitehorse's choices, then, separatist rather than reappropriated or inclusive?

The uniqueness of Native American art sensibilities, including a de-emphasis of individuality, informs positioning within these restrictive categories. It is useful also to keep in mind that individual artists may adopt any one of the strategies during the course of a conversation or during the course of a career. The movement between competing paradigms of reception is an essential component of what is viewed by the artists as a right to self-expression in the arts. In this sense, it could be argued that the reappropriation strategy is actually a higher-order variable, with artists appropriating separatist and inclusive agendas as they so choose.

Writing in *Locating Cultural Creativity*, David Parkin (2001:135) describes the tendency of marginalized artists to transcend consumer "rules" yet maintain a belief in the cultural authenticity of their works, as "paradoxical inventiveness." The paradox of parodying consumer demands and simultaneously claiming unique identities is conceptualized as a result of cultural change—to "constantly make use of new materials and styles as they become available" (135). This recombining and reincorporating carries the double danger of either reifying essentialist stereotypes opportunistically or accommodating "so many diverse cultural contacts and emotional ploys that their politically ethnic voice loses its distinctiveness. At the same time they proclaim their distinctiveness" (134). Parkin argues that a homogenization results from these endless borrowings, leading to the creation of a "cultural field" rather than any type of traditional ethnic culture. In his example, a Swahili cultural field results not as an essentialized entity but as "one according to which different communities, especially those distant from each other, may be similar in only one or two respects but contrast in many others" (142).

Having identified some of the ways in which indigenous arts are figured to be distinct, I wish to turn now to examining under what circumstances a "culture field" exists for debate in Native American representations. In particular, I am interested in the validity of pan-Indian or indigenous constructs and their usefulness in engaging the reappropriation strategies defined above. Is Parkin's homogenization evident, or does the concept of a cultural field allow for useful positioning in Native arts reception?

"That Dual World": Pan-Indian Debates

NANCY MITHLO: Can you tell me something about your background? How you grew up, when you first started thinking of yourself as an artist, if you were supported or not?

EMMI WHITEHORSE: I wasn't good at anything as a kid. I failed at everything. I was the most miserable student anybody could have in school, but I knew I could draw and work. And that helped me get going forward. Just knowing I could do that one little thing better than anybody else just helped me keep going. And the fact that I was stubborn, I guess.

I grew up on the eastern reservation of the Navajo reservation. It was very remote, almost treeless. It was like a moonscape, almost. I grew up with my mother and my grandmother. My dad was never around, so the kids sort of helped each other grow up, because Mother was never there. So we all had to fend for ourselves most of the time, and we were raised half and half…half at home and half at an institution that was a boarding school—a government boarding school. So, at an early age, we were already learning how to balance the two, the white world and Navajo life. I hated it very much—the fact that I was taken away at such an early age—but then at the same time, I was sort of glad that I learned how to live that dual world.

NANCY MITHLO: Was it like a skill?

EMMI WHITEHORSE: Yes. For me it became automatic. You clicked into place, you did this over here, and you clicked off and then did something else over here. So that early start, I guess, helped me also later on when I got to the university. It was sort of like back in boarding school. I thought…"I've been here before. I know what to do." So I wasn't really belittled by that university environment, because a lot of Native Americans, when they first come to the university, are just totally overwhelmed by the atmosphere, and they go one year and that's it, and they just drop out. I think that's what helped me stay in school.

NANCY MITHLO: Which boarding school was this?

EMMI WHITEHORSE: This was one that was provided by the US government, and it was on the Navajo reservation, but it was in Crown

Point, which was still quite a ways away from home for me. And when I was taken away, I was about five years old, and I remember the first day that I was taken...my mother took me to school to drop me off...I was so terrified, but I couldn't show it. I couldn't cry. I couldn't do anything. I just thought to myself, "I have to be brave, and I have to fend for myself, and I have to do this. Nobody's going to help me." Even then I was very inward and very quiet. So I hung out with some...I tried to make...you try to make friends very quickly, so that's sort of what I did. And I guess a lot of other kids...all of us had traumatic problems too.... They didn't know how to cope, either.

NANCY MITHLO: Would those same skills carry on in what you use to market your work now? Do you see the gallery scene...?

EMMI WHITEHORSE: Every system has...every business aspect of whatever has a system, and you just learn how to play the system. Yeah, I...if I could survive that, I could survive anything.[4]

M. Annette Jaimes, in "American Indian Studies: Toward an Indigenous Model," argues that a global perspective has led to a situation in which

> for all their obvious differences, indigenous peoples have certain things in common...1) ways of relating to the habitat which are non-disruptive, at least to the extent that they allow for the perpetual coexistence of humans and other organic life...and 2) the fact that virtually all of the peoples in question have been conquered, colonized and ultimately encapsulated within one or another modern nation-state. In short, the historical experiences of indigenous peoples the world over during the past five centuries show in many ways an almost overwhelming commonality. [Jaimes 1987:12–13]

This general conclusion is supported by Whitehorse's narrative, which not only demonstrates the suffering inherent in government boarding-school policy but also extends this observation to other Native American children, kids who "had traumatic problems too.... They didn't know how to cope, either."

Jaimes's argument for the existence of a Fourth World or indigenous identity in response to historical oppression is evidenced in the earlier work of Edward H. Spicer, in reference to Indians in the Southwest. Spicer's analysis articulates the importance of historical experience, identifying what he terms the most common form of this experience—"discrimination":

> The Indians…have, in every case where they survive with an active sense of identity, undergone distinctive experiences as compared with non-Indians. They have seen portions of their land appropriated by others, land associated with a mythology of the past and regarded as sacred. They have experienced the invasion of their communities by traders, bureaucrats, and missionaries, who insist on maintaining their own ways of life and pushing these ways on the Indians. They have been made aware of the ethnic classifications used by the invaders and have watched the success or failure of various plans for changing the Indians' ways…, in some degree the nature of the events and of the relations established with the non-Indians have been apparent to each generation.… It is in some form or other a part of Indian consciousness, but not until recently perceived by dominants. [Spicer 1972:26–27]

Tensions between asserting a communal identity referent (indigenous or pan-Indian) and championing an individualistic or tribal sensibility appear to exist in a continuous dialogue that extends to history, literary studies, sociology, anthropology, and political science. My aim here is to ground these resounding debates in the discussion of Native American women's articulations of their negotiations in the Western arts market. Whitehorse's narrative evidences the poignancy of historic events—events that were dictated by the US government and that extended to most, if not all, tribes of America. The boarding school experience, like LaMarr's relocation episode, was a political and social tool for assimilation of Indians into American society (Heyer 1990; Lomawaima 1994; Mihesuah 1993; Szasz 1974). These government initiatives impacted Native Americans specifically; they were "various plans for changing the Indians' ways" (Spicer 1972:26).

The existence of a pan-Indian sensibility has been critiqued both by Native Americans and activists who believe that tribal traditions are lost in the embracement of a homogenized identity and by intellectuals who deny the validity of this generalized descriptive. Authors Terry Straus and Debra Valentino discuss how concerns over the development of an intertribal "Indian" in the American Indian community were common in the 1970s, when pan-Indianism was understood inevitably to displace tribal knowledge, identity, and connection for Native Americans in urban areas: "Pan-Indianism, an artificial foil invented to facilitate federal policy, was seen gradually and insidiously to become accepted by Indian people as their own identity" (Straus and Valentino 2001:85–86). This tendency to accept dominant definitions of themselves as an "ethnic group" and a "racial minority" was interpreted at the time as internal colonization and a loss of self-determination.

Straus and Valentino conclude that detribalization, which was feared in the 1970s as a consequence of urban relocation, has developed into retribalization, wherein urban Indians forge relationships with their home communities from an urban base. Straus and Valentino's argument advances two parallel points: first, "the rift between urban and reservation Indian people is artificial and imposed" (Straus and Valentino 2001:86)—urban in this view is not a kind of Indian, but an experience that most Indian people have had—and, second, the concept of a tribe is an invention of the US government. "'Tribe' was neither a Native concept nor a native political reality. Tribes began in the conflict and negotiation with non-Indian governments" (86). Defined territories, political units, and tribal leaders were identified to facilitate the concession of lands and rights in the treaty-making phase of American history. This codification of tribal identities was further elaborated under the Indian Reorganization Act of 1934.

Straus and Valentino's second argument of historically determined identities is extended to critique the idea that intertribal identities are somehow recent and exist only in urban settings:

> While it is popular, politically correct, and in many ways important to note that Indian people did not think of themselves as Indians until they were so identified by others, it must be simultaneously asserted that intertribal exchange of items, ideas, and individuals occurred long before European presence in the "New World." [Straus and Valentino 2001:87]

A fluidity of identity—in which urban and rural Native peoples identify as Indians and as members of a particular tribe or tribes situationally and at different points in the life cycle—is advanced. This last point is important to the present analysis as artists situationally choose to align their work with separatist or pluralist ideologies.

The historic academic argument against pantribal identities is one of accuracy and of injustice. In *The White Man's Indian* (1979), Robert Berkhofer objects to generalizing from one tribe to all Indians and, conversely, to ascribing generalized traits of all Indians to one tribe. He summarizes:

> The famous reporters on Native American cultures in the colonial period of the United States, for example, invariably treated their tribe(s) as similar enough to all other Indians in customs and beliefs to serve as illustrations of that race in thought and deed. Even in the century that saw the rise of professional anthropology, most social

scientists as well as their White country-men continued to speak and write as if a specific tribe and all Indians were interchangeable for the purposes of description and understanding of fundamental cultural dynamics and social organization. Today, most Whites who use the word *Indian* have little idea of the specific tribal peoples or individual Native Americans to render their usage much more than an abstraction, if not a stereotype. [Berkhofer 1979:26]

He also emphasizes the "remarkable" persistence and perpetuation of the idea of the Indian despite "changes in intellectual and political currents and alterations in social and economic institutions" (31).

It is important to note how Berkhofer dismisses the general category of Indians while using the concept of whites unproblematically. Aren't both terms gross generalizations? His argument is historic and moralistic as he decries the injustice of white commentators both inventing and then using Indian stereotypes to prove their own sense of superiority. While seeming to advance Native American political causes, this argument simultaneously casts the Indian as an inactive and helpless victim to these mechanisms of white power. In Berkhofer's narrative, Indian people who embrace a pantribal identity for their own ends are seen as opportunistic and self-colonizing (196). This analysis effectively inhibits pantribal political organizing as a useful tool for social justice. Key to assessing Berkhofer's legacy is the consideration of the era in which he wrote—the late 1970s—when both Indians and progressive non-Indians protested the apparent loss of Native heritage inherent in a generalized Indian identity construct.

The year in which Berkhofer's text was written, 1978, was also the year in which the US Indian Claims Commission stopped hearing cases for compensation of lands seized, the year in which the Indian Child Welfare Act was passed to stem the flow of Indian children from being adopted out to non-Native families, and the year in which the American Indian Religious Freedom Act was passed to ensure equal access to religious practice. While each of these mandates certainly signals a more progressive era on the horizon, their very establishment is evidence of the vast neglect and discrimination of Native peoples immediately before. Could the conflation of pan-Indian reflexes with damaging stereotypes be the result of historical circumstance? Is it time now to untangle these clusters of meaning to allow a consideration of the progressive aspects of pantribal designations?

Pan-Indianism Revisited

More current works appear simultaneously to disavow the existence of a generalized Indian identity and then to use a pantribal referent or to recognize the use of both frames of reference strategically, as Straus and Valentino (2001) advance. Writing on Native American autobiographical traditions, Hertha Dawn Wong states that "defining a Native American identity is an especially treacherous endeavor, since such diverse native cultures and nations cannot be collapsed into one undifferentiated category," adding that "contrary to some romanticized version of communal identity, even within a specific tribe, individuality abounded" (1992:13). She then proceeds to make such pantribal generalizations, naming communal values, spiritual context, and identification with the land as central tenets of a Native sensibility. In response, Native writer and scholar Gerald Vizenor (1993:24) claims that Wong's "panoramic sense of tribal identities" lacks nuance and is overly romantic. He illustrates how the complexity of these constructs can be understood with the example of personal stories and visions, which were "heard alone, but not in cultural isolation or separation from tribal communities" (27).

Writing on Native American stereotypes and archetypes, Scott B. Vickers decries efforts "to deprive Indians of their heterogeneous identities and histories so that white colonists might more easily advance their Christian agenda of imperial homogeneity" (1998:9). In this analysis, homogeneity is acceptable on the tribal level but not on a pantribal frame of reference:

> The...traditional approach to Indian art is principally concerned with maintaining the homogeneous identity of the personal unconscious of the tribe, its unique symbols and images, while the emerging individuated Indian artist is more concerned with his or her relationship with the larger heterogeneous community of symbolic emotions that derive from the collective unconsciousness and are then filtered through that individual's consciousness. In addition, it should be noted that the recognition of one level does not preclude a recognition of the other, and that indeed both symbolic reservoirs can and do act together in creating individuated art. [Vickers 1998:114–115]

Interestingly, the movement between individuality and communal norms is deemed legitimate in Vickers's analysis only for the political construct of tribal identity and not for the political construct of pantribal sensibilities. This exclusiveness of acceptance seems inconsistent in the same manner that Berkhofer dismisses Indianness but takes whiteness as a given. Both constructs stem from the same inclination to segment disparate groups for predetermined purposes. Rather than assign ill intent or misguidedness to boundary construction and maintenance, a more productive analysis seeks to understand how the act of segmentation supports group aims. *Individuality, tribe, communal,* and *pantribal* all reference layered realities and relative points of departure that are utilized opportunistically by whites and Natives alike.

This analytical movement towards comprehending the logic of both mainstream and ethnic group claims is evidenced by Joel Pfister's (2004) observations on the centrality of individuality for American identity. Pfister argues that the concept of individualism is a historically constituted abstraction used to serve changing ideological needs. These abstractions also carry the potential for exploitation and oppression, as in the enforcement of individualism on Native American communities in the boarding school context. The ideological construction of both the individual and the communal says as much about American identity formation and maintenance as it does about Native American group sensibilities. Importantly for this analysis, Pfister notes how the imposition of identity (via government policy or in less obvious forms, such as stereotypes) is often mobilized opportunistically:

> Obviously, culturally contrived labels for persons or groups who did not originally classify themselves as one group eventually become real and influential when their social circulation is persuasive and meanings assigned to them are accepted as commonsensical. However, meanings ascribed to such labels can be altered to fit new struggles and circumstances. [Pfister 2004:20]

He adds:

> In the twentieth century...natives from many tribes self-consciously Indianized themselves in the process of redefining the White category of *Indian* through such means as the formation of pan-Indian political organizations, the publication of pan-Indian political magazines, the founding of schools, the writings of fiction and autobiographies, and the creation of art and music. [20]

Central historical studies on the history of pan-Indian organizations, such as Hazel W. Hertzberg's *The Search for an American Indian Identity: Modern Pan-Indian Movements* (1971), give weight to this type of critical analysis. In my own experience, I have found that reference to a Native American identity is challenged only when one cannot identify a tribal nation or family to which one belongs as a member. Upon arrival at the pantribal IAIA as a student in the mid-1980s, I was cornered by Jake (not his real name), an older Apache student who had attended the school years back and was only then completing his degree. Jake's seniority and age dictated that his determination of my status would be definitive in this new social environment.

"So, they say you're Apache," Jake ventured. "Where're you from?" Innocently, I answered, "North Carolina," the state I had moved from to attend the school. Obviously entertained, Jake smiled and shot back, "North Carolina? What kind of Apache are you?" I had understood too late the real meaning of his question and replied, "Oh! You want to know what tribe I am!" I went on to explain that our tribal designation was the Fort Sill Chiricahua Warm Springs Apache Tribe of Oklahoma but that my uncle would say that this was our "hang around the fort" name and that I should only say Chiricahua Apache. Jake was thrilled. "Who is your uncle?" he asked. It turned out that I was related to Jake by way of my great-grandfather, who was his grandmother's brother. From that time on, I was known at the IAIA as "that white Indian girl with North Carolina plates."

After having spent many years at the IAIA, as both a student and a researcher, my identity as an alumna would identify me as a Native person. But this pantribal identity would not be valid until I had established myself as a member of a specific tribe and family. As Nancy Shoemaker argues in reference to Indians in Minneapolis, "members of pan-Indian organizations always identified individual members by tribe, even though the organization labeled itself as Indian. One could not be Indian without belonging to a tribe or tribes" (1988:446). Her work demonstrates how the use of popularized images of Indian cultures by urban Indian organizations established a "common ground" that thereby allowed for the subsequent expression and reinforcement of specific tribal ethnic identities.

If Native Americans exercise some level of agency in choosing how to align or reject pantribal and tribal identities, in what ways are actions also restricted? Adopting Vizenor's and Pfister's premise that movement between individualistic and communal concerns is contingent and motivated, I wish to briefly explore how these boundaries are not only trespassed but also maintained. The area of my research where this concern was most evident was in the issue of censorship and self-censorship.

"Don't Do That": Restrictions in Native American Art

NANCY MITHLO: Who is an audience for you?

LAURA FRAGUA COTA: I think of a time, well—I have this one poster I did in commemoration of the 1680 Pueblo Indian Revolt.... We had the three-hundred-year anniversary in 1980, and I did this poster, and in it I have a woman and a man. The man is holding a spear, angry, facing one direction. And he's facing…in the background there is the Spanish flag. Because of all the tragedy that they conquered them and came, they had burned the masks of the religious dancers. And so in that poster I wanted to show that, masks…and have it on fire. There's the man and the woman and the Spanish flag and the church, and there's a priest. And I wanted to put that mask burning. I showed it to my Dad, and he kinda got upset, because he said, "You better not do that—better not show that mask burning." And I said, "But that's what happened." He said, "You better not do that. The people are going to be…they are going to say something." And that was the only one that I would say that I was told not to be making or had some questions about showing that particular depiction of that mask on that poster.

NANCY MITHLO: So do you figure that your family would be the most important—the people that you would answer to?

LAURA FRAGUA COTA: You see…there again, too, I think that even though I do work and I consider myself an individual, I am still a part of that people. And I will always be. Whether I live in the village or not. And there are things…just because I am away from the reservation does not give me the right to talk about whatever I want or show or make whatever I want to make. It's that responsibility. And I am sure there are those who don't take that responsibility. "Oh, I don't care. I don't live over there. What do they give me?" But that's not how I feel. I mean, there are things that I will fight if I feel that I have that right to do so. But there are certain things that I feel, because I am a part of this community, that I cannot do or I cannot show. And I feel that my dad was correct in saying, "Don't do that."[5]

I have presented an argument that Native American artists self-consciously choose aspects of ethnicity or individuality strategically to achieve aims and goals. All the artists with whom I worked had experience in the economic, social, and educational contexts of Santa Fe, New Mexico, the mecca of Indian arts commerce. So it is with a sense of sophistication and savvy that these artists maneuver through the artistic paradigms I have sketched here—individualism versus communalism, ethnicity versus autonomy, separatist versus inclusive. By articulating the paradigm of recontextualization, I hope to advance an alternative "third eye" approach to the strict classificatory boundaries that have defined ethnic arts for so long. The "third eye" approach references the ability to, as Rony states (1996:4), "view oneself as an object." Rony's central question—"What does one become when one sees that one is not fully recognized as Self by the wider society but cannot fully identify as Other?" (6)—is answered in the crucial awareness of self via the interrogation and creative adoption of conventional representations. Patterns of restriction typically follow the type of censorship by institutional forces documented at the beginning of this chapter. LaMarr's motivation in studying art at Berkeley was to speak to the disempowerment of Native American populations via contemporary Native art exhibits in mainstream non-Indian environments, such as museums. Yet even here she was restricted in her ability to convey cultural truths.

> So I went to Berkeley…it was right after the Third World strike, and Alcatraz had just finished, and Wounded Knee was still going on, and the occupation was going on. So I was doing art training, taking Native American studies classes—it was real important that I have this information there at work. But they wouldn't allow me at that time. They wouldn't allow any kind of cultural input or social commentary. [The artwork] had to be very abstract, so that's how I tended to work. I would lay down the foundation.… To me, it was a finished piece because it was an abstract, a color-field. So after I'd go through critique, I'd go back home and lay the rest of the stuff—the collage—and that's how I ended up working from then on. It…was a matter of layering, because this is what they forced me to do. Now this is what I do.

LaMarr's ability to respond creatively to the controls of her environment by manipulating the standards of abstract art with collage after her official university critique represents a classic form of reappropriation. But what of internal restraints, such as Fragua Cota's?

I intend to indicate a self-awareness and sense of agency. Reappropriation, however, is not a consistent strategy in the sense that not all things may be utilized—not all actions, objects, and forms may be adopted as a Native artist—even though economic or social consequences from the mainstream may result. As Fragua Cota notes, the consequences in terms of her community are greater than her investment in individually making a political and artistic statement. This allegiance to community is key to understanding the unique nature of Native arts production and circulation.

Writing in the *European Review of Native American Studies*, Armin W. Geertz (1991) notes how many contemporary Native American artists encounter quite different constraints than their Euro-American colleagues. He states that Native artists are culturally obliged to take into consideration the opinions of their parents and elders—more so than their Euro-American colleagues. In the example he provides, successful Native artists are often expected to take on the role of cultural spokespeople, "but, by their very youth, they do not have the right to be cultural spokespersons...cultural heritage is transmitted by knowers who are competent in their culture" (Geertz 1991:2). Competency in this regard is defined by wisdom, age, and cultural rights, not economic or social success in the mainstream.

I end this chapter with rather extreme references to censorship. I say "extreme" because I am not certain that *censorship* is the right term to utilize when describing the actions of artists who care about cultural constraints. Censorship in the arts connotes the withdrawal of public funding, the closure of offensive exhibits, the resignation of museum directors. All these connotations seem inaccurate, not only because these censorship activities usually involve the works of established artists in mainstream art venues but also because they imply an artist alienated from his or her own community, being attacked by that community. Are the events recounted in Jemez Pueblo artist Fragua Cota's narrative, then, to be considered censorship? A more useful term might be *refusal*, as articulated by Audra Simpson (2006). *Refusal* connotes a knowing denial of participation, a sharing in accordance with a higher good of communal values and beliefs.

Writing in Carol Becker's *The Subversive Imagination: Artists, Society, and Social Responsibility* (1994), B. Ruby Rich notes how those who organized against censorship in the arts in the late 1980s were mainly white and middle-class: "It was only these groups, in general, that had the sense of entitlement necessary to galvanize outrage at its withdrawal...members of other groups felt that they were already the victims of an on-going censorship that hid under the less formal banner of exclusion and was never protested" (Rich 1994:229). She advocates that the arts move from the isolation of the individual ego to the "call and response connection that links each one to some sort of community" (238). What, then, would Rich, the advocate of socially responsible arts, say in response to Fragua Cota's withdrawal of her commemorative poster, a poster that in many ways represents a pro-sovereign community statement?

Native artists often do not have a ready audience that understands these distinctions outside of their own tribal or pantribal communities. Even Native peers tend to shy away from discussing or taking a definitive stand on issues of the appropriateness of artistic choices that may be controversial, especially in terms of religion. A wonderfully rich and slightly humorous 1961 essay by Rosalie H. Wax and Robert K. Thomas titled "American Indians and White People" addresses these nuances. Refreshing for its candid nature (I imagine that a piece like this would be more difficult to publish in America's current nervous, race-conscious mood), the article addresses the importance of noninterference in Indian communities: "From earliest childhood he is trained to regard absolute non-interference in interpersonal relations as decent or normal and to react to even the mildest coercion in these areas with bewilderment, disgust and fear" (Wax and Thomas 1961:310). Noting that even "the most sensitive white persons who have lived with Indians are aware of this phenomenon," the authors conclude that "none have successfully described it in general terms" (310). They illustrate the noninterference behavior with examples (such as a passenger not informing a driver that he missed a turn), providing an antidote for cases in which individuals did not display proper decorum: "You do not take the words of an insane person seriously or get angry with him" (315).

The choices artists make within their own communities are thus particularly laden with complexities and not as subject to debate or discussion as issues of process, medium, or message might be (see plate 7). Navajo artist Gloria Emerson describes how the "tensions" in this area are conceived:

> The other thing I might have mentioned ten years ago is that Navajo, the early aesthetic was that women didn't paint or do figurative work. And there were very strong reasons for it. But in the time that I've been home, back on the reservation, I see more and more weavers doing the figures and the weavings and other kind of figurative work...the feeling of taboo or shyness about doing this, and I feel this real strong tension when I do figurative work.... And I often don't know why I paint the figurative work in the way I do, but I do feel this great tension because I know that Navajo women were not supposed to do this. And now I've moved into a new era where all taboos have gone out the window, so to speak.
>
> In the old way, the figurines were not done—they were done as a part of a curing, and they were done to heal a person. And so usually figures were made under that, as part of a ritual. They're part of ritual knowledge, and only the medicine people know that. And they then take those, and they place them somewhere out and bury them. The illness is buried and destroyed in that way so that the patient can be healed. And so that's how those figures—figurines—were used, but they were very properly placed away, given back to nature. And so here we are in our ignorance creating these figures without understanding what we are doing, understanding how, what taboos were associated with this.

NANCY MITHLO: Is it a double taboo because of not only the content but the medium as well?

GLORIA EMERSON: I don't know how to answer that, but...I, when I was painting here at SAR [the School for Advanced Research], I was thinking about sand painting, and I began to incorporate those sands from those places from the myths I created. So let's say Table Mesa—I went and collected the sands from Table Mesa, and then I incorporated it into the paintings that have to do with Table Mesa. And then that way it was grounding my work—it was making it more real, although the work, somebody might look at and think that they're nonobjective abstract painting, but the sands created that reality for me. But it also is referencing that tradition of ours, the sand painting tradition.[6]

The variables of individualism, gender, realism, religion, cultural change, and artistic medium all interrelate in this passage, which confounds the appraisal of most established art paradigms. The exercise of the "freedom" to depict images that were once restricted is not celebrated or even championed but is a cause for intense introspection and personal tension. Gender roles are altered not for a feminist agenda but because of a personal desire; the term *realism* does not conform to formalistic definitions but to definitions of material and process; religious mandates are not rejected but honored; change is accepted as inevitable. These counterintuitive readings may seem to imply that Native arts ideologies are, in Whitehorse's words, "foreign" to fine arts practices. As community members and individuals, Native women artists traverse ideological patterns in ways instructive to an understanding of how art works in community. These selective borrowings and reappropriations of process and products provide answers to exclusions and insights into restrictions, even self-imposed ones.

Notes

1. Quotations from Jean LaMarr in this chapter are from the author's interview with her, May 16, 1991.
2. Emmi Whitehorse, interview by author, May 8, 1991.
3. Whitehorse, interview, September 18, 2000.
4. Whitehorse, interview, March 15, 1991.
5. Laura Fragua Cota, interview by author, February 5, 1991.
6. Gloria Emerson, interview by author, December 7, 2002.

3 Born an Artist

NANCY MITHLO: I was reading over the interview we did last time, and one thing that I started talking about was your role as an artist and how you define that role—what motivates you, who your audience is, that kind of thing. Do you want to start there?

EMMI WHITEHORSE: [*laughs*] I don't know as to...exactly how to respond to that—I mean, the question of my role as an artist, because I'm finding out more and more...in a lot of the—according to Navajo philosophy, it's all one thing. They're not such separate things. It's still—I just still see it as pretty much lifestyle, just something that I feel like I was born into doing, not that I had a calling to do it. It's something that I feel like I was innately born to, born into, I guess.[1]

I began this inquiry about the culture of Native American arts by problematizing conventional domains of thought: Natives as passive victims, the universality of negative stereotyping, and the idea that culturally specific identities are the only authentic renderings allowed as sensitive and accurate image referents. A central concern of this book is the sense that contemporary Native American artists are falsely confined to regional and ethnic spheres instead of belonging to more universalist fine art realms. Talking seriously about any ethnic arts requires an engagement with notions of individualism and the collective. Ethnic qualifiers in the fine arts automatically connote a paradigm that privileges unconstrained individual freedom while rejecting communal imperatives (Fagg 1969). Ethnic artists who speak outside this agenda are rarely taken seriously under Western hegemonies of universal and objective fine arts criteria. Alternative agendas—carefully groomed and presented—are tolerated only within prescribed arenas of difference.

In the Native American arts market, these tensions may be described as the fine arts/crafts divide. Native American crafts are assumed to be communally based, historically accurate, and tribally specific. If Native American artists wish to exhibit under fine arts imperatives, they must become white by rejection of their tribal status ("I'm an artist first, an Indian second"). Alternatively, they can attempt to reconfigure the fine arts market by way of critique ("There's no word for *art* in my language") or choose to segregate themselves from the mainstream ("I live in two worlds"). These counter-ideologies are reactive, ineffective for social change, and ultimately reifying of status quo modes of reception.

I recognize that this generalized critique may appear overtly biased and resentful. I think such a polemical stance is required, however, in engaging narratives, such as Whitehorse's, that refuse to segment artistic practice as an exclusive enterprise but rather characterize the arts as a philosophical belief system. This insistence on a totality of life and artistic endeavors necessitates a reconfiguration of existing interpretative parameters. Clearly, my use of the social science concept of role did not match Whitehorse's cognitive reality. In what sense, then, can a more accurate reading be applied? What category of consideration is mobilized in lieu of the simplistic division of individual fine artist versus cultural group artist? What is the significance of arts training and professional arts identification for understanding the representation of Native American identity?

Confusion exists from the outset in examining the significance of being born an artist. In one sense, this testimonial could be read as a claim for intuitive knowledge, that Indians are naturally adept at the arts. The problem with this interpretation is its apparently uncritical embrace of essentialist categories—what Edward Said (1978) would describe as its "exteriority," the Western technique for representation that relies on traditions, conventions, and agreed-upon codes. To say that someone is born an artist in materialistic terms would imply that no formal instruction is necessary. It also would suggest that a biological connection is inherent between Native ancestry and skill in illustration. Although these arguments certainly exist in public discourse—and have existed historically (Gere 2004)—I propose that this interpretative stance misreads the more complex and intertwined rationales for its use. To be born an artist rejects the power of formal Western art training. To be born an artist argues that arts are inseparable from other aesthetic systems of thought. To be born an artist separates the production of art from its consumption. These rationales lie hidden from examination while the more direct, biological read proceeds right along.

A careful reading of Whitehorse's 2000 interview suggests some of these alternative understandings:

> I feel like this is what I was born into, until there isn't anything else that I can do outside of what I am doing now. But you never know, you know? If the bottom drops out of the art world, I could certainly go do something else just to make ends meet. I'm not afraid of doing that....
>
> I guess it's the freedom that it gives to me. It's a very particular kind of field for a certain kind of knowledge that you possess and something that you have to play with, be able to play in that particular playground. And some people have a very hard time being in that world or that kind of artistic energy. And it's a very special kind of energy. It's a very special kind...you feel as a gift for, or a profession, and somehow I feel that you are blessed with it in some way, shape, or form and only you can do that. And I think that makes it special every day. And you go into the studio and you do that. [It's] a special playground where nobody can go but you. I find that a very special, highly specialized area, and I think that makes it exciting, and I think maybe that's what gives motivation. That gives me the motivation to get up, do this every day.

In this passage, the economic returns of the market are deemphasized; Whitehorse could make a living elsewhere. Her craft is specialized—not in a biological sense, for she's not arguing that only Indians are born artists—but in the sense that she possesses "a certain kind of knowledge." Does this specialness indicate that she places herself purely outside materialistic concerns, as the prototype of the gifted artist, marginal, eccentric, removed? This classic interpretation of the arts, one characterized by Janet Wolff in *The Social Production of Art* (1981:10) as "a paradox posed as one of the timeless problems of the artist," is itself a fiction. Wolff convincingly argues, "The artist/author as some kind of asocial being, blessed with genius, waiting for divine inspiration and exempt from all normal rules of social intercourse, is...very much an ahistorical and limited one" (12).

Whitehorse actively moves between both ideological concepts critiqued here—one essentialist and biological, the other ahistorical and ideological. Art is not "above" social and political considerations as an archetypal role or as an inherent racial designation. These fictions are, however, real constructs that enable a testimonial of place and tribal philosophy. The strategic rejection of the Native artistic role does not indicate the uncritical acceptance of the Western genius artist role. Similarly, the description of the special nature of the artist does not translate into a distancing from values of extended community. Her engagement in one theoretical category—the fine arts world—should not indicate her rejection of another—Navajo philosophy. These realms of interaction may thus be simultaneously accessed and aligned with or rejected in an active and strategic manner.

In an analysis of Northwest Coast Native art, Judith Ostrowitz (1999: 16) refers to this manipulation of existing codes as a means of showing reverence for ancestors, as well as an exercise in authority—"to respond to the present as expressed through selective reference." Her argument presents the counterintuitive finding that reproductions in Northwest Coast art serve as "forceful assertions of ownership of the native past" (17). I use the term *counterintuitive* in reference to the prevailing notion that the new and unique are valued above all else in the fine arts, whereas contemporary Northwest Coast artisans producing replicas or commissions conceive of themselves as citing history and exercising authority, not recycling or imitating.

I want to apply this example of counterreading to the more cognitive features of Native arts production. Rather than interpret the use of dominant artistic paradigms in a straightforward manner, I wish to regard their appropriations in narrative forms as secondary readings. Matti Bunzl (2004:441) describes this reappropriation methodology as a "genealogy of secondary explanation." Specifically, Bunzl calls for the examination of secondary explanations as "historically specific fictions" that reproduce social and discursive differences (441). In this frame of reference, "the reality of cultural boundaries would emerge as the object of analytic scrutiny, requiring rigorous historicization in place of ethnographic naturalization" (440). This "history of the present" approach would then allow for the emulation of fine arts practice (including individualism) while simultaneously asserting an alternative perspective of inclusiveness that is rooted in unique philosophical belief systems (holism and the collective).

This alternative reading of social fictions and their appropriations may be productively applied to the arts-related narrative discourses identified above. The prototypical Indian art clichés "I live in two worlds," "There's no word for *art* in my language," and "I'm an artist first, an Indian second" are thus strategically put to use as modifications, and even rejections, of Western fine art concepts. The disavowal of the term *art*, for example, signals a critique of beliefs and attitudes that are seen as integral to Western arts culture, including primacy of form and aesthetic judgment; the manufacture of nonutilitarian objects; notions of upper-class consumption; and, most important, individualism. "I'm an artist first, an Indian second" argues the opposite assumption. This standardized appeal privileges the individualistic nature of arts production and exchange, elevating the economic value of the object as a noncraft product. "I live in two worlds" pulls back from this inclusive strategy to assert that Indian life is categorically separate and unique and that fine arts mandates may not be accurately applied.

Although these reappropriations may be interpreted as reifying dichotomies of the individual and the collective, I suggest that their performances serve as a means of owning, controlling, and redirecting existing interpretative frameworks for subjective alternative ends. Mimesis in this sense is "to live in a different way with the understanding that artifice is natural" (Taussig 1993:255). Taussig calls this "the unbearable truths of make-believe...a foundation of an all-too-seriously serious reality, manipulated but also manipulatable" (225). If all reality is make-believe, as Taussig argues, then appropriations of essentialized identities indicate not victimhood but its opposite—agency and control, "the power of the copy to influence what it is a copy of" (250). Taussig calls for a dialectical imaging, the give and take of appearance and reproduction.

I find Taussig's argument to be empowering and, in many ways, revelatory, yet his "constructionism" problematically concludes with the notion that there is no such thing as identity (Taussig 1993:254). How, then, to reconcile this postmodern sensibility with the appeals of Native writer and critic Louis Owens, who describes this reappropriative movement in terms of masks:

> The mask is one realized over centuries through Euro-America's construction of the "Indian" Other. In order to be recognized, and to thus have a voice that is heard by those in control of power, the native must step into that mask and *be* the Indian constructed by white America...to be seen and heard at all by the center...the Native must pose as the absolute fake, the fabricated "Indian." [Owens 2001:17]

In contradiction to Taussig's dialectical interpretation, Owens concludes, "The Native, in turn, finds no reflection directed back from the center, no recognition of 'being' from that direction" (17). I will explore this quandary of victimization and empowerment via image construction by way of subjective testimonials from Native women artists. My inquiry will ascertain the pertinent domains of image discourse and how they are constructed. The political nature of Indian arts, the impact of indigenous institutions, and the conceptualization of a land-based tribal sensibility serve as prominent themes in this discussion.

Stuck in Our Own Stereotypes

LAURA FRAGUA COTA: To me, I don't think the institute...the thing that I was drawn to the institute [for] was...the people. I don't think...for me it was the access to tools. Tools and the space—they didn't teach me the creativity. They didn't teach me how to express myself. They just gave me the tools.

I guess it depends on what kind of teaching you want. There are different teaching methods, and there are different students who require different teachings. There are students who need very close contact with the teacher. And there are those who need just to be free to do whatever they want. And I think, a lot of times, teachers just say, "Here are your tools. Go out," rather than "This tools is for this. This tool is for that. If you do this, that will happen." And I think that needs to be more stressed. Let them know what the tools will do. Let them know whatever medium is available and what it can do and how you can do it, rather than "Here are your tools. Go for it." It's like...I mean, they [the students] are afraid. They don't want to.... They are like little babies: "Teach me, teach me. I want to know. Don't think just because I am a student at the school, I know how to do it. No, that's why I'm coming to school—so you can teach me."

NANCY MITHLO: Do you feel that people do that from your background—from your Indian background? That people might say, "You must have learned this at home" or "You have a natural inclination"?

LAURA FRAGUA COTA: Yeah, but I think, too, we are stuck in our own stereotypes. "Well, you're an Indian; you know how to do this," you know. And no, I don't.

NANCY MITHLO: You mean that Indian professors would say that to Indian students like that?

LAURA FRAGUA COTA: I would think that sometimes they would. I guess, even in joking. I'll have some banners at the federal building, and they joke around and say, "Well, you're a Pueblo Indian. You like to climb ladders." [laughs] It's like, "You get up there!"[2]

I want to turn to a consideration of the formal response to a fine arts affiliation—arts training. While the social world of arts may be described in more holistic terms (by the assertion of being born an artist), testimonials of encounters in arts institutions, both Native and non-Native, reveal the tensions inherent in both using and reappropriating established arts hegemonies. Fragua Cota's narrative reflects the ideology that Native people are inherently artistic while also critiquing this essentialist stance. Her description of the Institute of American Indian Arts (IAIA), a tribal arts college, bridges the conceptual divides of the individual and the collective in complex ways.

For example, her assertion "They just gave me the tools" indicates an alignment with the idea that the arts are an integral part of a Native social world. Art school did not confer upon her a creative nature; her creativity is inherent in her identity as a Native person. Yet this somewhat biological assertion cannot therefore be extended to the practical matter of working with the materials—the media of artistic practice. Here, Fragua Cota's interview resonates with Wolff's premise that, above all, the arts are a materialistic practice. Arts production is inescapably tied to the collective labor of those who produce the materials, distribute the artistic product, assess the arts production, and consume the arts commercially. These factors and many others—the audience for arts production, the instruction in the arts—provide a context for considering the collective production of arts. Thus, institutional factors are essential to the demystification of the artist and "divine creative inspiration" (Wolff 1981:29).

The danger of being "stuck in our own stereotypes" indicates the lack of movement between competing paradigms—the lone creative genius versus the cultural artist, as well as inherent artistry versus instruction. These conflicting mandates are negotiated within the setting of the IAIA, making the school a fertile register for assessing the layered and nuanced aspects of Native identity and representation in the arts. As a federally funded pan-Indian arts institution, the IAIA has historically endeavored to recuperate the tribal by using the arts as a generative tool. Many, but not all, of the women artists I interviewed were either students or teachers at the IAIA. The political nature of the school—as a pan-Indian center, as an assertively transformative institution for Native identity—calls for further elaboration. My lengthy involvement at the IAIA—as a museum studies student, curator, and professor—necessitates that I situate myself within this contextual discussion.

It was through my work with the IAIA Museum in the mid-1980s that I first became engaged in the wider political efforts of Native American self-representation in the arts. Emerging national repatriation efforts, increased availability of tribal scholarship moneys, and a newly energized tribal cultural center movement defined a period of revitalization for Native arts and culture (Mithlo 2004). Significantly, the concept of the National Museum of the American Indian (NMAI) as a component of the Smithsonian Institution was taking shape, spurring national dialogues on the rights and legacies of Native North Americans (West 2000).

The initiation of a museum training program at the IAIA by museum director Charles Dailey in 1972 predated this museum revolution by a decade. A 1974 art museum survey captures Dailey's guiding principle: "Indians should be running their own centers and talking about themselves"(Newsom and Silver 1978:654). The authors of the survey succinctly concluded, "The institute's basic argument is that Indians are contemporary human beings with contemporary ideas and must be allowed to express this position" (656).

The IAIA was established in 1962 as a Bureau of Indian Affairs school. In the school's early years, its central premise was that art and culture are essential components of learning. The concept of self-actualization and regaining cultural identity as a means of enhancing cognitive skills was considered a new and experimental approach to Indian education. A prominent proponent (and in many ways the intellectual author) of this movement was Lloyd New, Cherokee artist and educator. As IAIA artistic director and later president, New articulated with grace and passion his primary credo: "Our first goal, basic to all others, was to give the student pride in his people, in his culture, and in himself" (New 1975:1). His full statement reads as follows:

> Our educational approach was based on the premise that if an Indian youth were given constructive orientation to his own culture and cultural heritage, he would inevitably tap the traditional roots of that culture as a basis for valid contemporary art statements. And further, that even a single successful experience in the arts and crafts would engender feelings of self-worth which in turn would motivate the student to pursue repeated success, thereby involving him in the pleasure of learning and the desire to do so. [New 1975:1]

The assertion that Indian people would benefit on a variety of levels (socially, economically, and psychologically) from an embracement and expression of cultural identity continues to inform Native American sovereignty efforts. The study of Native arts as a means of understanding a people's struggle for self-representation is an outgrowth of this educational theory. The school's curriculum in museum studies, creative writing, and two- and three-dimensional arts has for decades significantly influenced national dialogues in Native representation.

Assertions of political sovereignty in the arts have often been misinterpreted as nothing more than "art speak" intended to woo potential customers who desire an association with overt forms of political art, when the intent is really to reference a much deeper analysis. For example, Choctaw/Hopi beadworker and painter Marcus Amerman described his role as a "warrior for his people," getting honors through his accomplishments in the dominant society.[3] Other artists I interviewed, such as Chippewa painter David Bradley, argued that the alignment with the cultural identification of Native American is, in itself, a political act.[4]

The political significance of Native arts was clearly demonstrated by the passage of federal legislation regulating the production of Native American arts and the identity of the artists. Titled the Indian Arts and Crafts Act of 1990, or Public Law 101-644, this legislation was developed to safeguard Indian artists and their patrons from unfair competition in the form of fraudulent, cheap, imported goods. The legislation requires that a person selling art identified as being made by a Native American must be able to prove the artisan's identity. At the time this legislation was formalized, lengthy public battles ensued as many Indian artists who could not prove their status—or chose not to—objected to this federal policing of identity. Other Native artists welcomed the legislation as a means of exposing imposters (Dubin 2001; Sheffield 1997).

This heated public debate served to highlight the issues of identity I initially chose to research. The controversy surrounding the Indian Arts and Crafts Act of 1990 was an awakening of sorts to art historians, Native-art collectors, and tourists who had comfortably categorized the Native arts world as simply another "color of the week" ethnic phenomenon. The public nature of this controversy allowed me to argue that Native arts are unique because Native life is unique in America. Unlike other ethnic minorities, Native Americans have specific political standing (Snipp 1986; Thornton 1987). This legal, historical, and political status is one of the most misunderstood aspects of Native American life. For example, when explaining the governance of the IAIA, I commonly inform people that the president appoints the board of the school. "But isn't that unusual? Doesn't the president of a school normally work under their board?" they ask. "No," I counter, surprised by both my casualness and their confusion. "I mean, the president of the United States appoints the board of the IAIA!" Confusion surrounding the basic parameters of contemporary Native existence, especially the political aspects of Native identity, indicates how difficult an accurate reading of contemporary topics can be.

Now more than forty years in existence, the IAIA allows for an analysis that productively collapses the simplistic dichotomies that interpret all institutional training as inherently assimilationist. The archetype of naturally talented Native artists cannot logically survive in a context in which Native instructors are hired ostensibly to teach Native students in a Native way. Nativeness in this sense is not a natural attribute but a quality that can be taught and a quality that is characterized not by tribal designations alone but by a pan-Indian characterization. These attributes—an essentialized Indianness and a Western educational model—do not, however, negate alternative operative values exercised within these parameters. Many instructors and teachers do proclaim the inherent artistry of Indians; many others reject a pantribal sensibility. Discourses of fine arts practices and communal imperatives serve as useful tools of analysis for arts practitioners navigating these competing paradigms.

"Who Can Tell the Story of What Has Happened to Us and What Is Happening to Us"

I don't know enough about art...Indian art or art...to really be able to categorize it. I just paint. And I don't know if you've seen anything I've painted, but the reason I might say some of my work is individualistic is because, first of all, painting is new to Navajos. I mean, you don't paint. That wasn't our tradition. Using oils and acrylics is new, and I consider it an elitist kind of thing for Navajo women of my age to be painting. The reason I say "elitist" is because I can afford to buy paint, from oils to acrylics, and I have had more opportunity to travel than others have, who are more homebound, reservation bound. Now, if I gave, randomly, women in their forties and fifties canvases and oils, and so on, and asked them to paint, I'm sure that they would create new forms, real exciting, interesting... especially if they're less Westernized. I can't even begin to imagine what they might create.

But for myself...my personal reasons for painting [are] that I feel that there aren't many people of my age who have seen the tremendous changes taking place on my reservation, who can tell the story of what has happened to us and what is happening to us. And I had to find a way to do it. I've tried writing. I've tried poetry. I've tried a number of ways to describe the agony of our lives, and the ones of my age are going to die very soon. And they won't leave anything behind to tell, except maybe little pieces from letters or a story that might be remembered by the children—that sort of thing. And so that's my personal reason.[5]

My introduction questions whether images and representations in the arts are central specifically to an understanding of Native American realities and, if so, in what ways. This passage from Navajo artist and educator Gloria Emerson suggests that the legacy of colonialism in America requires a remembrance. Her choice to paint indicates that art serves as a tool of empowerment against forgetting "the agony of our lives" (see plate 8). This strategy of remembrance has a cost, however. The act of painting seems to require that the artist in many ways separate herself from the collective community, perhaps inhabiting one of the masks that Owens (2001:17) describes as "the fabricated 'Indian.'"

Emerson speaks poignantly about the elitism inherent in the practice of fine arts—the material costs and the physical separation. Regarded in a very fundamental way, can indigenous ideologies be conveyed while appropriating the tools of the colonizer, whether it is the use of the English language or fine arts production? "The master's tools will never dismantle the master's house," the much quoted line by activist/poet Audre Lorde (1984:112), casts doubt on this enterprise, suggesting that appropriation of Western ideologies inherently compromises anticolonialist endeavors.

Lorde's original call, however, was against the exclusion of sexual and racial differences in feminist academic discourse. She challenged white feminists to "make common cause with…others identified as outside the structures in order to define and seek a world in which we can all flourish" (Lorde 1984:112). What Lorde rejected as "the master's tools" was the tendency for white American feminists to reproduce racist ideologies in women's rights political struggles of the 1970s. In doing so, she challenged the material basis of their theoretical orientation, asking why "the women who clean your houses and tend your children while you attend conferences on feminist theory are, for the most part, poor women and women of Color" (112). Lorde's contention is that race and class variables are inseparable from gender oppression and must be actively engaged to secure real social change.

Lorde's applied antidote to feminist theory is of the same spirit as Emerson's self-awareness of class privilege by her participation in the fine arts world. This cognizance of interrelationships should not, however, be read overall as an inconsistency with Native values—a championing of the individual above the collective. The decision of Native American artists to adopt modernist art sensibilities appears incongruent or appropriative of the "master's tools" only from the perspective of an observer who is wedded to stagnant notions of authenticity, tradition, and tribalism. The critique of perceived inappropriate claims to modernity evidenced in debates concerning the authenticity of contemporary Indian arts casts Native subjects as helpless, naïve victims of—rather than active participants in—dominant economic and political power structures (Liddle 1990).

Historian Philip J. Deloria terms this juxtaposition of perceived traditional and modern norms as "Indian unexpectedness," stating that

> expectations underlie the objections when Native people pursue gaming enterprises (Indians should not have money), seek to develop wind-power farms (Indian environmentalism should be spiritual, not technological), make the rosters of professional sports teams (Indians cannot compete in such structured settings), craft careers as actors or writers, play blues, or mix jazz and powwow music together. [2004:231]

Deloria argues that the unexpectedness of participation in these Western systems stems from expectations of failure, an "innate limitation" on the part of Indian people.

The cognitive separation of Indian people from contemporaneous reality results in limited configurations of the Native presence. Both adaptation and acculturation are premised on the assumption that Native Americans are physically separated and bound in space and time, that they do not inhabit the same area or perceive the same experiences simultaneously with others. Deloria's argument repositions this one-sided paradigm by placing Native peoples of the twentieth century within an emerging American history, a history built upon the exploitation of Native resources, including land, minerals, and even cultural resources used in national symbolism. This appropriation itself places Indians within dialogues of modernism and globalization rather than outside them.

If one looks closely at the articulation of self and community highlighted in Emerson's passage, it is clear that she considers herself an active agent within society. Her decision to paint, while appearing to be beyond the borders of Navajo experience, is also a highly political act. Significantly, Emerson's entrance into art school (at the IAIA) was at a mature age; most of her adult life had been devoted to public service.

> I worked most of my life in social work, in education, administration, writing proposals—that sort of thing. And I always had been told by others that…the programs that I created or I administered were always creative and energetic, and so on. And I knew that somewhere along the way that I started to buy paints and canvas, and I started to work with clay, and so on, but never formally trained.

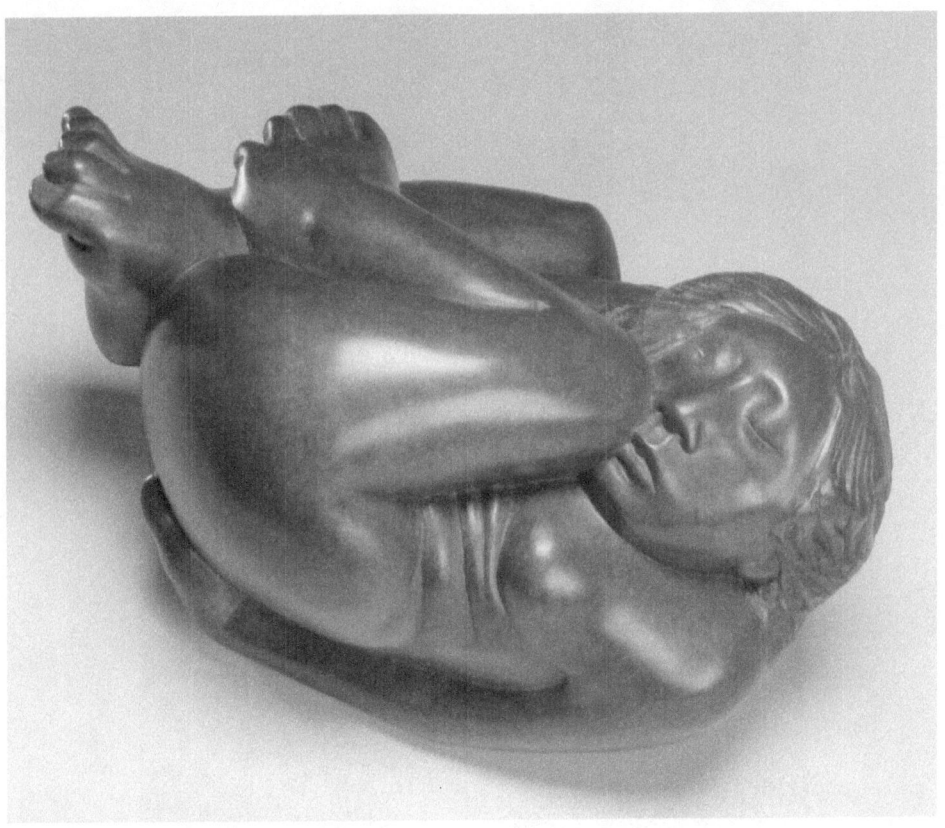

Plate 9.
Roxanne Swentzell: *Woman in Stone*, 2000. Stone, 10 x 9 x 8 inches. Photograph by Walter BigBee, The Big Picture

Roxanne Swentzell's *Woman in Stone* challenges the viewer to reassess the typical equation of the female nude's intended male gaze. This idealized figure conveys self-enclosure—the creation of an interior meditative space that concertedly defies exterior voyeurism. The serene facial features and massive feet suggest solidity and a secure sense of self, while the rippled stomach and full bust mirror an everywoman's body proportions. The use of round forms combined with the smooth bronze surface serves to enhance the Zen-like quality of the piece. This simplicity of line and sparse use of detail are characteristic of Swentzell's signature personalities, engaged in everyday human wanderings and musings. In a 1991 interview, the artist expressed how this sense of balance and acceptance is often in stark contrast to a non-Indian sensibility:

> Western culture...has this thing: if it gets hard, if life gets to be a struggle...they just pack up, and they move...they never really have to deal with the problems.... And I think, with traditional cultures...because they're so tied to a spot and a family and everything and somehow that's the whole world...you can't leave it...you're going to have to go through it, because you can't go anywhere. There's nowhere else to go. You are at the center of the world.

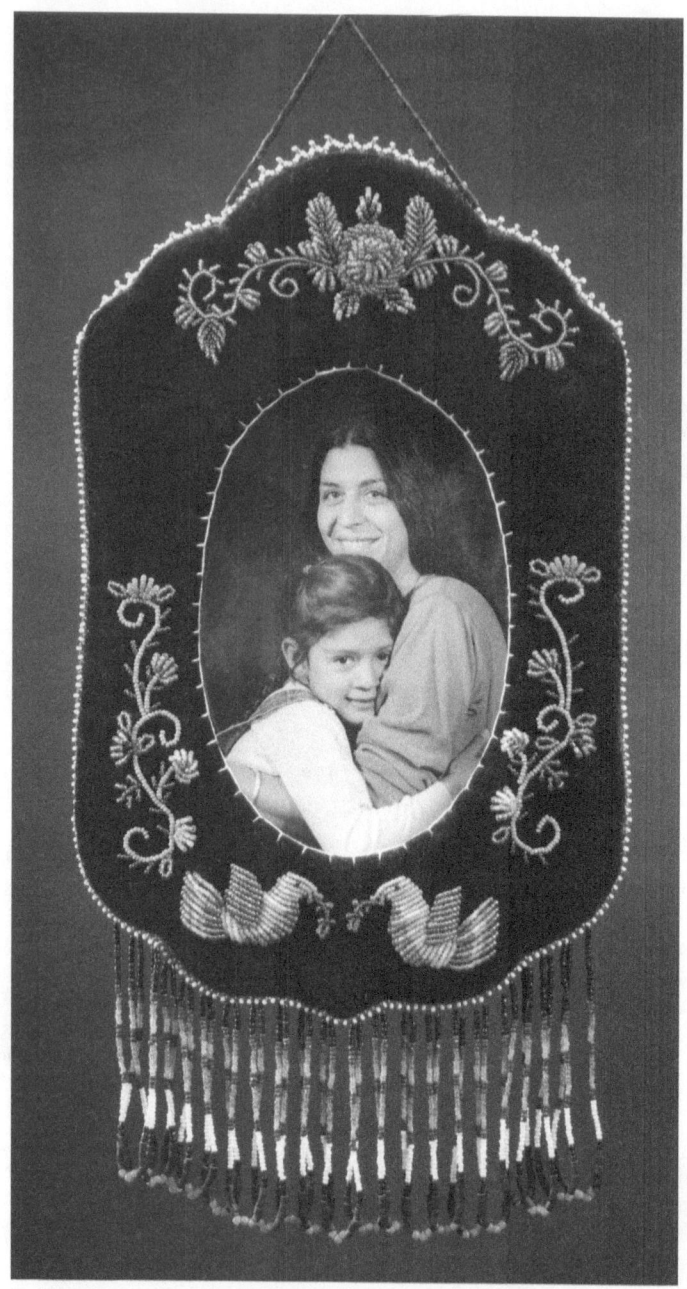

Plate 10.

Tammy Rahr: *Portrait with David*, c. 1986–1987. Velvet, glass seed beads, and photo (by Jud Cranston), 8 x 6 inches. Photograph by Eric Tadsen

"Home has to be first. There's no question about it. And for me, it's that simple. Home and my family have to be first…I'm two thousand miles away from my established family home, and I have one son, so in a way, I'm in it for him. Regardless of the other relationships that I've had in the past, the strongest one is always that connection that I have with David." (Rahr, interview with the author, September 13, 2000)

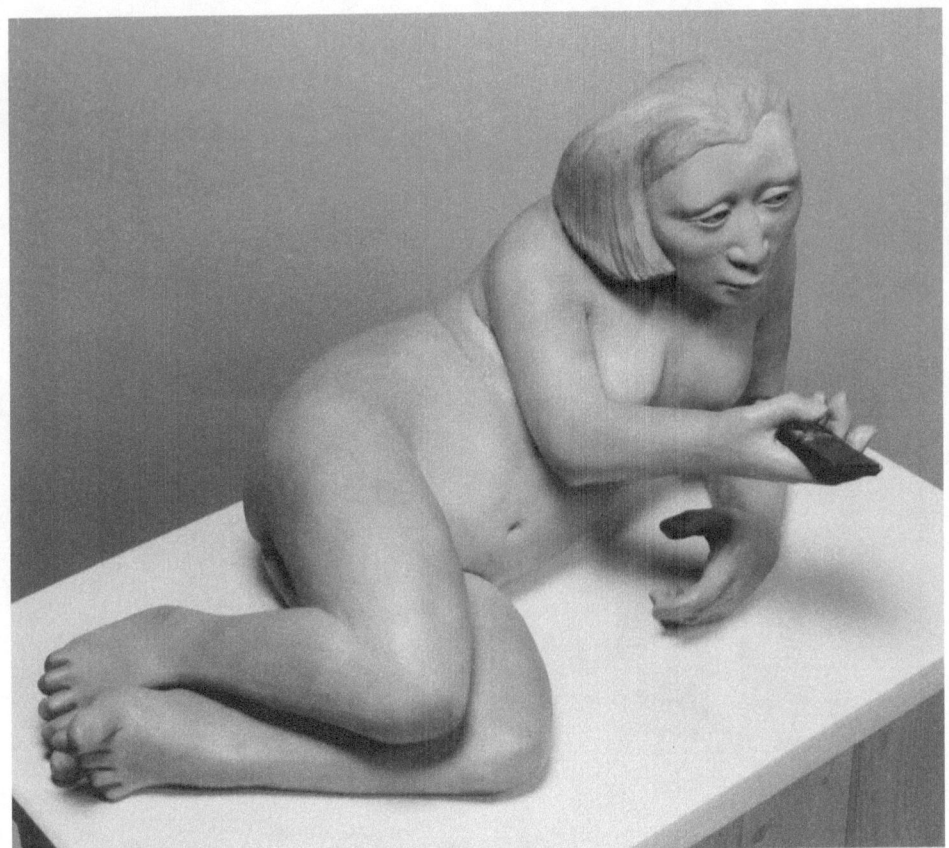

Plate 11.
Roxanne Swentzell: *Remote Woman, "I'm Getting that Far Away Feeling Again,"* 1996. Earthenware clay, 26 x 10 x 15 inches. Photograph by Walter BigBee, The Big Picture

The concept of alterity as a social tool that is practical, serviceable, and simultaneously mythical or symbolic informs works such as Swentzell's *Remote Woman*. In a practical sense, her female figure conveys the angst and alienation typically associated with consumerism, individualism, and capitalism. The half-cast eyes, drawn mouth, and slumping pose all indicate a disassociation with archetypical, earthy everywoman figures. *Remote Woman* serves as a type of anti-archetype in denying the viewer the pleasures of identifying with the earth-woman-goddess that Native female nudes often signify. Instead, in a mythical, tricksterlike fashion, earth goddess has succumbed to the corrupting forces of modern Western civilization—dependent upon crass commercial forms of mass entertainment. *Remote Woman* refuses to serve as an alternative refuge from these denigrating social influences and instead joins the pathos of the disaffected modern masses. She inhabits a space inappropriate for the symbolic earth-mother-goddess, thereby internalizing and rejecting the white imaginative process of othering.

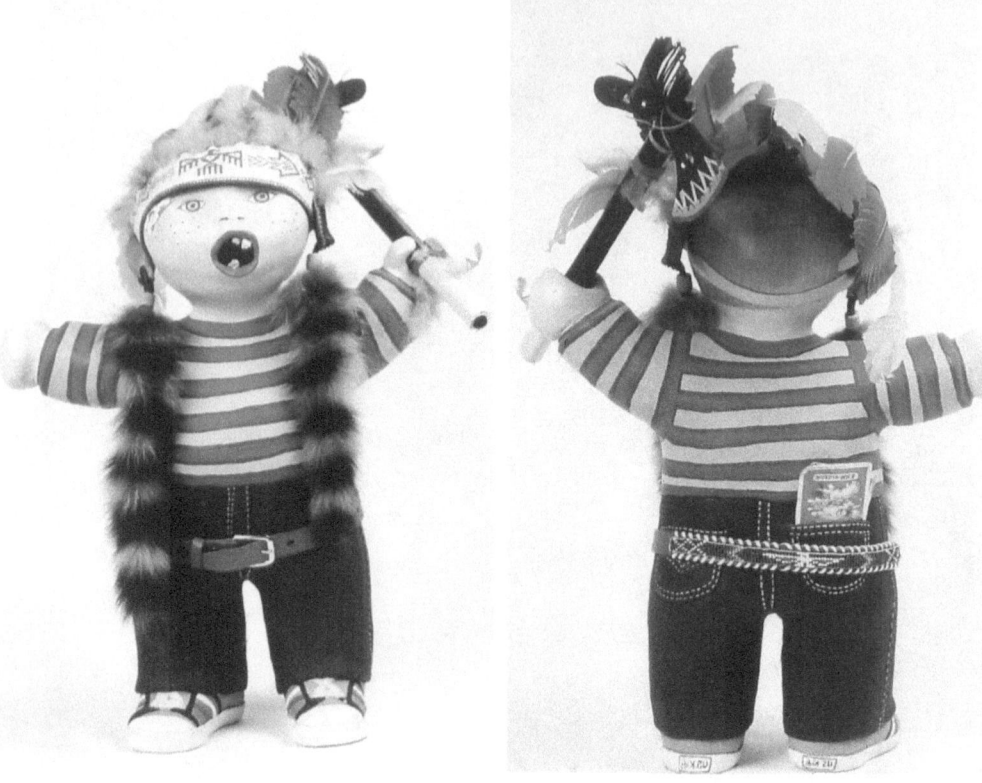

Plates 12a, 12b.
Laura Fragua Cota: *Just Because You Put Feathers in Your Hair, Don't Make You an Indian*, 1990. Mixed media, 19 x 16 inches. Photograph by Walter Big Bee, The Big Picture. Courtesy of the Institute of American Indian Arts

Fragua Cota's irreverent little boy serves as a caricature of white appropriation. This Indian stereotype of whites inverts the standard victim-informed analysis of white stereotypes of Indians. Utilizing humor, parody, and miniaturization as effective tools, Fragua Cota replicates and redeems popular caricatures of Indians—the plastic Indian, the cigar store Indian, the Halloween Indian—by shifting the point of view from one who observes Indians to one who observes whites.

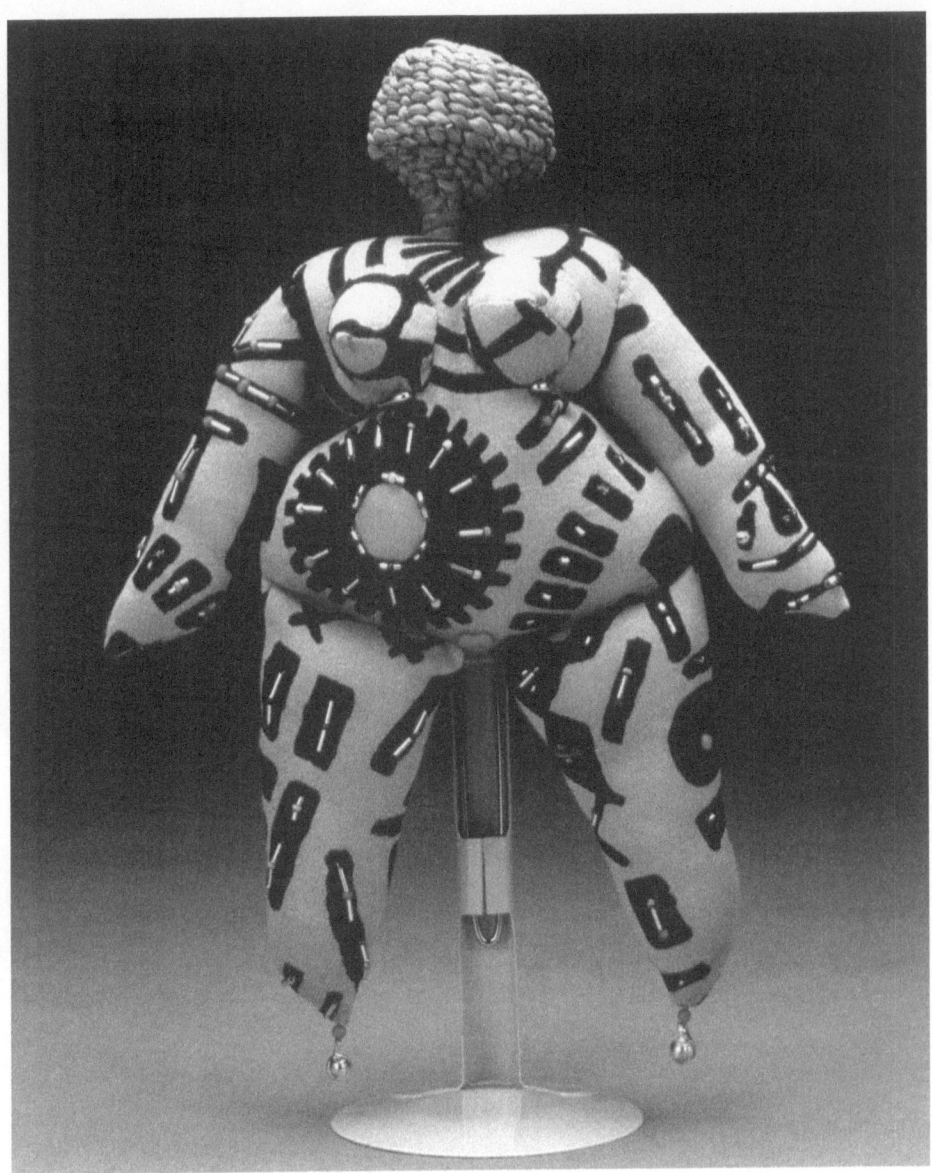

Plate 13.
Pat Courtney Gold: *Anti-Barbie Doll, Indian Version*, 2000. Cotton knit, twined cattail leaf head, and beads, 22.5 x 18 x 9 inches. Photograph by Bill Bachhuber

A central theme of contemporary American Indian arts discourse is negotiation of cultural difference by the use of inversion. In this iconic work by Pat Courtney Gold, signifiers of idealized beauty are reappropriated in the language of fiber arts. Indigenous materials and designs inhabit the space of Barbie beauty, confounding expectations with role reversal. *Anti-Barbie Doll*, as the product of a Native imagination, claims ownership by mocking the props and proportions of the commercial product. Courtney Gold retains the delicacy of the Barbie product with her deft design work, exposed breasts, and tiny hands and feet while simultaneously denying the replication of Barbie's signature blond hair and doe eyes. The basket, with its ceremonial and utilitarian referents, replaces the purely decorative fascination of the face, providing the viewer with a potent metaphor for the centrality of indigenous registers. *Anti-Barbie Doll*'s woven head thinks in an indigenous way.

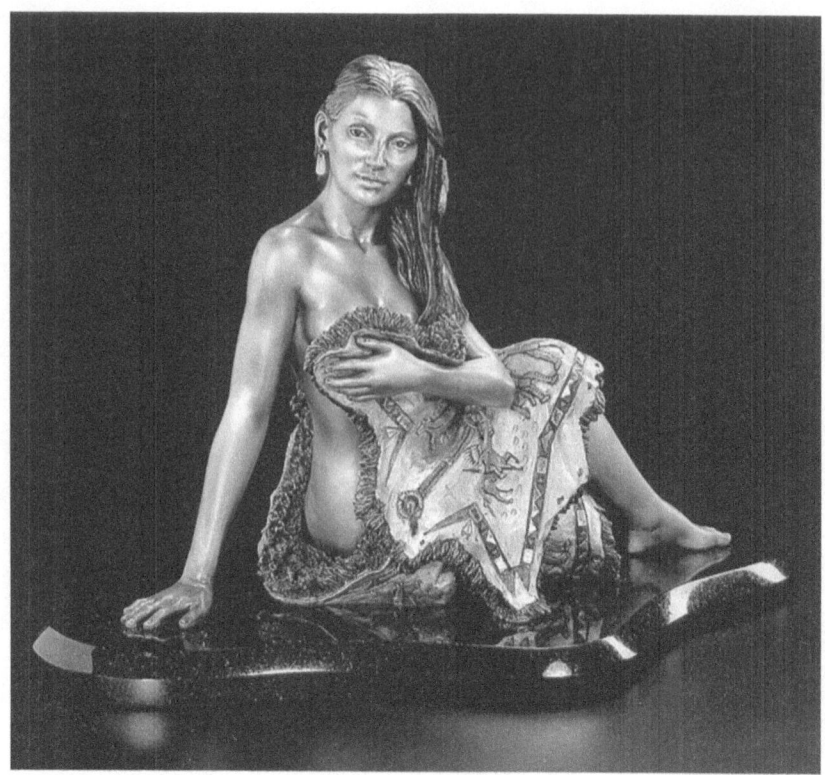

Plate 14.
Christopher A. Pardell: *Sacajawea*, 2001. Bronze, 13 x 21 x 12 inches. Photograph by Legends Studios, Fine Art Sculptures by Starlite Originals Sculptures and Statues

The description featured in the advertisement for this piece reads, "This sculpture depicts the strength and unbreaking spirit of Sacajawea, a guide and interpreter for Lewis and Clark."

    It is instructive to compare the bedding-wrapped, apparently nude Sacajawea with photographer Annie Leibovitz's *Vanity Fair* photos of American teen pop star Miley Cyrus, which caused a scandal in 2008. The images of a similarly sensually posed fifteen-year-old Cyrus wrapped in sheets resulted in major complaints from Cyrus's preadolescent fans and their parents. As with so many other popular depictions of American Indian women, Sacajawea—a teenage mother and guide on the Lewis and Clark expedition of 1804–1806—is memorialized primarily as a sexually available object. The variance of interpretations for visual signifiers in twenty-first-century popular American culture correlates with conventional notions of appropriate sexual behavior for young women and is informed differentially in relation to memory, history, and race.

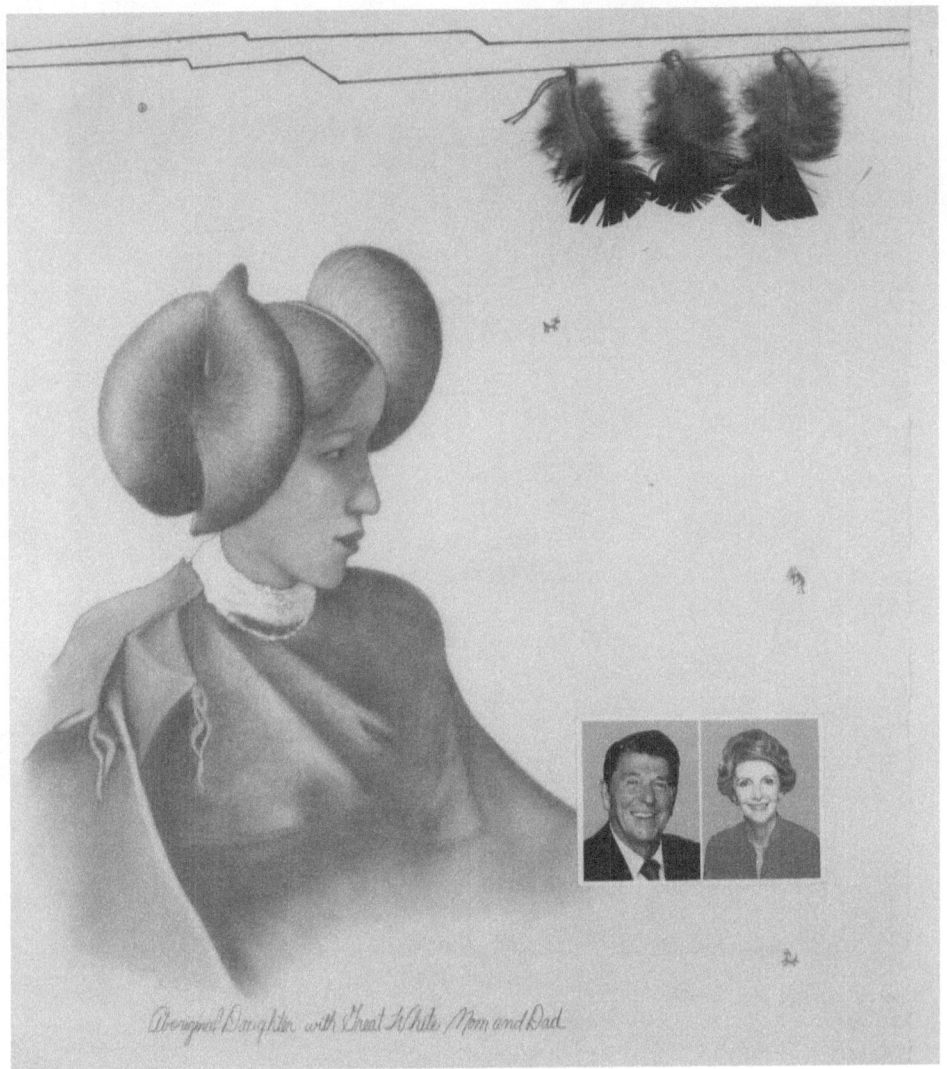

Plate 15.
Laura Fragua Cota: *Aboriginal Daughter with Great White Mom and Dad*, 1988. Pencil and mixed media, 26.5 x 13 inches. Photograph by Walter BigBee, The Big Picture

"Indian people have their tradition still. White fathers come and go. We still carry on our tradition. Nature is a part of tradition—feathers, spiritual medicine, birds. Nature is part of who we are, part of our tradition. Technology, computer, and Internet still have to be a part of nature. No one controls water and rain. It is part of what we have to work with. The woman with whorls in her hair is saying, 'We are here. We carry on traditions.' Why three feathers? Mind, body, and spirit. The three—the triad spirit. The lines are the petroglyphs and the earth mesa. Ram, Kokopelli, fertility petroglyphs are ancient symbols of what people saw. Whatever was their reality at the time, it was important to etch on rock. This is my reality—little figures on the rock. We are there forever." (Fragua Cota, interview with the author, February 4, 2008).

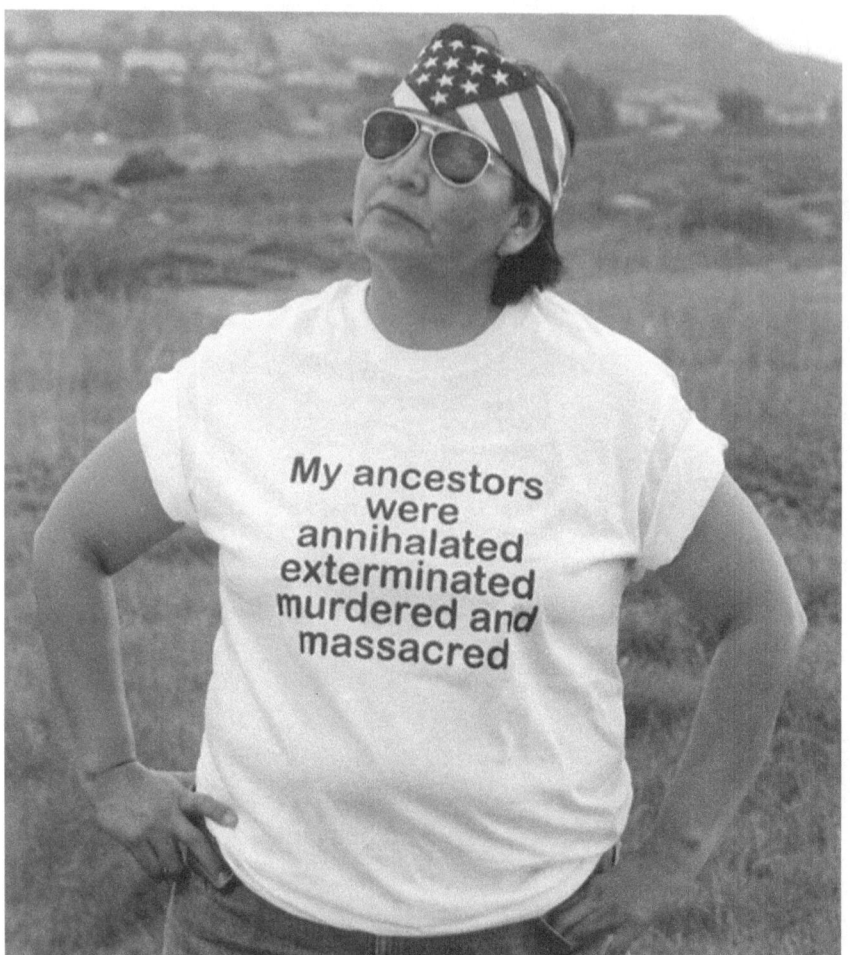

Plate 16.
Shelley Niro: *The Shirt*, 2003. Color photograph, still from *The Shirt* video. Shirt wearers: Hulleah J. Tsinhnahjinnie (pictured here) and Veronica Passalacqua

The Shirt is a short film that was shown at the 2003 Venice Biennale exhibition Pellerossasogna, sponsored by the Indigenous Arts Action Alliance and supported, in part, by the Smithsonian National Museum of the American Indian. It features a lulling soundtrack that guides the viewer on a serene drive past a frozen riverbank. Trees and electric lines glide past quickly, interspersed with close-ups of dripping ice and surging waterfalls. This northern habitat is interrupted with cutaway sequences of open green fields. The camera floats across the landscape laterally, delivering us to a close, almost confrontational shot of a strong Native woman striking a mountainlike pose against a serene blue sky.

Consecutive frames feature her sequentially modeling shirts that declare: "My ancestors were annihilated, exterminated, murdered, and massacred," "They were lied to, cheated, tricked, and deceived," "Attempts were made to assimilate, colonize, enslave, and displace them," and "And all's I get is this shirt."

The Shirt, as a film and parallel photo essay, employs humor and the environment in a playful political satire that appropriates and ultimately inverts the touristic gaze. The Native, not the white interloper, adopts the language of T-shirt communication. The shirt wearer is a silent but potent witness to extreme cultural loss and environmental degradation. Her message of cultural genocide is delivered obliquely, using the very tools that are employed to contain and minimize the impact of wholesale extermination policies. Rather than eradicate this tragic history and its social weapons, Niro reworks and reappropriates derogatory language by using creative and proactive measures. Consequently, the 2003 Venice exhibition Pellerossasogna, translated as "Red Skin Dream," serves as a remembrance of intolerance.

> And it just started to grow on me during the eighties that I really had to do something for myself, because everything that I had done was outwardly oriented. And I thought it was time for me—time to turn inward and to explore the inner world...not me as an individual, but me as a phenomenon, me as a part of a tribe and the changes we were going through. So while I feel I am a case study of what's going on throughout the reservation—and I needed to get that out and to document it in some way—I think my whole family feels that way.

Emerson's desire to capture, to convey, her experience as a tribal person is clearly not an individualistic endeavor. Her embrace of a tribal sensibility in this regard would not present the same tensions that Owens describes as inherent in the production and circulation of American Indian literature, for example. In sharp contrast to Owens, Emerson expresses little interest in audience. Thus, the desire "to be recognized, and to thus have a voice that is heard by those in control of power," which most concerns Owens (2001:17), is not the compelling motivation for her; documentation is. Emerson describes her artistic practice as an internal, personal one, yet this process is politically significant as well. She is, in her words, "a case study of what's going on throughout the reservation."

A crucial aspect of Emerson's professional arts identification is her training with an indigenous arts institute, the IAIA. This setting privileges not simply individual artistic freedom but also exploration of a specifically Native American aesthetic sensibility. The institution also allows for the production and circulation of images for an American Indian audience, in contrast to educational settings where this identity is marginalized or ignored. As Tuscarora scholar Richard W. Hill Sr. has observed, "Indians express themselves through art because the social, political, and religious education received at the hands of White Americans has not always allowed Indians to be themselves" (Hill 1990:3).

The IAIA training Emerson describes is not entirely informed by a communal sensibility but is determined by gender and power variables, specifically what Emerson terms the "patriarchal painting school." When I questioned her about her evaluation of her own work in 1991, shortly after her IAIA education, she replied, "I'm not sure about my own criteria because I've learned my criteria from male teachers." She related how this recognition of a distinctly male influence came about by her exposure to feminist critiques of art education programs. Her moment of awareness is recounted in the following conversation in 1991:

GLORIA EMERSON: I had an experience where I had tried to do the colors of the Navajo creation story in a flat, two-dimensional way as an abstract painting, and it was black at the bottom—black, red, blue, and yellow. So when my painting instructor saw this, he told me that I should turn it upside down, because the yellow was very strong, and that it would work better. I accepted his judgment. The white woman…friend…looked at this painting and asked me what it meant…what was my reason for doing this?…what did it mean? I said, "The significance of this is that this is a creation story." She said, "Well, then why did you turn it upside down? You have to stick to your guns. If it doesn't work aesthetically, you have to stick with your guns. You have to deal with the problem. It's a technical problem. But you have to set your own criteria." And it frightened me that I had become so used to accepting my instructor's point of view. And I hadn't learned how to challenge yet—at that point. And I hadn't learned to set my own standards. And I still haven't, in some cases. When I had my first show, I brought my…I put everything into a pickup and brought them all the way from Shiprock to Santa Fe to have two male art teachers who happened, I thought, to be the best art teachers in the school to review my work. And only until they had selected the juries did I feel comfortable to go.

NANCY MITHLO: Would that be true, regardless of gender? Because I know when I talk with some artists, there's this debate about whether it's helpful to be in a mentorship role with an established artist or whether it's a hindrance.

GLORIA EMERSON: That's possible. That's very possible. And that's why I think it's important to have real diversity in your institute. At that time, there weren't enough women instructors who were very strong. Now, I would be able to get a more balanced perspective—both with gender and also with tribes and then non-Indian. But I feel that within this institute, we really want to build toward more of a global perspective. We also need art instructors from other world cultures.

Emerson's proactive response to her recognition of male bias in the IAIA setting was to organize a seminar at the school with her white woman friend and other IAIA women art instructors, such as Otellie Loloma and Wendy Ponca. Emerson's narrative indicates how an adequate analysis of identity expression in Indian arts cannot be pursued only from a Native/non-Native standpoint but must also consider other attributes, such as age, gender, and class components. The segmentation or separation of Native arts from the arts of any other community has been labeled "an odd kind of segregational racism" by critics (Lail 1991:11). The terms *ghettoize, stereotyped,* and *political,* for example, were mobilized in critiques of the 1991 traveling exhibit Our Land/Ourselves: American Indian Contemporary Artists, curated by artist Jaune Quick-to-See Smith. Writing for Albany's *Times Union*, art reviewer Thomas Lail enacted the standard contradiction of both demanding that the work look Indian—asking, "Where's the culture?" —and simultaneously decrying the premise of an exhibit that features only Native American art. He asserts, "The very idea of presenting an exhibit such as this is controversial since it works to segregate and ghettoize the works rather than present them as works on equal standing with other works" (11).

Native artists traverse these contradictory and often unmanageable demands by strategically opting into either the "reject culture" or the "embrace culture" ideology. Often it is the former of these two options, a distancing from ethnicity, that is most rewarded in critical arts theory. Curator Jean Fisher outlines this quandary in an either/or fashion:

> To present traditional Native American art, when a White audience cannot "read" its signs and is ignorant of how it functions culturally, is to risk the work's appropriation to exotic ethnicity, intensifying the Anglo's desire to preserve the least challenging aspects of Native cultures as safe museum relics. To present work that is not inscribed with recognizable signs of "Indianness" is to either face accusations that it cannot be "Indian" art, or to be confronted with a cultural arrogance that dismisses as irrelevant what does not conform to the codes of avant-gardism. [1987:9]

The Indian art cliché "I'm an artist first, an Indian second" invalidates the advancement of ethnic specificity, raising as it does the currency of the individual above that of the collective. A parallel development in African American contemporary arts is the coinage of the term *post-black* by curator Thelma Golden in her 2001 exhibit Freestyle (Cotter 2001). This denial of cultural poignancy in an age of globalized influences has variously been cast as universalism, hybridity, the quality debate, identity politics, multiculturalism, and the dialectical perspective.

While offering apparent freedom from constrictive categories imposed from the outside, a negation of ethnicity also implies a negation of history. This is the sense in which art historian Michael D. Harris (2003:257) asserts that "post-black" descriptives are problematic: "To suggest that race is no longer visualized, meaningful, or problematic seems incorrect and fanciful." The apparent danger is forgetfulness of the power that race exerts, even in the denial of its existence. In this manner, the "abandonment of an ethnic frame...move[s] the artist into a frame that, by its seeming invisibility, closely resembles the way naturalized whiteness functions" (248–249). Harris's insistence on a situated identity resembles Bunzl's (2004:441) call for a "genealogy of secondary explanation" inasmuch as the reasons for the segmentation of race must be retained in order to deconstruct the negative impact of racism, sexism, or homophobia. Bunzl's "historization" and Harris's "rootedness" share the logic of Emerson's remembrance—to remember is to keep the agony alive, even as one must experience the pain of its existence in its retelling.

The demon of reification is, I think, a preferable choice to the naturalization of race in all its negative impacts, including the invisibility of whiteness. Just how one reifies, and with what motivations and intents, informs the interpretation of one's claims to ethnic identity as authentic or inauthentic—or, adopting Harris's (2003:216) references, "signifyin'" or "shining." "Signifyin'" connotes self-awareness, an agenda, an appropriation that is successfully subversive. "Shining" implies playacting willfully, selfishly, and with potentially harmful consequences to others.

If the motivation of effective arts practice is entering the debates of race and ethnicity to question and potentially alter oppressive societal norms, Harris's advocacy of rootedness is essential: "Art rooted in the center of that identity is often more effective in confronting the conflicts on the periphery because, rather than facing hostility or problems by adopting their modes, contexts, and definitions, artists can use their own sensibilities to devise strategies that preserve their own artistic personality"(2003:248). Just how an artist's "own sensibilities" differ significantly from mainstream norms remains unclear. While the use of paints in Navajo culture may be seen as elitist and foreign, for example, the commitment to memory is far from an alien concept in indigenous ideology; in fact, it is a central tenet.

Writing in the heyday of 1990s debates on multiculturalism (and during the time that many of my interviews took place), art historian Thomas McEvilley cites historicism as a central methodology for unraveling the postmodernism turn in the arts. He states, "In the move away from Modernism (colonialism), of course, post-Modernism (postcolonialism) does not begin with a clean slate. The idea of a historical change that leaves causality behind is a contradiction, since an acausal moment would of necessity be ahistorical" (1992:131).

McEvilley's analysis highlights a concern that has remained integral yet elusive to debates on appropriation and agency in the arts. He cites how non-European arts practitioners have been perceived as ahistorical beings:

> In the Modernist period, when whites saw history as exclusively their own, African, Indian, Chinese, and Amerindian societies were regarded as ahistorical because they weren't dominated by the need to feel that they were evolving toward some ultimate consummation. Colonialism was justified as a means to drag the supposedly ahistorical into history. [McEvilley 1992:132]

This perceived lack of contemporaneous identity necessarily characterizes all ethnic arts as stagnant in place and time, with effective agency of the artist denied or subsumed under the weight of cultural mandates. The effect of this invalidation process is that "appropriate" histories are authored outside subjective experiences. Yet it is the subjective—or in Emerson's words, "the story of what has happened to us"—that is desired most by artists as a means of recuperating traditions as they quickly alter under Western influences. McEvilley sees the arts as a forum for the rewriting of history, both of the self and of the other: "Peoples clinging to their own heritages, traditions, languages, and styles of self-hood insist that they be written into history as themselves, and that their picture of us, with elements we might not relish, be written into that history too. Even more, they demand that they will write the history" (132).

The ability to document, to witness, to offer testimony in the arts requires, in a Wolff contextualization sense, the material supports for arts instruction and the access to materials. As Emerson so clearly describes, this fine arts process is, in itself, an elitist endeavor. To be an artist born into a way of thinking and believing is one component of this remembrance. For an artist to acquire certain skills in an institutional manner is another. The justification of expressing a cultural self in the arts unique from the universality of all human experiences—a cultural self bounded in many ways by place and belief—is an endeavor often rife with negative connotations of separatism.

"You Are at the Center of the World"

> Everything about my life is my family and my aunts and uncles and everybody like that. I think when you grow up around family all the time, you take it for granted that that's your whole life and that's who you belong to, until you sort of move away. If you go to New York or something, suddenly you're…you can never…home is here, home is with your family, no matter how much you hate them. Home is there, and something is missing if you're not there. I don't

know if that answers your question, but it's got to affect the artwork.

It's got to also…I was thinking about how many cultures…or at least Western culture…has this thing: if it gets hard, if life gets to be a struggle—or, say, they bump into a hard relationship and it becomes unfun—they just pack up and they move. Or they…It's sort of like this jumping around where they just go…they go to the spotlights all the time. They hop from one spotlight to the next, and they never really have to deal with the problems. When the problem comes, they just split. And I think with the traditional cultures… because they're so tied to a spot and a family and everything and somehow that's the whole world, why do you…you can't leave it. It's right there, and the spotlight is there—everything's always there, and whenever you're hit with the problems, you're going to have to go through it, because you can't go anywhere. There's nowhere else to go. You are at the center of the world. I think that probably helps them to be able to go through stuff. That enables them to see different worlds of existence—because they have to. They have to over and over again. Or you die.[6]

Cree activist Sharon Venne has argued, "Often it is written that Indigenous peoples have a spiritual relationship to their territories. This is not a myth. The myth is that Indigenous peoples can survive without their lands and territories"(2004:130). Roxanne Swentzell's passage asserts the primacy of location as an indicator of her philosophical orientation (see plate 9). Her "rootedness," as Harris would describe it, informs her art practice. As she puts it, "it's got to affect the artwork." Far from being a barrier to arts expression in a Western fine arts, individualistic sense, Swentzell's communal sensibility and orientation of place are described as assets. Traditional cultures are enabled "to see different worlds of existence" in their rootedness. In contrast, Western cultures "never really have to deal with the problems."

Efforts to embrace a more fluid and shifting globalized perspective in the social sciences have historically minimized the importance of bounded and discrete cultural groupings as colonialistic and dated. The shift in anthropological understandings of fieldwork as a practice defined by geographical features to the idea of ethnography as an inquiry of "location" has been explored by Akhil Gupta and James Ferguson in *Anthropological Locations: Boundaries and Grounds of a Field Science* (1997). While presenting a somewhat redemptive project in terms of countering positivistic knowledge and "evolutionist and colonial ideas of 'natives in their natural state'" (1997:38), the authors nevertheless propose an ideology that minimizes subject interpretations that value discrete place and identity. Thus, their statement that their "focus on *shifting locations* rather than *bounded fields* ...sees anthropological knowledge as a form of situated intervention" (38) suggests that valued cultural knowledge lies in the intersection of political ideologies, not in the physical properties of land-based societies.

Although the effort to practice a "decolonized anthropology" certainly has merit, the collateral assumption that we inhabit a "deterritorialized world" (Gupta and Ferguson 1997:38) is problematic from the perspective of place-based peoples whose connections to specific land bases inform their sense of identity and safeguard their sovereign political status. One cannot imagine simply choosing to be an Indian, for to do so would be committing ethnic fraud. The decentering of the field as a site of privileged knowledge has the consequence of elevating the concept of "situated knowledges" seen as "interlocking...multiple social-political sites and locations" above subject assertions of cultural particularism (37).

A positioning that diminishes discrete identities is reflected in such phrases as "a set of labels that pins down one's own identity and perspective" (Gupta and Ferguson 1997:37) and "the prison house of essentialism"(17) and in efforts "to challenge this picture of the world, one made up of discrete, originally separate cultures" (35). Gupta and Ferguson's statement that what they "object to is...the implicit presumption that 'Otherness' means difference from an unmarked, White western 'self'" (14–15) blocks both traditional researchers and traditional subjects from using these constructs for anti-imperialist aims.

How does one then interpret these conceptual differences—one that rejects the mandates of place and one that advances place? Can a "postexoticist anthropology" (Clifford 1997:193) validate what anthropologists may consider the self-exoticism of their subject others? Writing in *Anthropological Locations*, James Clifford begins to address this issue by asking, "In local/global situations where displacement appears increasingly to be the norm, how is collective dwelling sustained and reinvented?" (212) Clifford's work on oppositionality has informed my research in considering the self-expressed binaries of Native women artists as a topic of inquiry. Although Clifford notes how binaries are often naturalized "along lines of gender (female, domestic space versus male travel), class (the active, alienated bourgeoisie versus the stagnant, soulful poor), and race/culture (modern, rootless Western versus traditional, rooted 'natives')"(212–213), his analysis ultimately converges with those of the editors in stating, "Home is not, in any event, a site of immobility" (213).

The aim of my inquiry is not to ascertain identity formation, but to examine how identity is communicated in the production and circulation of

Native American arts. The literature on ethnicity and identity has historically interpreted cultural differences along a spectrum, from culture as a "determining force" to culture as a "reified ideological fantasy" (Eriksen 1993). From Fredrik Barth's *Ethnic Groups and Boundaries* (1969), which positions a natural state of difference, to the constructivist agendas of Benedict Anderson ([1983]2006), identity debates have centrally engaged notions of causality. Although this body of scholarship has clear application to the debates I am forwarding, what I am trying to accomplish in this text is direct engagement with the signs of cultural difference and their interpreted meanings. Constructivist theories of identity serve to diminish the claims of indigenous peoples to specific locations in a similar manner, and popular "identity politics" writers such as Richard Rodriguez (1994) negate discrete identities on the charge that they deny "the basic fluid experience of our lives." In *Brown: The Last Discovery of America* (2002), Rodriguez champions a celebratory "blending" of America. Citing the mascot controversy at Stanford University, in which Native American students successfully petitioned to have Prince Lightfoot removed as the school's sports symbol, Rodriguez complains, "The Indian, as much a puritan as any Puritan, as regards identity, never gets a handle on parody or, indeed, on self-parody" (2002:70). The ability to blend creatively, to construct varied cultural attributes at will, and to negate ethnic classification as deterministic is advanced under the argument that the freedom to choose subject markers should be exercised by all, even those whose cultural attributes have been marginalized by colonialist mandates. To choose to do otherwise by retaining ownership of a discrete identity is deemed puritanical.

Native American legal activists such as Venne interpret this blurring of boundaries as an opportunistic effort to extend colonialism. In reference to Canadian and US efforts to control tribal membership, she claims:

> If the colonizer's legal system can define who is an Indigenous person and who is not, then control of lands and territories is the next step. Those Indigenous peoples not recognized by the colonizer cease to have any legal rights to their lands and territory, leaving the lands open for use by the colonizers. [Venne 2004:127]

In this sense, anthropologists, social theorists, and politicians share the same practice of negating boundaries, even as their aims differ. While anthropologists seek to alter dated theoretical conceptualizations of culture that may serve to bind subjects falsely in time and place, identity critics wish to open up possibilities of imagining alternative selves, and politicians may wish to control allocation of resources, all can be said to be diminishing Native efforts to mobilize collectively as land-based peoples.

Fluidity's effects are that no one position is privileged above another. Academics who champion a fluid identity in Native America are seen by indigenous spokespeople as opportunistic in terms of knowledge capital, undermining the discursive authority of indigenous values. An example of this conflict is the "invention of tradition" debate in Hawaii, where contemporary discourses of cultural identity (including sovereignty and cultural revitalization movements) are characterized as being reappropriated in selective and inauthentic ways as political tools. Sociologist Leilani Holmes notes that anthropologists' writings about Hawaiians may be politically influential enough to "[limit] the right of Hawaiians to define their own past, present, and future" (Holmes 2000:48), adding that the debate ignores the "present-day studies of everyday talk and action on the part of Hawaiian people" (49).

The editors of the volume from which Holmes's essay was drawn define indigenous knowledge as one intimately associated with the land: "We conceptualize an 'indigenous knowledge' as a body of knowledge associated with the long-term occupancy of a certain place" (Dei, Hall, and Rosenberg 2000:7). The ability to reappropriate is also a central construct of this approach—as opposed to the negative reading of these interventions as opportunistic. Stating that "anticolonial theorizing rises out of alternative, oppositional paradigms, which are in turn based on indigenous concepts as analytical systems and cultural frames of reference" (7), the editors advance a concept that legitimizes essentialization on the basis of historicism: "The notion of 'colonial' is rooted in imposed relations and power inequalities engendered by history, tradition, culture and contact" (7). Given this configuration of extremes—pluralism and cultural specificity—how can one productively incorporate the complexity of contemporary identities "in a world of globalization and transnational capitalism, a world that is created by markets as much as by movements of people"? (de Alba 2004:106). The negotiation of land-based identity with global capital exposes operative identity constructs.

"'I Am Walking Away. I'm Going Back'"

> NANCY MITHLO: What happens when you have conflict either between your work and home or your work and your belief system? Can you give examples where you've had this kind of conflict and how you resolved them?
>
> TAMMY RAHR: Well, you can't drag homework with you, that's for sure, and home has to be first. There's no question about it. And for me, it's that simple. Home and my family have to be first. Have to

because, well, for a number of reasons...parenting. I'm two thousand miles away from my established family home, and I have one son, so in a way I'm in it for him. Regardless of other relationships that I've had in the past, the strongest one is always that connection that I have with David. In a way, a lot of other people don't have the dualities that Native people have. We do have that communion; we do have that inner strength to say, "I am walking away. I'm going back. I'm going to jump the creek, and I'm going to be who I really am." And I think that a lot of people think that is a disadvantage. They put us down for being late. They put us down for having Native traits. But those can be really strong advantages. How many people can do that in this life? Maybe it's a little bit of arrogance with the notion of "This is my island." This whole place is my island. This is my home. It's where my great-great-great grandmother is from. And even though we're only given a fraction of what we once had, still, we have home there on the other side of the creek.[7]

In an effort to understand the relationship between place, identity, and gender in aesthetic development and production, Alicia Gaspar de Alba (2004) has theorized that multiple systems of "place-based aesthetics" exist. These include race-based, diasporic, indigenous, and feminist aesthetics. Although each of these aesthetic practices is rooted in specific constructs of place, de Alba (2004:108–109) problematizes the meaning of *place* to extend to race, religion, community, and the body as "sites of identity." She concludes that indigenous aesthetics are distinct from race aesthetics: "In contrast to race-based aesthetics, which looks outward from the colonial experience to a collective memory of a homeland that will most likely never be seen, indigenous aesthetics is born from within the colonial context and looks inward into a collective experience of the homeland's colonization" (113). Referencing the loss of tribal territories, she continues, "In this aesthetic system, community becomes the signifier for place or homeland...the native community more than the land base—becomes that place of attachment, that common ground in which indigenous identity is rooted" (113).

This conceptualization of place shares certain affinities with the "invention of tradition" debates in that de Alba's problematizes the ways colonized peoples reclaim culture—or "fill in the gaps of the self" (de Alba 2004:104) through the "myth-symbol-image" (119) power of cultural representations. Her reading of various artistic responses to dispossession of land bases both celebrates and critiques various strategies for positioning identity in the arts. Ultimately, this proactive reading of invention questions the efforts of dispersed communities and artists to imagine utopian constructs, such as Chicanos depicting Aztlán, the mythical lost land. Even as de Alba advances artistic representation, she simultaneously asserts that place means more than geographical location, that "place of origin does not explain or define identity" (106).

Rahr's statement questions this permeable definition of place and home by declaring all of North America part of "turtle island," or indigenous people's territory. Residing in the Indian arts capital of Santa Fe, New Mexico, far from her home in New York State, Rahr is cognizant of her vulnerability and distance from family (see plate 10). And yet the whole continent is conceived of as home—"'my island.' This whole place is my island. This is my home." The "arrogance" with which she makes this assertion is evidence of the ability to see the alternative perspective that Swentzell describes—"to see different worlds of existence." For Rahr, it is a manifestation of the dualities of Indian life.

I am compelled to provide a homegrown example of Rahr's reference of "jumping the creek." In my many years of teaching Native American students, I have dealt with the difficulty that admissions offices like to term "retention." The challenge for administrators responsible for Native students in higher education settings is not only recruiting them and encouraging them to leave home communities—whether rural or urban—but also helping them to thrive in an academic setting, retaining them for the full four-year period in order to complete their degree requirements. As a professor, I am both pained and proud when a student decides to leave an academic environment that he or she experiences as oppressive. Midsemester, a week after classes have begun, two weeks before the end of the year—at any point, it is conceivable that a Native student can simply decide that enough is enough and elect to leave—to "jump the creek," as Rahr says. I remember one October weekend when Judy (not her real name), a mature student with a six-year-old, called her boyfriend and asked him to drive overnight and come take her home. I bought an old dresser from her, helped them load, hugged the child, and waved farewell. Months of support and negotiating on campus in her behalf were gone. Passing her adviser in the hallway at school the following Monday, I asked whether she knew that Judy had left. The adviser asked casually, "Well, when will she return?" My reply was, "She's not coming back. She's gone. She went home." Silently, to myself, I cried, "That's it! Don't you get it? She'd had enough. She left!"

I indulge in this illustration to try to convey the absolute power of indigenous claims to land, place, and people. W. Richard West Jr., director of NMAI, describes this as "the rich intermesh between person and place in Native life" (West 1998:11). He further claims the centrality of place as "one of the most defining elements of Indian life," determining who we are and establishing "our relationship to everything around us" (11). Lest this insistence on land base be misconstrued as idealist and unrealistic—and given the mobility of indigenous peoples in the United States and Canada—curator Gerald McMaster, writing in *Reservation X*, insists, "A contemporary community is no longer a fixed, unified, or stable place; it exists in a state of flux" (McMaster 1998:20).

McMaster's words seem to reflect the imaginary spaces of de Alba's conceptualization of place as fluid. Yet de Alba's claim that the people of a community—specifically, indigenous communities—hold more importance than a physical location seems mistaken. In her words, "the native community more than the land base—becomes that place of attachment, that common ground in which indigenous identity is rooted" (de Alba 2004:113). This representational construct fails to capture the unique status of Native Americans as sovereign nations. As Venne argues, "Being 'Indigenous' is a political identification and not a racial indicator. Indigenous peoples identify with their lands and territories. It is not the color of the skin or the state government's racial criteria that makes an Indigenous person" (2004:127). In reference to the arts specifically, McMaster (1998:29) claims, "Anyone can become an artist, but not anyone can become an Indian." So while the identity of an artist, as well as cultural identity, can be mobile and unfixed, the two together result in an equation that is "not quite balanced." McMaster (1998:29) terms this weighted positioning "the makeup of a complex subject of the modern age." His full statement is, "Contemporary artists place greater value on self-determination, a willingness to be an individual yet unconsciously tied to place" (29).

Although I agree with McMaster that contemporary artists place a greater value on self-determination in addressing these constructions, I question his assertion that the attachment to place must be unconscious. This rationale seems to replicate the false binaries of individual/collective that have overdetermined artistic motivation and production. I favor the rather overt political positioning reflective in Venne's statements that push the status of sovereignty to the center of discussions. To be unconsciously tied to place seems to evade the more difficult agenda of interrogating ideologies as false constructs. It is toward these ideologies that critiques must be directed, not the institutions that train artists, the markets that circulate arts, or the rejection of communal classifications used as descriptives of Native arts.

The conflicting ideologies of place-based affinities and fluid identities suggest patterns of binary classification. These conventional representations—the West and the rest—draw upon active contrasts of traditional/

modern, communal/individual. An overview of how alterity is utilized in Native American ethnographies and the application of alternative theories (tertiary classifications) is provided in the next chapter.

Notes

1. Quotations from Emmi Whitehorse in this chapter are from the author's interview with her, September 18, 2000.
2. Laura Fragua Cota, interview by author, February 5, 2000.
3. Marcus Amerman, interview by author, March 21, 1991.
4. David Bradley, interview by author, February 21, 1991.
5. Quotations from Gloria Emerson in this chapter are from the author's interview with her, May 31, 1991.
6. Roxanne Swentzell, interview by author, July 10, 1991.
7. Tammy Rahr, interview by author, September 13, 2000.

4 "Art Stars" and Other "Honorary Whites"

> I think women have not been as separated from everyday life as men have been, and it just makes them deal with their careers real differently than men. A long time ago in traditional cultures, it was not so much that way, but boy, it sure is now, and to go out and become somebody and to become famous and have a career and all that seems to be much more of a pressure on men than it is on women, because women seem to be more content with having a nice house. I love my house. I love my kids. They [men] get caught up in many more things...I think that's why the men will pursue the spotlight more, just because they're counting on it for their identity. The women seem to still be more identifying with the home than the men are, especially in the pueblos, especially in our...these traditional cultures. Most of these Indians...the women, they're making their pottery on their kitchen table, and then at dinner they move it and bring out their food, and then they bring back their pots, and then they'll go take care of their grandkids and their kids and go sweep the yard.... It's all a part of what you do in a day. It's not "I'm an artist. I am R. C. Gorman. I am whatever."[1]

Santa Clara sculptor Roxanne Swentzell's observations clearly demark how Native men and women confront societal expectations differently, complicating the binaries of Indian and non-Indian in ways that illuminate the impact of modernity and its inherent intrusion of Western economic patterns. Individualism, competition, self-promotion, and adherence to exclusive spheres of interaction—public and domestic—are articulated in comparative terms, in relation to both history and gender. Here, the domestic woman is championed as more authentic in terms of her connection to community and children and the care and feeding of a family than her male counterparts, who become "Honorary Whites" by pursuing notoriety. Gender is compared in how and where one practices art—from everyday kitchen art practices to the public "art star" represented by celebrated and commercially successful male Hopi artist R. C. Gorman (Monthan 1990). The concept of tradition is widened to include a historic sense ("a long time ago in traditional cultures"), as well as a contemporary one ("especially in our…these traditional cultures"). And important to this study, identity in the fine arts market is cast as something that is constructed—"they're counting on it for their identity"—interpreted in a negative sense in contrast to "all a part of what you do in a day."

I want to cast this comparative positioning in reference to Native American ethnography, relating the situation of Native American artists to the ways in which oppositional characteristics aid and enhance readings of their lived realities. The concept of alterity is examined in this chapter for its usefulness in articulating how key differences are perceived and mobilized by self and others. I hope to problematize standard readings of "oppositional" reference terms in ways that expose the intersection of lived practice with theorization. A concern with power and its application, as well as social change, must be considered in any appraisal that makes binary divisions its central interest. In the academic literature, descriptives such as *dialectic*, *alterity*, *constructivist*, and *dichotomy* enjoy relatively unproblematized use, while other, related concepts such as *binaries* and *oppositional* connote now-outdated academic paradigms such as structuralism, essentialism, and positivism. I will play with these various positions as I examine Native American identity constructs through time.

I continue my discussion of imagery by revisiting the analysis set forth by Robert Berkhofer in *The White Man's Indian* (1979). My impulse is to rectify earlier assumptions about the ways in which stereotypes work. Native ideologies are incredibly complex and deeply configured. The holistic and multivalent character of indigenous studies does not lend itself easily to established disciplinary or philosophical inquiries. Key theoretical assumptions are frequently applied to American Indian studies in a surface fashion, leading to inadequate or even inaccurate conclusions.

Central conclusions, developed in historically specific contexts, can lead to decades of misdirection and confusion. This is clearly the case with Berkhofer, whose conflation of pan-Indian ideologies and stereotypes has contributed to a freezing of the Native American contemporary arts field, prohibiting as it does the mobilization of counterimagery for politically progressive ends. One of the reviewers of the manuscript for this book queried why I use a source that was published almost three decades ago as a primary theoretical resource. The fieldwork for my dissertation occurred from the mid-1980s to the mid-1990s, during the height of multicultural debates. This politically charged era produced scholarship that has since become rigidly established, forging a limited set of interpretative directions in identity scholarship that requires reanalysis.

My central contribution in this regard is the dismantling of key premises that have handicapped a contemporary analysis of Native American visual registers—specifically, the crusade against stereotypes. Debates about stereotypes operate on the assumptions that (1) all stereotypes are bad, (2) stereotypes are largely bad because of pan-Indian ideologies, and (3) eradication is a necessary good. I open up the possibilities that (1) not all stereotypes are bad, (2) pan-Indian ideologies are inevitable and can be put to socially progressive ends, and (3) eradication inhibits the more productive work of rehabilitating imagery constructs by inversion based on alterity. I hope that exposure of these debates will be both relevant and useful. [See plate 11]

To talk about Berkhofer, one must first address Roy Harvey Pearce, his scholarly predecessor. My starting point, then, is Pearce's examination of Native American imagery from contact to the mid-1800s, *The Savages of America: A Study of the Indian and the Idea of Civilization*, originally published in 1953 and revised in 1965. Pearce's contribution ([1953]1965:ix) is the double use to which the image of the Indian could be put, in both positive and negative terms. He identifies the various depictions of the noble savage and savagism in the agenda of American conquest, concluding that "the American's need to compare himself with the Indians whom he knew is as deep and basic as his humanity" (136). This selective representation of the native is essentially self-serving:

> Studying the savage, trying to civilize him, destroying him, in the end they had only studied themselves, strengthened their own civilization, and given those who were coming after them an enlarged certitude of another, even happier destiny—that manifest in the progress of American civilization over all obstacles. [Pearce (1953)1965:ix]

Pearce's study is expanded by Berkhofer's. Like Pearce, Berkhofer argues that white imagery tells more about white desire than Native reality. His terminology and analysis broaden those of Pearce two decades earlier, especially in reference to visual culture: "I mean by image the more literal, even pictorial representation people had of the Indian in their minds...stereotype designates any image we today no longer find accurate in light of our knowledge" (Berkhofer 1979:xvii). The essentialness of negative comparison for whites constructing images of Indians is affirmed: "Since Whites primarily understood the Indian as an antithesis to themselves, then civilization and Indianness as they defined them would forever be opposites" (29). Berkhofer concludes, "the history of the White images of the Indian leads one to cynicism about the ability of one people to understand another in mutually acceptable terms" (196).

In applying these earlier sources, I question how the same premises might look outside the totalizing victimhood in which Pearce and Berkhofer place Native Americans. Given that American extermination policies of the Indian Wars period pre-1900 can be said largely to have failed and that the American assimilationist policies of the twentieth century were compromised, if not altogether rejected, then how does one conceptualize contemporary Natives as actors and agents? Drawing from Pearce's and Berkhofer's premises, I question the counterpropositions. If white stereotypes of Indians express white identity, do Indian stereotypes of whites convey Indian identity? If, historically, whites used negative images of Indians to justify conquest, do Natives use negative images of whites to justify indigeneity? Is it true that when we engage in others' otherness (even in opposition), we become them by matching their criteria? Is avoidance of be-coming an "art star" or "Honorary White" (Bonilla-Silva 2004) a reification of these categories or a statement of sovereignty?

By now, I am in a position to state more clearly a thesis that informs an important area of this narrative discourse analysis. Succinctly, I propose that white stereotypes actually serve to strengthen rather than dissolve tribal identity, and Native stereotypes of whites (and "Honorary Whites") often help shape the expression of Native self-identity (not the formation of identity, not the expression of *all* Native self-identity, but a type of communication of contemporary self-identity). Further, this type of expression of self-identity relies on contrast and occurs when the social parameters are defined by outside, traditionally Western, forces and negotiated by the contrast principles expressed in pursuit of both internal self-resolution and external control of social tensions. The ways in which these self-expressions of identity are utilized further—either to define personhood or to hold relationships together by way of conversation and engagement, for example—suggest compelling areas of inquiry.

In advocating for agency rather than victimhood, I realize that I face at least two immediate criticisms, both of which may likely be advanced by Native communities themselves. The first is the proposition that by assigning self-reflectivity, power, and action to marginalized communities, I am on some level denying that racial oppression continues. According to this argument, I am naïve in my assumption that the targets of racial stereotypes are willing and safely able to mobilize similar conceptual attacks of essentialized representations. In response to the charge of naïve optimism, I claim guilt—I do think opportunities to talk back exist, perhaps more often in elite and mobilized populations and certainly more often for the two generations raised since the 1960s civil rights era. The existence of continued oppression is certainly evident in the research presented here, yet the women quoted continue to dream as optimistically as I do about the future our children face as Native people.

The other criticism that begs recognition is that by indicating an apparent cause-and-effect proposal for white stereotypes and Native identity, I am minimizing—or worse, championing—racist caricatures of Native Americans. Further, in simply talking about stereotypes in any positive light, I am minimizing the work by Native activists who champion erasure of mascots and stereotypical representations in all forms of the media. Am I saying that demeaning stereotypes are actually not so demeaning after all if they offer an ultimately positive outcome for Native communities? Clearly, I am not. As a point of clarification, let me remind the reader that I am forwarding my idea of stereotypes not as an inherently demeaning term or action but as a generalized descriptive with no intrinsically positive or negative attributes. Stereotyping thus is only the act of signifying otherness. Current writings on the "other" (described in more detail later in this chapter) suggest that the act of othering, of dividing, is inherently oppressive (but as you will see, I disagree). My argument is that engagement in these terms and actions is the only way for demeaning, oppressive imagining to be rendered real and made available for debate. Erasure as a political strategy for eradication of mascots has not been proven as the most successful strategic approach. Politically, engagement is a sound alternative to demands for erasure alone in achieving social change. In relation to cause and effect, I suggest only that white stereotypes of Indians often help shape the communication of Nativeness via contrast and comparison, as one method among many.

I hesitate even to declare that my proposition of Native agency has been fully demonstrated, for to ascertain this thesis conclusively, I would need to observe how contrast is utilized in white-defined social situations other than the Indian art world described here. Additionally, I would need to clarify whether contrast is expressed in the public, as well as the private, sphere and whether it is used primarily for internal or external needs. Most important, I would require a model that allows for internal complexities. While addressing some of these shortcomings, I suggest that Native agency in image manipulation or reappropriation of stereotypes offers a potent model for examination in other social contexts. As an effort to this end, I will briefly examine three related Native American ethnographies that suggest parallel lines of inquiry.

Patterns of Alterity in Native Ethnography

Keith Basso's 1979 *Portraits of "The Whiteman"* argues that the internal humor of the White Mountain Apache men builds upon a metanarrative that positions "the Whiteman" as a symbol of what "the Apache" is not. By internal humor, he refers to the fact that "Whiteman" humor is not directed toward non-Indians but rather is performed among Apaches as a form of linguistic play. Usually, "portraits of the Whiteman" in joking form are performed by adult men, and the objects of the Whiteman jokes are adult men (Basso 1979:32).

Basso engages analyses of sociolinguistics, humor, and performance in his understandings of Apache value systems that privilege personal characteristics such as privacy, respect, reserve, and noncoercion. An Apache man engaging in this humor may imitate a fellow tribesman by talking in a boisterous, loud manner, calling him by his given name, taking him by his shoulder to force him to sit down, and inquiring about his health—in general violating every sense of good comportment as defined by White Mountain Apaches.

Although the content of the Whiteman symbol may vary from tribe to tribe and from generation to generation, Basso generalizes this performative genre as belonging to all Native American cultures: "It appears to be the case that in all Indian cultures 'the Whiteman' serves as a conspicuous vehicle for conceptions that define and characterize what 'the Indian' is not" (Basso 1979:5). He notes, however, that "'the Whiteman' comes in different versions" (4). Jokes parodying white men can also be used to comment on other ethnic groups—"Blacks, Spanish-Americans, Orientals, and other Indian groups"—indicating an impressively flexible genre (100).

My analysis finds congruence in and also departure from Basso's ethnography. Most obviously, Basso's text investigates this form of binary opposition as specifically male humor; women are conspicuously absent. This lack of analysis could be the result of there being no comparable female joking behavior, simply a different fieldwork focus, or a lack of entry into women's behavior linked to Basso's position as a male ethnographer. This last variable is not sustained in the ethnography, for many of Basso's sources are female— the history of Whiteman jokes is, for example, related by an older Apache woman (Basso 1979:29–30). However, according to Julie Cruikshank (1990), these distinctions are important to note; access is not all encompassing. In her ethnography *Life Lived like a Story: Life Stories of Three Yukon Native Elders*, she is explicit about how her position as a female ethnographer has impacted her research efforts: "The kinds of long-term collaborative working relationships I have developed with older women are simply not socially appropriate for me to have with older men" (Cruikshank 1990:19). As a decidedly gendered form of alterity and reversal, Basso's "Whiteman" humor would seem to suggest potent applications of comparative analyses between male and female joking behaviors.

In terms of methodology, my research is grounded in analysis of taped and transcribed conversations, not observations of the type that Basso utilizes in descriptions of joking performances. I interviewed women from a variety of tribes, not a single tribe set in a regional context, as Basso did. Our talk often veered from the research at hand to other, more personal topics rooted in our shared womanhood, such as health, children, and relationships, confirming Cruikshank's observations concerning the impact of gender in fieldwork situations.

In reference to the theoretical arguments presented in Basso's work, I find his use of Alfonso Ortiz's writings on role reversal compelling. According to Ortiz (1972), Pueblo imitations of culturally dissimilar people (whites and other ethnicities) occur most conspicuously in the context of public ceremonials (Basso 1979:102). In the context of Native women artists working professionally in Santa Fe, one may fruitfully apply this parameter in observing how Native actors conceive of public spaces in the Indian art world. Does contrast occur more often in non-Native settings? For example, Emmi Whitehorse describes her positioning as an artist in terms similar to those used to describe her experience in boarding schools (see chapter 2). Both involve public situations in which Native and non-Native behaviors may clash severely.

Basso postulates that conceptions of the Whiteman are primary in understanding what an Apache is saying to the Apache with whom he is joking. There exists a present relationship of two Apache men engaging in playful banter; but more important, this present relationship is based on an absent relationship that is a critique of how non-Indians behave. He provides an example in which a young Apache girl playfully grabs a puppy by the tail and is nipped. After screaming, "You're nothing!" in Apache, she turns and addresses the dog in English: "You bad boy! Why you do that—make trouble for me? You stay here…don't go outside, get punish what you did it. Maybe you going to other classroom. I tell you mother what you did it" (Basso 1979:10). The puppy in this example is serving as a present reference to the absent relationship of a scolding schoolteacher (who we assume is Anglo). According to Basso, "to know what an Apache is saying about his relationship with someone he is joking, one has first to know what he is saying about Anglo-Americans and their relationships with Apaches. Conceptions of 'the Whiteman' are primary" (17). Thus, the primary function of Whiteman jokes is to make sense of what Basso terms "a complex human 'problem'" (17). He summarizes: "Jokers use jokes to make sense of Whitemen"(18).

The Native women artists I interviewed did not impress me as being concerned with understanding Anglo behavior so much as discerning how Native people themselves should behave. Their narratives do not engage performance or joking behavior but are more characterized as narrated self-reflection, using a negative comparison to frame positive attributes. Consider the following passage from Tessie Naranjo (who earned a PhD in Sociology from the University of New Mexico) on Western education:

> I had a real difficulty doing it, and it's amazing that I got as far in my education as I did. I had a real struggle with it because, you know, you need discipline. I think I had persistence, but without discipline. And other things that are very Western-like...playing up to the teachers or raising my hand. It was my Pueblo nature or Pueblo personality that didn't know how to compete, so that my grades were very mediocre. I don't value competition. I don't value individualism. I value the communal sort of thing. I really value the communal, collective sort of thing. So I felt unsuccessful with my Western education, and very slowly I was able to...in my own way, I guess...able to work it so that I would get as far as I did.[2]

Naranjo's narrative does not seem to evidence an overriding concern with how to get along with white men so much as a concern with how her own personality functions and is compromised by the external system she must navigate. This intersection of formal education and Native values is a powerful source for examining how Natives configure themselves in response to Western norms. The boarding school experience in Native North America is a rich area in which to examine the intersections of white and Indian behaviors, as Tsianina Lomawaima's text demonstrates.

Lomawaima's 1994 ethnography, *They Called It Prairie Light: The Story of the Chilocco Indian School*, examines how assimilationist Indian boarding schools inadvertently created a new pan-Indian identity, both by conceptualizing all tribes as one discrete "Indian" entity and by bringing previously isolated tribes together. Lomawaima argues for recognizing the power of individual students as active creators of their positionality in this process, not as hapless victims of a federal system. Chilocco boarding-school alumni (from 1920 to 1940) reveal in their memories of school life how they created a school culture influenced but not determined by the bounds of federal control (Lomawaima 1994:xi). "Schools often strengthened rather than dissolved tribal identity" (xiii).

Lomawaima (1994:xiii) rejects both deterministic ethnic theories that postulate a "natural opposition of human groups" and the idea that ethnic identity "emerges" in such a setting. Stressing the internal complexities of boarding school student life and the importance of attending to the concrete details of personal narratives, Lomawaima advocates a more nuanced approach than the formation of Indian identity only in opposition to non-Indian authority.

My argument stresses similar themes to Lomawaima's work: the Indian art market generally and Indian images and stereotypes specifically may strengthen rather than dissolve tribal identity. Likewise, I agree that identity formation is too strong a conclusion and suggests a lack of diversity of the in-group referenced. I stress the communication of identity as a means of individuals clarifying their own self-perceptions. These convergences between the Native arts world and the boarding school experience are likely due to the similarity of the study group (pantribal male and female respondents), as well as the interview format (life history narratives).

Cruikshank's *Life Lived like a Story* presents several useful avenues of analysis for Native women's life narratives. Cruikshank suggests that Yukon women's autobiographies should not be interpreted as factual evidence but as a means of understanding and explaining contemporary events (such as the construction of the Alaska Highway): "The genre…may be more closely associated with conventions of oral narrative than with positivistic evidence about the past" (Cruikshank 1990:2). The manner in which oral histories are used by the women in explaining their own communities and lives (the context of the telling) drives Cruikshank's inquiry, not the content of the narratives themselves as a type of archival record. Her work presents evidence similar to Lomawaima's in that the life stories do not entirely form identity but communicate identity through the process of the telling.

Addressing the theoretical distinctions in the field of anthropology, Cruikshank argues against the typical divisions that address storytelling—notably, "expressive forms" and "adaptive strategies"—stating that these separate categories "may be inappropriate in situations where people see storytelling as central to their culture" (Cruikshank 1990:354). She suggests a more holistic approach to the interpretation of storytelling, arguing that conflicting social norms (the adaptive strategies approach) may be dramatized in storytelling but the narratives should not be interpreted solely in this functionalist manner. Neither, then, should the stories be considered apart from the telling as artifacts or examples solely of "expressive forms."

For example, the "stolen woman" tale that involves a woman's opposing loyalties to her brothers and to her husband's family expresses social tension but is not rooted exclusively in these contradictions. Cruikshank argues that this reductive approach (structuralist in nature) does not fully account for the ways in which narrators actually use symbols as models for their own lives. She invites a play between the social significance of stories and the allegory of social interaction that takes place in the story of the myth.

In advocating that structural oppositions alone should not drive interpretations (Cruikshank 1990:342–343), Cruikshank presents an analysis similar to Lomawaima's, in that she argues for attending to individual talents and experiences. Cruikshank's more recent (2007) research examines how the establishment of territorial boundaries divides indigenous peoples who were formerly connected. Additionally, this more physical boundary making has the effect of informing identity constructs across northwestern Canada and Alaska. The content of narrative as socially significant thus should not be dismissed in privileging an analysis of identity formed in response to conflicting norms.

All three ethnographies (Basso, Lomawaima, and Cruikshank) draw from the concept of oppositionality or alterity. Basso's linguistic play utilizes role reversal, Lomawaima's boarding school narratives draw meaning from the dialectic between institutional requirements and individual identity formation, and Cruikshank's life histories present symbolic dichotomies between societal norms and individual actions. Basso and Lomawaima treat the division of Native and non-Native norms, while the Yukon women's stories focus on supernatural characters that illustrate internal social tensions and resolutions that are referenced in light of external societal demands. In all three cases, the importance of both the content of the narrative (how to behave) and the form of the narrative (jokes, narratives, storytelling) is essential to communicating values, allowing researchers to explore the possibilities of how oral expressions in the forms of joking, life histories, and storytelling work as cultural processes rather than as cultural descriptions. The comparative forms of the narratives (positioning accepted values of an in-group with the stigmatized values of an out-group) then operate as tools or grammars for conveying beliefs.

It is important to note that these assumed, inert conventions or tools may be expressed and interpreted differently in terms of gender. Cruikshank suggests that the narrative conventions of Native women may differ significantly from those of Native men and non-Native women. While men's life stories tend to be heroic, "women's autobiographies rarely present a coherent polished synthesis" (Cruikshank 1990:3). Diffusion and diversity, as well as relationality, have been explored as themes in feminist women's autobiography (Smith and Watson 1998). Basso's analysis of a particular cultural form in joking behavior is discretely marked by code switching, with circumscribed beginnings and endings. Cruikshank's analysis of women presents a more indirect, even discontinuous, presentation of women's stories, suggesting that this narrative style could be interpreted as a gendered norm. She explains, "From the beginning, several of the eldest women responded to my questions about secular events by telling traditional stories. The more I persisted with my agenda, the more insistent each was.... Each explained that these narratives were important to record *as part of* her life story" (Cruikshank 1990:2). Could Basso's emphasis on performance in Apache humor thus be seen as a gendered norm rather than as a marker of White Mountain humor overall? Clearly, the authority of ethnographic accounts that privilege either male or female perspectives should be investigated for the presence of these types of generalizations.

If stories help Yukon women cope with change and conflicting demands, as Cruikshank's text argues, can this ethnography be extended to the broader analysis of contemporary Native stereotypes? Cruikshank's work suggests that the concept of a border—the event of engagement with others—may actually fuel the articulation of self-identity. This parallel suggests that stereotypes may fruitfully be conceived of as modern myths.

The use of stereotypes as symbolic reference points or myths suggests early structuralist positions that interpret myths as inherently contradictory. Social tensions are played out in oppositions such as life and death, nature and culture, granting a temporality to events that are timelessly atemporal. This resolution of contraries, sanctioned by the work of scholars such as Claude Lévi-Strauss (1963), suggests a functionalist reasoning that denies the active engagement with meaning and convention championed here.

Yet the benefit of aligning stereotypes with myth is that it would permit an unencumbered analysis that bypasses the solely negative definition of stereotypes utilized by Berkhofer, for example. In other words, stereotypes as myths permit the use of these essentialized constructs as a type of grammar or tool for conveying substantive narratives of proper behavior. If this corollary is drawn, then it becomes possible to examine whether constructions of "Whiteman" behavior (stereotypes) provide Native women with a tool with which to withstand change and stay culturally centered in a manner similar to the way Yukon elders use storytelling as a tool for action and instruction.

On a broader analysis, we can ask whether all oppressive characterizations, racist beliefs, and essentializing behaviors provide grounds for enactment of Nativeness. Are these performances only a reaction to moments of cultural discord in an external and reactive fashion, or do they serve to enhance the articulation of identity in a manner that is beneficial to discrete communities? If the use of "Whiteman" stereotypes is solely in reaction to essentialized formulations of the "Redman," then can it be said that indigenous values are at play? Mia Bay's *The White Image in the Black Mind* (2000) suggests that African Americans were "inexorably drawn into a debate over the character of the races," primarily as an attempt to "rebut and refute" white claims about blacks (Bay 2000:6). The danger in this approach, as she points out, is a form of black chauvinism that mirrors the racist logic it opposes: "Racism could be reversed more readily than it could be controverted" (45). Extended to a consideration of Indian claims by whites, does the use of white stereotypes indicate submission to racist ideologies in reverse or the adaptation of a language that enables the expression of values? Clearly, the related ethnographies referenced above indicate the latter of these two considerations.

Are Stereotypes Modern Myths? And If So, Are They Inherently Moralistic?

> Conflict, yes. Because one of the things that is discouraged is that you don't boast about yourself and you don't stand out. You always try to be very humble—as much as possible—and I do feel very uncomfortable on the front covers of newspapers. I do feel very embarrassed about it. But at the same time, it is a part of the business, and you do have to be visible if you want to sell your work, and you've got to be out there every day. I just sort of see it now as something I've got to do to put food on the table. That sounds terrible.
>
> It is very hard for Native Americans to treat this like a business and to plan and to do this. For a white person, it's easy—that's the first thing they think of...image building. Take a look at Jeff Koons—that publicity he's used just to get where he is. It's unbelievable. None of us will ever do that because...it's not part of our upbringing. It's too evil. It's something like that. For me, it is.[3]

Whitehorse's pragmatic approach to her career demonstrates how conflicting values of artistic identity are articulated by contrast. The Native American experience is generalized from tribal specifics, defining behaviors that are deemed proper ("you don't boast about yourself") or improper ("you've got to be out there every day"). Simultaneously, however, this analysis is claimed by Whitehorse as an individual alone, for to speak for others is also a weighty matter that could be considered presumptuous. In the end, she qualifies her statement that the shameless self-promotion of such famous celebrities as the Pop artist Koons is akin to something evil by saying, "For me, it is."

This honest self-narrative presents several compelling points of departure for this discussion. Does "Whiteman" behavior as illustrated by the career of Koons serve as a symbol? Can the shameless self-promoting of this non-Native be considered a modern myth of "Whiteman" behavior? Does this comparison between Native and non-Native values act as a tool of identity expression? Are these moralistic considerations? Are stereotypes inherently moralistic?

John LeRoy's *Fabricated World: An Interpretation of Kewa Tales* (1985) presents research on tales (*lidi*) among the Kewa of Papua New Guinea. Like Pearce and Berkhofer, LeRoy utilizes concepts of negative comparison to offer illustration and instruction of ideal values: "Kewa tales deal with difficulties within the social domains. That is, they refer to specific conflicts or *oppositions*" (LeRoy 1985:15). He states that, unlike Lévi-Strauss's binarism (which he defines as cognitive or logical), the oppositions he discovered were moral or ethical:

> Each social domain I shall consider to be mediated by ideas about the propriety of action. Notions of "good" or "bad" do not express some vague desire about what wishfully ought to be the case. They might more usefully be thought of as predicates that define positively and negatively the domain in question. [LeRoy 1985:15]

LeRoy's analysis presents the good/bad contrast as dialectical, as well as definitional, oppositions corresponding here to practical problems experienced in everyday life. Although LeRoy describes the use of lidi narratives in terms of structural theory, he also recognizes that the "movement of the narrative is not so much to 'resolve' the original opposition or conflict as to simply express it—to subject it to cultural mediation and meditation" (1985:15–16).

This analytical approach would seem to indicate that the communicative aspect of stereotypes is central to working out identity orientation; the cultural mediation described by LeRoy mirrors the related Native American ethnographies discussed above. These ethnographies suggest a dynamic approach to the use of alterity—a social tool that is practical, serviceable, and simultaneously mythical or symbolic. Thus, Whitehorse's use of the white man as something akin to evil is not simply a biased rejection of all non-Natives but is a means of communicating her own personal values defined generally as Native values. Do cultural mediations of this type serve primarily internal (moralistic in terms of conformity to community standards) or external (ultimately peripheral to community) needs?

The question of how binaries serve different constituents has long been viewed in the anthropological literature as involving general issues of classification and boundary maintenance. Classification would appear to indicate a problematic of in-group referencing, and boundary maintenance, an issue of one's relationship with others. The earlier literature on alterity and ethnicity was particularly concerned with how groups maintained difference in light of assimilationist efforts and acculturation trends. The classical work on cultural boundaries is Fredrik Barth's *Ethnic Groups and Boundaries* (1969), which proposes the importance of dichotomies for maintenance of ethnicity. Barth states,

> The nature of continuity of ethnic units…depends on the maintenance of a boundary. The cultural features that signal the boundary may change, and the cultural characteristics of the members may likewise be transformed, indeed, even the organizational form of the group may change—yet the fact of continuing dichotomization between members and outsiders allows us to specify the nature of continuity, and investigate the changing cultural form and content. [Barth 1969:14]

A concern with continuity is echoed as well in Edward Spicer's work on persistent cultural systems (1971). In the ten systems investigated, all actors shared a common trait—the tendency to develop well-defined symbols of identity that differentiated them from other groups, especially those groups they opposed. Spicer states that the formation and maintenance of persistent identity systems are "intimately bound up with the conditions of opposition," adding that "it appears that the oppositional process is the essential factor in the formation and development of the persistent identity system" (Spicer 1971:797).

Related early works of alterity studies dealt with the topic of inversion in ritual, such as role reversal or institutionalized clowning. In *The Reversible World: Symbolic Inversion in Art and Society* (1978), Barbara A. Babcock expands the anthropological concern with inversion in ritual alone, defining symbolic inversion as "any act of expressive behavior which inverts, contradicts, abrogates, or in some fashion presents an alternative to commonly held cultural codes, values, and norms, be they linguistic, literary or artistic, religious, or social and political" (Babcock 1978:14). Rather than serve as functional boundary-maintenance references alone (what I am terming external or reactive uses of binaries), symbolic inversions came to be seen as mechanisms whereby culture is enabled to "speak about itself" (21), thus indicating a concern with self-classification, psychological and internal social order.

Illustrating this reversal theory in the same volume is Renato Rosaldo's analysis of colonial descriptives, "The Rhetoric of Control: Ilongots Viewed as Natural Bandits and Wild Indians." This essay explains how the terms, or "verbal portraits," used to describe the Ilongots are "polar" and "imply an opposite, such as 'criminal' versus 'lawful,' and 'filthy' versus 'clean.'" (Rosaldo 1978:242).

> If civilized people were said to be sedentary, the Ilongots were to be regarded as nomadic; the civilized thesis generated its savage antithesis. Like ethnocentric and racist perspectives on "the other," the colonists' formula—as symbolically potent as it was distorted—was to take a characteristic regarded as morally ideal in their own society and verbally endow the Ilongots with its opposite. [Rosaldo 1978:254]

The use of distortion echoes themes presented earlier—Cruikshank's insistence that life narratives cannot be used as simple truth statements but as symbols of right living and Basso's presentation of humor as distorted and exaggerated antinorms. Moral ideals referenced in contrast are utilized by colonial powers in the act of making colonial subjects the other (boundaries) and by the colonized in ordering their own moral universes (internal self-classification). It is this internal use of binary classification in a moral and ethical sense that I am most concerned with, as demonstrated by patterned references to Whiteman behavior in the arts, whether that be self-promotion, marketing, or education (see plates 12a, 12b).

Given the utility of symbolic inversions in a nonfunctional, communicative manner, why is it so difficult to redeem stereotypes? Why is it that binaries are dismissed as only functional? Critiques of binaries (and thus structuralist modes of thinking) are typically based on two arguments. One is the obviousness of the approach as "the oldest classificatory toolkit of men and women, juniors and seniors, and maybe even early hominids from this side as opposed to that side of the river" (35). The other is the inability of binaries to express "the richness and sophistication of 'other' people's taxonomies" (Baumann 2004:35).

An additional argument launched from the perspective of indigenous researchers is that the use of borders and binaries results in "essentializing discourses of liminality" that "delimit the work of decolonizing research" (Mutua and Swadener 2004:12) both spatially and temporally. This approach sees the application of these older conceptual divides as inherently essentializing and therefore damaging. A researcher's engagement in these narratives is thus reactive and limited by an "oppressive colonizing language developed within a colonizing oppressive research tradition" (12).

In defense of utilizing terms of engagement that may be characterized as oppressive and colonialist, I argue a line of reasoning similar to my rationalization of referencing stereotypes: (1) the language and the theory of alterity exist and are manifest daily in the academy, media, and politics; (2) a sustained engagement in this vocabulary does not necessarily indicate a particular alignment of my position with other uses; and (3) eradication or avoidance as a political strategy has not proven particularly effective as a means of social change.

Othering as the New Stereotype

> Well, I don't think monetary achievement is my ultimate goal, even though I would like to feel comfortable. I hear a lot of Indian artists [say], "I want to be rich, and I want to be the R. C. Gorman, or the Fritz Scholder, or the ultimate." To me, that's almost a white man's philosophy or a white man's artist goal. But I am building my own studio now, and what I'd like to do…I want to finish my studio this summer, and eventually…I want to be able to create a freedom… that means low overhead and very little cost. I want to have a reputation as a Native American graphic arts center, so people can come in and have fellowships and work with me for a couple of weeks and produce prints.[4]

Pitt River Paiute artist Jean LaMarr expresses her orientation as a community member via her commitment to educating others and providing a space for their creativity as Native American artists. She enacts this positive expression of her own values in contrast to the values of "known" male Native artists who have achieved financial success, an indication here of non-Native values perceived as a Whiteman orientation. Whiteman as a symbol enables articulation of Native norms. Importantly, Whiteman is not a racial but a behavioral referent; a Whiteman is competitive, individualistic, and capitalistic (Haozous 2005). A Native person is noncompetitive, communal, and not engaged in excessive consumer practices. The definition of one stereotype enables the definition of another.

Recent scholarship has utilized the concept of "othering" to describe the parallel uses of "oppositions" and "binaries" by an earlier generation. This literature emphasizes the fluid nature of identity constructs, rejecting earlier structuralist arguments that proved too rigid for application in modernist global settings. Othering has replaced stereotyping as a means of describing in less judgmental terms how groups of people struggle with articulating and understanding difference. This softer analytical approach emphasizes agency rather than victimhood and incorporates the dynamisms of rapid change and movement across regional divides. Thus, classificatory schemes, boundary maintenance, and even moralistic stances are less a concern than providing conceptual structures that avoid essentialist approaches.

An example of this approach is provided by Raymond Corbey and Joep Leerssen in the compilation *Alterity, Identity, Image: Selves and Others in Society and Scholarship* (1991). They take as a "pre-given fact" that subjective identity exists "in a constant confrontation with a sphere outside its cognitive purview (Corbey and Leerssen 1991:xviii), positioning alterity not as a new insight in the manner of Berkhofer's *White Man's Indian* but as a given. Associated responses of guilt, shame, or other moralistic reactions to the outcomes of stereotyping are excluded in an effort to examine only the theoretical processes at play: "Otherness...is a categorical fact of life, and as such ethically neutral" (xviii). Alterity thus is inherently neutral—"alterity does not *by definition* imply a denigration of the Other" (vii).

Ernst van Alphen, a contributor in the same volume (1993:3), presents alterity as a "code" and "a device of meaning-production":

> The only way to know the other is by letting the other speak about me, by giving the other the position of "I." When "I" speak about the other, I remain in fact caught in the process of defining or demarcating my self-image. The other is used as a screen on which ideals or terrors can be projected, or as locations to which problematic feelings about self can be displaced. [van Alphen 1991:15]

Van Alphen's essay highlights the work of German artist Anselm Kiefer, who is noted for controversial pieces in which he evokes Germany's Nazi past, at times dressing in military garb and performing, insinuating a "disturbing nostalgia." Kiefer has said, "I do not identify with...Hitler, but I have to reenact what they did just a little bit in order to understand the madness. That is why I make these attempts to become a fascist" (answers.com). This quote has striking similarities to explanations provided by artist Kara Walker in defense of her use of plantation imagery: "I decided to offer up my side-long glances: to be a slave just a little bit.... So I used this mythic, fictional, kind of slave character to justify myself, or to reinvent myself in some other situations" (Saltz 1996:86). Both artists adopt derogatory images as their artistic palette not to celebrate but to memorialize. Kiefer's work is described as "a sustained reflection on how mythic images function in history, how myth can never escape history, and how history in turn has to rely on mythic images" (Huyssen 1989:27). Stereotypes in these examples are often misread in a primary sense rather than in a reflective, mirroring, othering capacity (see plate 13).

Anthropologists Gerd Baumann and Andre Gingrich (2004) refined the concept of alterity studies by articulating a structural approach to the field and utilizing the concept of multiple grammars. In explaining their adoption of this "unfashionable" approach, they propose "flexible classificatory models employed in, and for, social interaction" as a pragmatic solution to the divide between essentialism and "helpless reduction of all social facts to contextual contingency" (Baumann and Gingrich 2004:xiv). Like Corbey and Leerssen, they see the fact that "every selfing involves an othering" as an "unproductive, and essentially moralist, truism" (x). Unlike these authors, however, they value the implications of their research as a means for understanding extreme forms of collective and genocidal violence (xi).

Baumann and Gingrich advocate a multidimensional approach to othering rather than the binarism that tends to reify and essentialize people and communities. Their structuralist approach compellingly argues for three different types of self/othering processes or grammars: orientalization (reverse mirroring), segmentation (contextual inclusions and exclusions), and encompassment (hierarchical subsumption). Baumann additionally demonstrates that each of these othering grammars adheres to a ternary structure rather than the self-evident binary divide, arguing, "Binarisms inevitably raise the possibility of tripartition" (2004:35).

This ternary approach to self/othering is made evident by reference not only to the classical notion of the liminal phase—a transition between life and death, for example—but also to language whereby each self and other implicates a third or absent party. Ambiguous categories—creolization or hybridization—are also considered within these grammars as individuals and groups of individuals are variously segmented or amalgamated.

Baumann and Gingrich's working definition of identity is characterized as multidimensional and fluid and encompasses power-related ascriptions by selves and others, "simultaneously combining sameness, or belonging, with alterity, or otherness " (Baumann and Gingrich 2004:). Thus, essentialist or moralistic connotations suggested by "strong" concepts of identity are rejected in favor of "weak" concepts of identity studied in context and with attention to agency (x). This abandonment of moral considerations is circumscribed by Baumann, who, while admitting that "moralizing about othering is boring and useless," also suggests that a value-free social science does not exist, stating in particular, "I have yet to see an academic not frightened by violence" (Baumann 20004:45). Moral and ethical concerns are thus retained in light of the implications of extreme forms of othering—the type described by Baumann as "anti-grammar"—"We are good, so they are bad" taken to the genocidal conclusion, "We must live, so they must die" (42).

The Politics of Othering in Indian Country

Having traversed a somewhat chronological discussion of alterity and identity via history, ethnography, philosophy, and anthropology, we can productively ask how these approaches to defining difference in contrast contribute to an understanding of Native American representations and, specifically, the situation of Native American women's lives. After revisiting the propositions I introduced at the beginning of this chapter, can it be said that white stereotypes can be redemptive for Native Americans' self-imaging? This premise was advanced on the example of Native stereotypes of whites as a form of inversion of white stereotypes of Indians. Additionally, my proposition was restricted to the usefulness of communicating identity via the modern myth of stereotypes, not to an argument for total identity formation. This expression of self-identity was further interpreted as utilizing contrast and occurring in contexts perceived as non-Native. Demeaning uses of stereotypes as racial hate slogans are recognized as an extreme and damaging form of stereotyping in general and are not normalized in this scenario.

Drawing from the scholarship of Baumann and Gingrich on alterity and identity, I argue that the grammatical/structural approach they advocate can apply partially to the case study presented here. Native women referencing both Native men and white men as displaying "art star" or Whiteman behavior adhere to the grammar of orientalizing and, consequently, to the work of Edward Said (1978). This "binary opposition subject to reversal" (Baumann 2004:20) appears to mimic similar arguments positioned decades earlier by Pearce and Berkhofer, with the crucial difference being new considerations of agency and a dialogic process of communication. In many ways, the mirroring of this social practice can be said to resemble the symbolic inversion studies of the late 1970s and, as such, address psychological concerns.

Baumann and Gingrich's grammar of segmentation most powerfully speaks to the case at hand as we see Native women artists positioning themselves as independent entities at the level of individual or tribal member and also as members of the more generalized identity of Native American. For Swentzell, this was expressed as "these traditional cultures"; for Whitehorse,

"Native American cultures." Both examples represent a fusion of individual tribal entities in opposition to the Western ideal of artist, thus advancing the argument of white stereotypes strengthening rather than dissolving Native identity.

The third grammar identified, encompassment, though suggesting perhaps a practical solution to the tensions of "art star" versus communal artist, does not readily transfer directly to Native American art dialogues. Encompassment seems a close match with assimilation, a practice attempted by the federal government and primarily rejected by tribes who have resisted this encroachment on their sovereign status. Considered on a micro level, encompassment works in a negative fashion as those "Honorary Whites" who seek and accept "art star" status conform to values deemed amoral in the narratives presented.

The suggestion that identity/alterity debates that appear to be binaries at surface level may actually reference multidimensional or ternary aspects holds real possibilities for application in Indian Country. Although Baumann and Gingrich demonstrate this dimension of the debates primarily in reference to language, similar arguments have been advanced productively by feminist scholars, who advocate new considerations of how differing is weighed politically and morally. Val Plumwood (2002:45) claims that feminism "seems to require a concept of women's difference and women's presence as positively-other-than rather than as other-than-the-male." Stating that the fields of gender and racial studies have been divided in "problematic and oppressive ways between a privileged, dominant One and a devalued or subordinated Other," she argues, "there are other ways to make this conceptual division that provides the basic logical framework underlying genderized and racialized identities" (46).

Rather than debate the numerical variants of othering, Plumwood asserts that the problem is one of conflating two distinct terms: dichotomy and dualism. She positions *dichotomy* as an inert term that registers only the act of severing. Dichotomy and alterity, thus, are larger concepts indicating "the mode of division of a field" (Plumwood 2002:47), while the concept of dualism has been employed problematically "to indicate a polarized, oppositional, and oppressive form of differentiation" (47). Plumwood advances recognition of the distinctions between "differentiation itself and oppressive forms of this operation" (47). She summarizes, "The assumption that dichotomy is automatically a polarizing function is fallacious. A separation is not the same as a polarization" (49).

Plumwood's arguments clarify the Baumann and Gingrich grammars lexicon by disassociating the action of otherness (alterity) from the consequences of othering (polarizing identities). Translating these concepts to the narratives of Native women, it can be argued that the stereotypes referenced are, by their nature, actions of alterity—or, as I have advanced, tools of communication. The use of Whiteman stereotypes is orientalizing by inversion, produces segmentation, and resists encompassment—but by means of "positively-other-than," in Plumwood's words, rather than the reverse racism of which Bay warns. Negative characterizations are thus a potent tool of self-expression, not simply another event to which oppressed actors must respond with either quiet dignity or angry backlash. Plumwood summarizes, "The idea that negative characterizations are automatically oppressive and must be avoided at all costs if we are to attain liberated discourse is widespread among intellectuals of various kinds. It can seriously distort and limit expression in a variety of movement contexts, not just in feminism" (Plumwood 2002:53).

The avoidance of discussions deemed dualistic and therefore oppressive may be limiting in Native arts contexts as well. If the construction of Whiteman stereotypes is predicated on contrast with white stereotypes of Indians (by way of inversion), then this form of narrative construct could not occur without segmentation or, as Plumwood terms it, dichotomization. The fact that this register of identity narrative does seem to occur in contexts perceived as non-Native (boarding schools, art markets) lends itself to the generalization that this tool of communication is generated by encounters in which mutual grammars of reference are not readily available. Thus, Western symbolism (essentializing stereotypes) is adopted as a ready means of bridging conceptual gaps in mutual value systems. The incorporation of this form of othering by Native communities could be considered alternatively as creative indigenous adaptations or as reactive behaviors triggered by contact and blurred boundaries. These varied interpretations will depend upon the contextual circumstances of their enactment and the orientation of the observer, predisposed to either interpretation of agency or victimhood. The history of the literature suggests that attention to both Native and white stereotypes can contribute to more accurate readings of this symbolic analysis of narrative forms.

Notes

1. Roxanne Swentzell, interview by author, July 10, 1991.
2. Tessie Naranjo, interview by author, April 18, 1991.
3. Emmi Whitehorse, interview by author, March 15, 1991.
4. Jean LaMarr, interview by author, May 16, 1991.

5 "They've Got It All Wrong"

Uses and Abuses of Indian Representations

I saw this Hopi, a sculpture of this maiden with a butterfly whorl. And that's a maiden—that's a young girl. She's a virgin. And they had this...this sculpture was this woman, but she must have had a bustier on, and it pushed her boobs up, and she had a big old cleft, and her manta came down, and it was slit down to the middle, and she wore her hair all...Hopi maiden! That's a maiden! It doesn't look like a maiden to me! [*laughs*] See, those kinds of...come on, a young girl, unless she grows fast, develops really fast. For a Hopi young maiden, she wouldn't be...that big...she wouldn't be that developed...her manta wouldn't be slit down to show her cleavage. And you know, because they don't know that culture, it's like they are making a mockery of it. They are cheapening it. And when I saw that, it was like, "No. That was sick."... Because you are a part of that culture, you know...the dos and don'ts. And because the people who do the artwork depict Indian people doing things, they've got it all wrong. And that's when people will come in and see that and [say], "Oh, that is beautiful. Oh, are all the Hopi maidens dressed like that?" No, no we don't! That's a maiden. A young girl would not be dressed like that. She's not a young maiden. Look at how big she is. That's a woman.[1]

Artist Laura Fragua Cota of Jemez Pueblo expresses the frustration of many Native artists who are forced to address dominant and competing images of Native culture that operate out of a frame of representational references separate from their own. In the imagination of the consumer, the sexualized female primitive is a ready reference, an inert category of artistic registry that poses no significant negative consequences to the communities represented. The incorporation of certain tribal forms, particularly the hair done in the traditional butterfly whorl, may be seen as an innocuous adaptation of a cultural attribute. Yet for a Pueblo person, this free borrowing of a social signifier for virginity in tandem with overtly sexualized dress and exaggerated breasts represents something "sick"—a cultural insult.

Anthropologist Peter Whitely (1997:186) uses the phrase "primitivist cathexis" to describe the allure of this aesthetic appropriation, arguing that voyeuristic attributions of beauty "effectively [discharge] human obligation and [divert] any real social concern" (see plate 14). Thus, staged cultural identities evident in the sculpture of a Hopi maiden enable outsiders "in the seclusion of their imaginations" to divorce their experience of Hopi culture from other material realities—including, in this instance, religious and cultural values. In this world of Indian art production and consumption, "complicity in domination" is denied by placement of art in a category apart from material politics. These "abuses of representations" are seen as inescapable: "Contemporary Hopi life is indetachably positioned within the political-economic and aesthetic-cultural interests of a national polity and its local forms under the control of Anglo-Americans" (187). Whitely thus concludes, "Aestheticization defuses social responsibility" (186).

While Whitely argues for an inherent corruption of social morals in aesthetic sensibilities, my premise positions artistic production as a means of overcoming social irresponsibility. It is precisely the aesthetic qualities of representations that render them powerful; this potential is conceivably available to both Native and non-Native communities to appropriate to their own ends. Artists, as image producers, are uniquely positioned to intercede in these dialogues via the tools of representation. The manner in which identity politics are expressed through Indian arts exposes often subtle orientations; aesthetics may enhance exoticism as well as self-determination. In what ways does self-representation, then, differ from the forms of representation that are considered appropriative, racist, or demeaning? Importantly, can the preconceived attributes of non-Indian image producers be reappropriated in meaningful ways? To return to the questions posed at the beginning of this work, how are certain identities privileged, and what do actors/image makers do with these monopolized images?

Given that complete agency is often exercised within material constraints, is it realistic to think of ways that images such as the sexualized Hopi maiden may be redeemed? I have suggested that eradication is not a particularly productive avenue for asserting social justice, presenting as it does a simultaneous disavowal and embracement of image making as consequential. I have advanced the thesis that forms of inversion (Native stereotypes of whites) serve as one avenue of asserting positive self-representation and that dialogue with demeaning racist stereotypes can serve as a platform for indigenous self-representation. I recognize that these strategies assume the ability of those marginalized to enact change—possibly a naïve, privileged, and overly optimistic position to champion.

Kamala Visweswaran (1994:8) warns that identities, no matter how strategically deployed, are not always chosen but are, in fact, constituted by relations of power and always historically determined. Additionally, Richard Handler (1994) and others have suggested that the concept of identity itself as a reference for the complexities of hybrid, changing, and globalized lives may be unproductive and restrictive. Is this argument for positive self-representation, then, futile (in terms of historical precedence) or even wrong (as an exercise in essentialism)? I argue that the complicity of stereotyping, the construction of a pan-Indian identity, and the basis of comparative posturing may offer multiple dynamic means of understanding how power is conceived, exercised, and manipulated to various ends. Importantly, the circumstances of Native women's lives serve as a type of testimonial to the struggle image producers face in constructing alternative realities, providing an applied platform for the exposure of these various theoretical orientations.

Returning to Fragua Cota, we can productively gain an awareness of her positioning from her description of her motivation as an artist:

> When I see a relationship that...how someone treats an Indian person out on the Plaza makes me want to say, "Now what can I say about that scene there—the way they treated that Indian lady?" What can I do as an artist to say, "This is what happened, and I do not like it," other than going out there and cussing out that lady? "What are you doing here?" You know, what can I say that would still be legal and yet safer? Those kinds of things inspire me to do something—to create something that I want to say. Then there are times when you see beautiful sunsets, and I've got to go paint that, you know. Either way, you are saying something that you want, you see something that you want to paint, you see the reaction of these two people, you are angry, you want to put that anger out. 'Cause

you can't go over there and push that lady around, sock her, even though that's what you want to do.

This expression of cultural responsibility and use of art as a cathartic means of expressing rage at cultural appropriation identifies the art-making process as situated in understandings of a broader community and the artist's place in that community (see plate 15). Earlier studies on race and ethnicity utilized the concept of role theory as a means of articulating the worldview of unique communities in contrast to Western norms. Role, then, served as a precursor to identity as a theoretical approach. Charges of essentialism may be directed at both role and identity as theoretical applications, primarily because of the difficulties inherent in conceptualizing and articulating ideas about discrete community formation and maintenance. Theorist Paula Moya rightly notes that a rejection of identity constructs is often based on contradictory claims. While critics may point to the ways in which the "instability and internal heterogeneity of identity categories" make it difficult to claim, for example, a universal "women's experience," this disavowal simultaneously results in the impossibility of identifying applicable criteria to understand women's actions. "As a result, 'women's experience' can only be understood as an arbitrary construct" (Moya 2000:3). This rejection of cultural identities ignores the fact that "goods and resources are still distributed according to identity categories" (8). A denial of identity is therefore a denial of the ability to name and acknowledge structures of inequality. These debates take on added poignancy in reference to both art and Native American topics.

Art is commonly perceived in reference to modernist sensibilities of individualism. The pantribal designation of Native American appears to negate the salience of both individual tribal identity and personal individuality. This study seeks to position the concept of race (the Native American variable) alongside modernist (and therefore individualistic) aesthetics. It is essential to discern, however, the difference between an adoption of visual modernist icons (nonrepresentational imagery, performance art, and installation art) and the ideology of modernism (complete freedom as an individual, no cultural restraint). Although contemporary Native American artists may produce works that suggest modernist sensibilities in their visual and aesthetic forms, it is critical that the conceptualization of the artist's role in society (the old role theory, the new identity theory) is understood as a separate and autonomous consideration from artistic imagery.

This separation of conceptual categories (distinguishing the look of contemporary art from the lives of the artists) is a complex undertaking, for it is but one dimension of understanding identity debates in contemporary

Indian art worlds. The exterior aesthetic of a work of art (its medium, content, genre) serves as a primary and immediate level of engagement. As illustrated by the Hopi maiden example, the physical properties of art can only present a platform for further assessments of meaning—variously, either consumer fantasy or discussion of conflicting role attributions. The engagement with praxis is the connection that Whitely (1997:186) calls for—attention to the "human obligation" and "real social concern" that links art with artists and their communities. Consideration of these processes within tribal sensibilities results in mixed readings. Many Native people contend that there are more important things on which to spend capital (emotional, physical, or political) than addressing image politics. Others argue against the nature of debating representational issues from a pan-Indian positioning and for engaging with tribes as sovereign and separate political entities. Still others may enact the essentialism that seems inherent in categorization, embracing self-stereotyping and stereotyping of others in contrast. Even more confusing, the imposition of identity classifications imitates oppressive governmental and colonialistic practices that effectively silenced the free exercise of self-representation. Identity in reference to authenticity or blood quantum is thus suspect, weighing discussions of self-representation in Native communities in unique and often burdensome ways.

I engage three primary dialogues that may serve to clarify these various levels of debate in image representation: an analysis of the character and prevalence of Native American stereotypes as expressed in key testimonials by Native women artists, the strategies these artists employ in response to stereotypes, and the relationship between these two variables. This last discussion—the intersections of how essentialized images are perceived and therefore how subject others choose to respond to their existence—also entails a consideration of context, the relative age of the actors, their locations, and their communities. Each of these variables has the potential to clarify how the engagement of internal and external imagery serves to expose prevalent conceptual frameworks. The dialectic process itself can then be seen as the means by which identities are conceptualized, communicated, and sometimes integrated into concepts of selfhood. This proposition suggests that communal identities (tribal, pantribal, ethnic, racial) are expressed in relationship to anticommunal expressions, assertions, and even legislation. Communal identities are thus championed as valid platforms, despite their dismissal by both critics of damaging stereotypes and current postmodern trends. The arts serve as a particularly potent realm from which to construct these questions, given their visibility, accessibility, and seemingly innocuous character.

The Squaw/Princess Will Not Die

This book began by asking how contemporary Native women artists respond to societal notions of their role as bearers of tradition (the squaw) or exotic others (Indian princess). I advanced a theory that claims that the act of othering in identity politics, stereotypes, and role referents can be an essential component of self-inscription. This processual view sheds light on the communicative aspect of identity but stops short of claiming that identities are formed entirely in relationship to contrasting exterior assumptions of selfhood. Thus, Roxanne Swentzell's "barefoot Native" narrative (presented in my introduction) serves as one of the possible narratives available as identity referents. The conflicts inherent in the dysfunctional public image of Native women are made evident and available for critique in the retelling of the stereotypical myth. Importantly, this use of the "barefoot Native" narrative is referenced in a context in which the social parameters are defined by outside, traditionally Western, forces—the Santa Fe Indian Market. Active contrast (mobilization of alterity) is thus enacted in an effort both to resolve internal self-resolution "pressures" and to control external social tensions ("people's ideas of who I am").

The inescapability of image politics is evident in Swentzell's disavowal that "it wasn't done for an image. It was only practical reason," wherein she positions this contrasting worldview (primitive Native image) as simultaneously outside her own frame of reference and erroneous. Yet what are her options? To present herself otherwise to her consumers—"if…I showed up …in some heels"—also carries consequences: "People would be very upset that I'm not keeping to my image of what they have of me." The addition of gender and age as variables deepens the analysis, for the consumption of her identity is directly linked to her femaleness and remains invariable as she ages. "Our little Indian woman" can be owned and controlled endlessly in image politics, reinforcing the idea that squaw/princesses do not die.

Analyses of stereotyping in general and Native American stereotyping specifically have alternately assessed the prevalence of negative portrayals (by examining the general public's perceptions) and identified the political strategies for addressing these harms (by considering the target group's response to stereotypes). An example of the former approach is Jeffrey R. Hanson and Linda P. Rouse's "Dimensions of Native American Stereotyping" (1987). While the authors argue that stereotypes are "deeply embedded in American historical and contemporary consciousness" (Hanson and Rouse 1987:34), as evidenced by their continued presence in several domains of American culture (arts and literature, education, mass media, sports, recreation, and commercial advertising), they also argue that a new pluralistic understanding of Indians may be emerging alongside more "traditional" stereotype paradigms. Several aspects of their study are relevant here: the researchers' identification of distinct kinds of stereotypes, their conceptualization of a pantribal identity as detrimental, and an articulation of the disjunction between the existence of negative images and the viewer's subsequent interpretation of those images.

Two opposing paradigms are presented in Hanson and Rouse's study—"traditional" (historic and unitary) stereotypes and "emerging" (current and pluralistic) stereotypes—with the aim of showing that all stereotypes are not consistent but are dynamic and variable over time. Traditional or past stereotypes are seen as inherently "negative, inaccurate, misleading, and insensitive to Native Americans" (Hanson and Rouse 1987:34). Past stereotypes conceptualize Native Americans as homogeneous, static, primitivistic, and unable to exist in contemporary American culture. Emerging stereotypes are contrastingly interpreted as heterogeneous. An acceptance of biculturalism is evident, as are understandings of Native Americans as discrete tribal entities. This emerging stereotype is seen as "more neutral than negative" (57). The authors conclude that the emergent stereotype "coexists with, but is more prevalent than," negative traditional stereotypes (56).

Of particular interest is the authors' reference to Berkhofer's *The White Man's Indian* (1979). Key among the criteria that Hanson and Rouse cite as major components of historic and negative perceptions is the centrality of pan-Indianism—"the typological lumping of Native American cultures and peoples into one homogeneous 'other' category" (Hanson and Rouse 1987:36). They adopt Berkhofer's argument that the monocultural idea of "the Indian" denies "the manifold lives of Native Americans" (Berkhofer 1979:196). The category of pan-Indian referents is seen to be a major informing factor of inaccurate and demeaning stereotypes. The premise is that the eradication of pan-Indian referents will necessarily result in a more pluralistic and therefore tolerant reception of Indian America. Hanson and Rouse's 1987 findings indicate that demeaning stereotypes will be less prevalent in direct correlation to the diminishment of pantribal, homogeneous representations of Indians.

Subsequent investigations by Hanson and Rouse (1991) demonstrate that although respondents may recognize that American Indians are culturally diverse, specific knowledge of American Indian history and culture has remained low. Even in areas where respondents were better informed about American Indians because of proximity, negative stereotyping continued because of status-based prejudice associated with competition over scarce resources. The results of this study showed that actual knowledge itself does not alter negative appraisals if one ethnic or racial group is competing with another for social and economic resources. The controversy cited by the authors involved Chippewa treaty fishing rights in Wisconsin, where emotional anti-Indian sentiments were expressed by non-Indian commercial and sports fishermen. Negative personal stereotypes (Indians are lazy and lack ambition), though in the minority generally, were articulated in higher percentages in areas with greater Native American populations.

The enduring nature of stereotypes—despite their alteration over time in terms of content and regardless of direct contact with and knowledge of Native Americans—appears to lead to the conclusion that essentialized images are vital in the interaction of diverse groups. The tendency for this essentialization to be viewed in primarily negative terms, as the majority of the literature on stereotypes does, inhibits alternative interpretations of its use. Simulatneously, Hanson and Rouse's work offers valuable insights into the complexity of identity politics and confounds key issues. In an effort to avoid a "partisan" interpretation, the authors have relied on quantitative data culled from questionnaires instead of utilizing the qualitative method commonly associated with both current anthropological methods and the holistic Boasian anthropology they champion. They adopt a healthy and, I think, more useful approach in their critical stance, wherein they question the monolithic nature of stereotypes through time. Additionally, they make the important distinction of questioning the public's uncritical acceptance of stereotypes' truth-values, stating, "The fact that the movie industry recycles movies containing inaccurate and misleading Indian stereotypes from earlier eras does not necessarily mean that audiences universally embrace them" (Hanson and Rouse 1987:39). They question the assumption found in many qualitative research methodologies: "The presence of negative stereotyping in one cultural domain (e.g., educational literature or movies) is an automatic indicator of its presence in others" (39).

The research is seemingly uncritical, however, in its correlation of emerging or pluralistic imagery with the demise of negative and oppressive typecasting. Clearly, Hanson and Rouse's 1991 study seems to indicate that particularistic identities do not prohibit prejudice. Stated positively, status-based prejudice in this study is directly linked to resource allocation, not to monolithic ideas of identities. The culprit of enduring stereotypes is not, then, pan-Indianism or a lack of educational or accurate media, but intergroup competition based on resource allocation. This conclusion speaks to arguments made in chapter 1, which cites Robert Bieder's theory (1981) of "mentalists" and "realists"—with mentalists positioning imagery as primary and realists privileging political and social acts. I advocate keeping these categories at play and avoiding a deterministic agenda that seeks to discern primary causes.

My aim in this instance is to dismantle the pervasive foil of pantribal or essentialized images as the culprit of social oppression. Imagery and ideas do exert pressure on exoticized others and should be considered as real constraints. Why, then, are images classified as only mental? Why are politics and economics labeled as realistic and not mental? The segmentation of imagery as separate and ethereal as compared with the material conditions of social, political, and economic interests serves to mask the potency of stereotypes. Academics and activists who seek to stop or at least intervene in the repercussions of stereotypes certainly recognize that this is the case, but they often do so on grounds that accept the characterization of images as solely mentalist. Social psychology, cultural studies, and ethnic studies may examine attitudes and impacts of derogatory stereotypes, yet these efforts retain the mentalist characterization. What actions are required for images to achieve a realist description? What would the consequences of this reformulation mean to the image producers who are the subject of this inquiry?

A return to the ability to classify and characterize distinct communities as legitimate categories of consideration may move image debates into more realist discussions. Current ideologies of postmodernism, hybridity, or "free-floating signifiers" surely cannot accommodate this approach, but sovereignty, indigeneity, and pan-Indianism can and do embrace group characterizations. It is apparent that escape from perceived restrictive categories of essentialism alone will not ensure social justice. Thus, Berkhofer's early work, which projected an emerging heterogeneous and culturally relative identity for Native Americans, failed, just as Rouse and Hanson's early study faltered because of their assignment of homogeneous identities as the culprit for harmful stereotypes. The existence and use of broad, generalized categories of reference, in themselves, are not inherently damaging and can be usefully mobilized in inter- and intragroup dynamics. Hanson and Rouse's (1991:2) assertion that "differences between ethnic groups...can be accented and/or exaggerated by racial and ethnic stereotypes" makes sense in this analysis only if we consider the additional possibility that these differences, as expressed by stereotypes, have other potentials, including self-inscription, political mobilization, and the enhancement of communication between disparate groups.

Inversion, Eradication, Reclamation

While academic studies examining the prevalence of negative portrayals expose key theoretical issues in consideration of how stereotypes are received and conceptualized by a largely non-Indian public (Fenelon 2003), the adoption of various political strategies by Native populations offers essential insights as well. A particularly valuable analysis for this study is C. Richard King's "De/Scribing Squ*w: Indigenous Women and Imperial Idioms in the United States" (2003). This examination of the political struggles over the use of the term *squaw*, including the move to change place-names, highlights the "colonial legacies and postcolonial predicaments of naming, representation and language" (King 2003:2). King identifies three prominent oppositional strategies evident in efforts to assert rhetorical sovereignty: inversion, erasure, and reclamation. These applied strategies will be considered in concert with the more theoretical approaches taken, for example, with the discussions of inversion from chapter 4.

As a political strategy, inversion disrupts veiled racism and sexism by making obvious the oppression inherent in the use of the term *squaw* (commonly perceived as referring to a woman's genitalia). For example, activists who wish to convey the humiliation associated with the use of *Squaw* in place-names may suggest that Squaw Valley be renamed Cunt Valley or that Squaw Creek be named Twat Creek (King 2003:8–9).

Barbara Babcock's research on symbolic inversions (1978) suggested that reversals are closely tied to the examination of classificatory systems. The shock of recognition may be particularly effective in this political usage of inversion precisely because it places pornographic terms in the same classificatory category as place-names most consider to be inert descriptives. This reasoning argues that if *cunt* is simply another term, then why can it not be used as a public name?

Eradication is perhaps the most common strategy utilized by individuals and organizations opposed to the state-sanctioned use of *Squaw* place-names. King (2003:5) reports that more than nine hundred place-names contain the *Squaw*. Legislation banning state-sanctioned use of the term has been passed in Minnesota, Montana, and Maine. As King points out, although eradication may address the formal use of the term *squaw*, it fails to prevent the more pervasive and popular uses that are spontaneous and informal.

By contrast, reclamation strategies seek not only to control but also to revive indigenous practices and naming. King provides the example of the Narragenset word *eskwa* (of which *squaw* is thought to be an abbreviated form), a descriptive term meaning "woman" that carries no derogatory connotations. Eradication of the word *squaw* would mean loss of the ability of indigenous peoples to name themselves. King summarizes that regional histories will continue to inform both how indigenous women experience the use of the term and how activists choose to respond.

Although King's essay is directed specifically to the use of the term *squaw* only, I have found that the three strategies King identifies can be productively applied to the use of stereotypes in general. For example, inversion has been used in a parallel fashion by American Indian activists in the protest against Indian sports mascots. A well-publicized inversion strategy was the establishment of the University of Northern Colorado's Fighting Whites intramural basketball team in 2002. The "multiethnic, multiracial" team members sought to focus attention on nearby Eaton's Fighting Reds team logo by using humor and satire. The Fighting Whites's team slogan is "Every thang's gonna be all white!" (Johansen 2003).

Like King, I find the implications of eradication less than ideal in terms of addressing popular and widespread uses of derogatory terms. If we apply eradication, for example, to Swentzell's "barefoot" narrative, we then deny her active agency to impart and understand how identities are imposed and how she can feasibly respond. Similar to the use of the word *eskwa*, use of the phrases "the pretty little Indian princess" and "our little Indian woman" allows indigenous women to critique colonial legacies and assert ownership of their own self-representation. This reclamation strategy thus claims ownership of the language of the oppressors in order to mobilize new understandings of self.

Eradication as a political strategy to address perceived harmful stereotypes is commonly utilized not only in political strategies but also in academic texts. In a similar manner to studies that seek to ascertain the prevalence of stereotypes, these works also identify pan-Indian descriptives as the political target and central problem. An example of this approach is Scott Vickers's 1998 publication *Native American Identities: From Stereotype to Archetype in Art and Literature*. Vickers argues that

> during the last five hundred years of colonial expansion in what is now called the United States, what Indians have long considered to be their heterogeneous identities (for each Indian tribe has developed its own tribal identity) have slowly and methodically been restructured, by "the myths of historians," into a more homogenous identity that groups all Indians into a single amalgamated "tribe." This amalgamation has been accomplished by the "outside" influences of the colonizing culture.... In accomplishing this end, it has been necessary to create a single Indian entity out of many, a process that has in turn necessitated the formulation of stereotypes that replace historical Indian identities with an easily manipulated sameness. [Vickers 1998:3]

This analysis enacts the same essentialism that Vickers decries. Restricting Native self-reference to specific tribal allegiances alone prohibits the formulation of pan-Indian identities. This limited perspective collapses the possible referents Native people themselves may activate into only two mutually exclusive categories: Indian or their specific tribe. A one-dimensional characterization results that denies the mobility that many other ethnic groups may exercise.

Additionally, this protective positioning victimizes Native populations by casting them as passive recipients of harmful stereotypes, their experience here defined by Vickers as a process of "dehumanization and deracination" (Vickers 1998:5) as well as "denigration" and "brutalization" (27). Vickers's platform demands that

> Indian stereotypes, whether noble or ignoble, must be defused, both internally within Indian communities and individual psyches, and externally through critical theory, vigilant demythologization, and a resurgence of Indian "autohistories" and individual Indian voices in the arts and literature, as well as in politics. [Vickers 1998:44]

This approach assumes that Native expressions in these fields will be free of reference to stereotypes themselves as a central concern and reference point for political struggle. An engagement with stereotypes as a form of cultural identity is not solely oppressive—it can also be socially enabling. Moya reminds us that "progressive social change is predicated on an acknowledgement of, and a familiarity with, past and present structures of inequality—strictures that are often highly correlated with categories of identity," adding that "this correlation undoubtedly accounts for why identity has been a fundamental element of social liberation as well as social oppression" (Moya 2000:8).

Even in works that accept the existence of a pan-Indian identity, stereotypes are uncritically perceived as the primary cause of oppression. Donald L. Fixico's *The Urban Indian Experience in America* (2000) argues that the real source of urban Indian problems is non-Indian attitudes. Abusive characterizations are seen as primary to self-reference:

> Negative stereotypes about Indians of the past have stigmatized the real "Indian in the city" situation. "I believe these images are very hostile to our problem," said Noel Campbell of the American Indian Association in Los Angeles. "Until these images are done away with, we aren't going to improve any of our standards."... The power of images fostered by stereotypes has caused psychological damage to

American Indians in cities and will continue to do so until attitudes of non-Indians change. [Fixico 2000:30]

Fixico's analysis expands on Vickers's eradication platform by suggesting not only that negative stereotypes should be eradicated but also that positive Indian stereotypes should be simultaneously reinforced as a means of overcoming low self-esteem. In this scenario, stereotypes are viewed as concurrently damaging and redemptive, indicating an alignment with King's eradication and reclamation strategies. A concern with how external stereotypes, in general, impact Native American self-perceptions allows for consideration of images as central to identity constructs. Stereotypes (and by association, imagery and image producers) are championed as progressive strategies in their potential to advance healthy representational politics, while they are also suspect in generalized terms as harmful influences. Fixico's work thus maintains a belief in the usefulness of positive stereotypes even as he decries the existence of negative imagery: "The identity crisis will persist until a positive image of American Indians is established and accepted by the public and by urban Indians themselves. A positive self-image would encourage equalization of education and socialization where Indian children are concerned" (Fixico 2000:41–42).

Fixico's work is fairly mainstream and representative of many urban Native community concerns. The inherent irony in advancing image production while damning its potentially destructive qualities is as veiled in this work as it is in the minds of many, if not most, concerned with representational politics. The characterization of all stereotypes as damaging, the censure and criminalization of pan-Indian identity constructs, and the advancement of eradication as a political strategy indicate a general reactionary stance that not only fails to incorporate but also denies the existence of proactive essentializations, multiple identity referents, and indigenous creative reinventions of self that draw from the established referents of the mainstream. The implications of this clustering of attitudes and strategies are a narrowed field of strategic movement politically, socially, and personally, as well as a constriction of Native identities in time.

The fluid and shifting nature of stereotypical perceptions demands responses that are similarly characterized by shifting strategies that recognize the historic and the current implications of these image politics. Whereas dismissal of the potency of imagery calls for eradication, and denial of homogenous referents freezes debates and actions in time and place, reclamation of image totalities has the potential to move debates forward while also recognizing the harms of prejudice and discrimination based on these same premises. As King (2003:10) suggests, these reclamations have the potential to "facilitate revival, continuing control, and remembrance."

Humor and the Dynamics of Social Power

If eradication as a political strategy is dismissed, then what forms the contours of how reclamation of essentialized stereotypes can productively be put to use? If image politics are championed as powerful, possibly inescapable, and potentially useful in positive self-representations, then to what ends must these actions be directed? Who defines what may conceivably be viewed as exploitation in engaging with ideologically laden images and notions that were created in a context of racist oppression?

David Pilgrim, founder and curator of the Jim Crow Museum of Racist Memorabilia at Ferris State University, located in Big Rapids, Michigan, lectured to an audience at Stanford University in 2005, asserting, "There are three places where 1920s racism is still active. The comedy stage, eBay, and the porno store." While eBay and the porno store connote direct commercial interests, comedy signifies less the power of the dollar and more the popular, spontaneous, and informal uses of stereotypes—uses that King (2003:10) indicates are largely immune from censure through eradication. An engagement with humor via artistic appropriation of stereotypical images offers an illustrated means of understanding the history of derogatory appropriation and the possibility of diffusing its power by remembrance and reclamation.

Pilgrim's stand of teaching tolerance with items of intolerance has led to a lifetime of collecting demeaning racist and sexist objects. Like stereotypes in general, these materials—tourist souvenirs, children's toys, household items, KKK paraphernalia—are often intended to evoke humor through such typecast characterizations as exaggerated physical characteristics; distorted cultural traits; and misappropriation of such cultural signifiers as food, dress, religion, and environment. An abundance of car license plates, salt and pepper shakers, and commercial and sports logos assaults the viewer with their crassness, seemingly cruel intent, and inhuman treatment of racialized others. Black mammies, Uncle Toms, and Aunt Jemimas are displayed alongside drunk Indians, Jamaican potheads, and kung fu fighters (Ferris State University).

Clearly, Pilgrim's intent is to overwhelm with quantity while achieving shock through recognition of the pervasiveness, longevity, and adaptability of racist kitsch. He argues that activism is not the enemy of objectivity; the stated mission of the museum is to promote scholarly examination of historical and contemporary expressions of racism. Pilgrim's agenda suggests that negative portrayals do have redemptive qualities because of their confrontational nature—as direct, often bigoted, and racist images, they offer an unmediated space to examine patterns of subjugation constructively. This space is not immune to criticism, as Pilgrim's statement here makes evident. Pilgrim is not an advocate of eradication—he chose not to support an open ban of eBay's trading in offensive materials. However, he does question the ability of contemporary comedians (including African American comedians) to engage in racist discourses unchastised.

An example of how humor can operate within this discourse nationally is black comedian Chris Rock's 1996 routine "Niggas vs. Black People":

> Who's more racist, black people or white people? Black people. You know why? 'Cause we hate black people too. Everything white people don't like about black people, black people *really* don't like about black people. There's some shit going on with black people right now. It's like a civil war going on with black people. And there's two sides. There's black people, and there's niggas. The niggas have got to go. Every time the black people want to have a good time, ignorant-ass niggas fuck it up.... I *love* black people, but I hate niggas. Tired of niggas!...
>
> And I see some black people lookin' at me. "Man, why you got to say that? Why you got to say that? It ain't us—it's the media.... The media has distorted our image to make us look bad. Why must you come down on us like that, brother? It ain't us—it's the media." Please cut the fuckin' shit. Okay? Okay? Okay? When I go to the money machine tonight...I ain't looking over my back for the media. I'm looking for niggas. Shit, Ted Koppel ain't never took shit from me. Niggas have. You think I got three guns at my house 'cause the media's outside? "Oh, shit! Mike Wallace! Run!" Get the fuck out of here, man. Tired of this shit. [Chris Rock Enterprises Inc. 1996]

Is this raw criticism an acceptable form of social change? Should in-group members engage in internal stereotyping and derogatory commentary for a largely white audience? Is Rock immune from condemnation because he is black? Bernard Saper poses the question of in-group stereotypes in his 1993 article "Since When Is Jewish Humor Not Anti-Semitic?" He concludes that Jewish humor is acceptable when it "is told by Jews to Jews about Jews" (Saper 1993:71). Saper also concurs with the noncensure status, stating, "Because the Jewish joke, meant to be told within the in-group, might furnish ammunition for the non-Jew to use against the Jew does not mean that such humor should be totally abandoned" (75).

Conceivably then, prohibitions of racist or stereotypical images (the Jim Crow Museum) or acts (Rock's humor) could inhibit the positive effects of self-inscription. Obviously, Rock may freely engage in self-deprecating humor because he locates himself within the larger group being criticized, yet his audience may likely not be all black. Can his performance then be sanctioned under Saper's definition? Investigation of producers and consumers of media imagery as separate considerations is a critical step to understanding fully how these constructs function in whole environments.

Rock's defense of the media classifies him clearly as a noneradication proponent. His statement, "Shit, Ted Koppel ain't never took shit from me. Niggas have," places him in the position of largely defending a realist category of interpreting stereotypes. Materialistic causes, not mentalist media images, are the source of oppression. However, Rock is a product of the media, and in many ways his position defending images as innocuous could be interpreted as largely self-serving. Are media images, including stereotypes conveyed orally in humor, protected from criticism more by those who are their producers? Do heavy consumers of media images tend to see them as more harmless than those who are less involved in this field? Importantly, in what contexts are these displays of identity performed, and how does that placement inform the utilization or rejection of reappropriation and eradication strategies?

I want to briefly consider two Native women artists who are active in these debates: Charlene Teters, known largely for her installations and antimascot activism, and Shelley Niro, noted Canadian Mohawk artist and filmmaker. My intent is not to compare the women's careers or orientations in terms of artistic works but to show how their personal orientations, while similar, have led to their adoption of different image strategies as defined by King. In concert with my general overall approach, I will focus only on their narratives as testimonials to their lives as Native women artists. Teters's interviews were conducted from 1994 to 1996; Niro's interviews date from 2002 and 2003.

Niro explored the terrain of questionable reappropriation as an exhibiting artist in the 2003 Venice Biennale exhibition Pellerossasogna (Red Skin Dream). In deliberations preceding the exhibit's opening, members of the sponsoring organization (Indigenous Arts Action Alliance, or IA3) debated the wisdom of referencing the derogatory term *Red Skin* as an exhibit theme. Their comments were ultimately edited as a poem by coexhibitor Diné poet Sherwin Bitsui and formed the exhibit's catalogue submission (Bonami 2003). Niro countered concerns about the appropriateness of *Red Skin* by invoking a sense of generational history:

> I think every generation probably experiences lots of that real direct

racism or hatred. I use my parents quite a bit as an example. They'll tell stories, and it was just the way they existed on a day-to-day basis... having to work for farmers and be janitors and fruit pickers and all that sort of thing. And how they had to live more or less hand to mouth, and they...basically kept us in a section where they were the slaves...they were the workers. And because of that, they had to really take a lot of abuse. And in a way, it's sort of been a reminder to my thought that this came from a time that Indian people weren't treated that well. It is like a little burr on my skin or something to say..."I know where it's coming from, and I know what it's supposed to mean, but it doesn't hurt me." For some reason, you just have to keep those things alive, in a way.[2]

I have argued elsewhere (Mithlo 2005) that this honoring of the past by engagement in stereotypical language and imagery is indicative of an indigenous perspective. While justification of keeping racist qualifiers alive often connotes psychological self-determination and emotional orientation for the individual, as argued by Saper, for example, Niro cites her parents' generation's oppression as the source of her actions, suggesting an interest in the benefit to the community as a whole by remembrance (a "burr on my skin"). In a similar fashion to the Abenaki activists cited by King, the erasure of derogatory terms also has the capacity to erase colonialist histories, leading to the adoption of reappropriation strategies.

Niro's film submission to the Biennale exhibition was a critical and wry commentary on Western capitalism and exploitation titled *The Shirt* (Niro 2003; see plate 16). Her positioning in this examination of place, the female body, and indigeneity is explained in the following passage: "It is important to acknowledge the foundations of positive forward action. I created *The Shirt* thinking of ancestors, comrades, and the future generations" (personal communication with author, July 8, 2003). Engagement in stereotypes that were created with the intent to harm may serve, in King's (2003:10) words, as tools of "revival" and "remembrance."

Commonly, the rationalization to engage in deprecating humor is justified in terms of individual functional and emotional ends. Saper asserts that Jews developed their comic bent because "it helped them to find peaceful strategies for dealing with prejudice and persecution; to take the edge off tragedy; to maintain their dignity, integrity, equilibrium, and sanity; and to get along and get ahead" (Saper 1993:82). This individualistic and personal fulfillment reasoning should be highlighted as separate and distinct from consideration of reappropriation as a tribute to a previous generation. Although both humor and appropriation of stereotypes may resolve conflicting notions of difference, it is crucial to remember that these manifestations may spring from different causes and aims.

Spokane artist and activist Teters occupies a leadership position nationally in the eradication of stereotypes. As a cofounder of the National Coalition on Racism in Sports and the Media, she has clearly adopted an eradication strategy in the manner of King's description of changing *Squaw* place-names. Teters's involvement in this cause began in 1989, when she enrolled at the University of Illinois at Urbana-Champaign (where she ultimately received her MFA), home of the Fighting Illini (Rosenstein 1997). As a result of her commitment to changing the Chief Illiniwek mascot, Teters was attacked by brutal campus police, spat upon by jeering sports crowds, and demeaned by campus officials eager to see her reputation destroyed. After three decades of sustained protest, the university discontinued its use of Chief Illiniwek (Zeller 2007).

Teters's narrative relates how she was first drawn into the mascot debates, when she took her children to a University of Illinois basketball game:

> My kids sank into their seats because they were just so embarrassed.... Because they go into this frenzy when the mascot comes out. They're all, "Chief! Chief!" They go into this wild frenzy... yelling, or they have their own little war whoops and things like that...which they always billed as an authentic dance. And he does this gymnastics routine and just jumps into the air and does flips and stuff like that, wearing the traditional regalia. And [my son] was trying to laugh, because that was the only way he could respond. And with me, it was just a sadness. It still doesn't leave me. It's a very powerful image to experience that. And that sadness turns to anger, just like that. So that was the catalyst for me... watching how it impacted my kids. And they are people who know where they come from. They are not insecure about who they are. They know they are Indian. What is it doing to our Indian youth who don't have a strong connection, who are still going through that identity crisis that a lot of us are? What is it doing to them? Those are the ones who are losing.... So I realized at that point that I couldn't be there and not address it. Because if I don't protect the integrity of my cultural identity, then how are they going to know that it's something important to protect?[3]

Like Niro, Teters justifies her involvement in image politics by its relation not to herself personally but to her extended family. In this case, it was the racism not of a generation past but of future generations that concerned her most:

> This movement is being led by our children. It really is. And I have to say it's true. You know, when I think back to my own situation, it wasn't me, really. It was my kids telling me that they're really uncomfortable with this. So I as a mother was responding to their uncomfortableness and their humiliation, and so forth, because I've been conditioned to tolerate it—like all of us have been conditioned to tolerate it.

This passage indicates that for people of her generation, the implicit racism of mascot caricatures is a poignant and painful experience, but one that Teters has been trained to tolerate. This acceptance could be interpreted as an attribute primarily associated with age and previous personal experience. Yet her relationship with extended family and tribal communities ultimately takes precedence over this conditioning of tolerance, an orientation that is shared by Niro. Although their primary motivations (non-individualistic and communal) are similar, Niro and Teters have articulated different principal strategies for engaging in the dismantling of oppressive imaging as outlined by King. Niro's adoption of reclamation can be seen to contrast with Teters's calls for eradication.

A consideration of context is key here. Teters's political involvement in the eradication of Indian sports mascots as stereotypes began in the decidedly public arena of university sports. Teters was an art student at that university, and she ultimately incorporated her experience into her art practice. Her 1993 exhibit Into Indian Country reproduces images of Chief Illiniwek in her installations (Villani 1993). Thus, it could be argued that while Teters's primary political narrative is one of eradication, her artwork nevertheless reflects more of a reappropriation orientation.

I have argued that varied stereotypical perceptions demand strategic responses that are similarly diverse. My application of King's fundamental strategies (inversion, eradication, and reclamation) should not be interpreted as an effort to restrict all potential responses to only these three options or to insist that Native actors—and in this instance, Native women artists—utilize only one response pattern. While inversion typically disorients, eradication demands an action. Both strategies start and end from the viewpoint of those perpetuating essentialized images. As the primary strategy advanced here, reclamation privileges the perspective of the subject other without undue concern for audience. The actions of shock, demand for change, or proactive movement forward may each be adopted at various times for unique aims. Correspondingly, strategic actions may be the same but with different motivational aims. Niro can be said to share in the strategy of humor and reappropriation of stereotypes that Saper describes in his analysis of Jewish humor, but with separate intentions—Niro's being community reintegration and Saper's, individual equilibrium.

This example serves to demonstrate how complex the interpretation of stereotypical images can be. Considerations of motivation, audience, ethnicity, and time inform how individual image producers may adopt or reject available political strategies. The dynamics of social power should be considered, above all, as contextual and shifting in relevance to community norms, individual experience, and mainstream practices.

"Those Strategies Visually Root Us in Our Oppression"

I want to move away from a strict analysis of verbal texts to consider some ways in which oppositional strategies are utilized in visual culture analysis. My aim is to highlight where and when the boundary crossing of reappropriation is deemed suitable and when it is considered exploitative. I have found art historian Michael D. Harris's text *Colored Pictures: Race and Visual Representation* (2003) to be valuable in articulating how black artists respond to stereotypical images, particularly the recycling of derogatory images. Harris presents an argument that both supports and questions the legitimacy of the "recycled" artistic strategies he terms inversion, recontextualization, reappropriation, and deconstruction. An advocate of dismantling racist stereotypes, he also reminds the reader that engagement in derogatory images may reify rather than critique racist stereotypes. Ultimately, these representations bring up the question of agency—how to achieve self-inscription outside the all-consuming references of the Western mainstream. Harris (2003:192) asks, "Are these strategies truly effective or merely diversionary chimera?"

It is helpful, I think, to consider the conceptual underpinnings of diverse strategies as indicative of the context in which they are employed. Harris's orientation in these debates is informed by his belief that the self-representation of blacks is directly linked to how whites represent them. In this respect, his work resembles Berkhofer's (1979:196) prediction that "the future of the Indian as image must be determined by the preconceptions of White cultural premises." The fictions of race thus define the experience of self-identity: "Blackness is a fabrication that has been refabricated by African Americans. Both black and white identities are fictions, but fictions do exist" (Harris 2003:37).

As Berkhofer argues for the primacy of white imagery, Harris interprets black participation in image construction primarily as a reactive exercise. He states,

> Despite their conceptual opposition, white and black identities share a mutual dependency. The construction of white ethnicity has been dependent on an opposition to blackness, while black ethnicity has been dependent on the threat of white racism. White is more describable by its contours and what it is not than by what it is, and its normalization also standardizes the opposition to, and de-valuation of, nonwhiteness.... Whiteness and blackness are inextricably linked, mutually dependent, and always mediated by power. [Harris 2003:18–19]

The inescapability of essentialized images is linked in Harris's text to the dynamics of social power. Popular culture is "enlisted" in order to verify racial constructions. Thus, racial identities are ideological, but with material consequences. Stereotypes as social mythologies assist in the maintenance of asymmetrical power relations (109).

Although the primacy of the white imagination offers a firm footing for Harris's discussions in reference to alterity, he also expresses unease with this equation. Nowhere is this discomfort more visible than in his analysis of Kara Walker, an artist whose work is located "deeply within white racial perceptions of blackness" (Harris 2003:197). Other representations discussed within Harris's text, such as appropriation of the Aunt Jemima icon, are interpreted rather positively as ironic reversals and "complex visual rhetoric[s]" that serve to effectively destabilize "fantasy constructions of blackness" (116). These reversal strategies "signify"—they are a deliberate, discursive double play—"we played with their racism to 'play' them" (6).

Yet Walker's work clearly crosses a boundary with Harris, and this transgression appears to have everything to do with a white audience whose notions of exoticism are, in Harris's mind, reinforced via Walker's imagery:

> By casting herself in blackface as a Negress slave, and by subjecting black women in her work to extreme degradations and stereotypical exaggerations, she has locked herself into the racial discourse she is attempting to subvert. By identifying with slavery, she seems to trivialize it, and this has alienated her from preceding generations who

> have profound memories of racial violence and oppression and therefore a deep empathy for the crushing and violent consequences of slavery. [Harris 2003:222–223]

There are strategies of resistance to damaging stereotypes that are acceptable and some that are questionable. The dividing line is thus cloudy and alters with time, circumstance, and—important for Harris—audience. Angry Aunt Jemimas produced in the 1970s signaled a collective disruption of veiled racism that was consistent with larger political movements. Harris argues that Walker's highly sexualized images, her implication of herself as a Negress (as a form of blackface), and her postmodern nihilistic sensibilities do not align her with any larger community sensibility (Pan-African, African American, or black militant). Tellingly, he implicates her mostly white curators and collectors as perhaps being more entertained by the work than politically sensitized.

Harris remains deeply ambivalent in his analysis of recycling, inverting, and deconstructing racist images, stating that "those strategies visually root us in our oppression" (Harris 2003:222). He decries collecting racist kitsch and calls for nothing less than "transformation of the consciousness" (222) of those represented. His dissatisfaction with forms of reactive self-definition (in relation to slavery, racism, and victimhood) is linked negatively with the ability of African Americans to define themselves in reference to African conceptual and historical foundations (222–223).

Certainly, Harris's critique of collecting racist memorabilia places him at odds with Pilgrim's project, which seeks to use these materials for transformation of racist beliefs. As an artist and a curator, Harris's position may be said to be compromised by a primary engagement with the reception of these works in the often elitist world of arts consumption and display. Pilgrim's positioning as a sociologist and a collector of memorabilia from swap shops and garage sales is informed by a desire to encourage dialogue in reaction to these disturbing "hateful things." The white audience looms prominently in Harris's critique of reappropriation strategies, concerns less evident in the work of the Native women artists who are the subject of this study. Perhaps the reception of black art in mainstream art practices, as compared with the marginalization of Indian arts in these same contexts, influences Harris's concern with white influence and power. His longing for preslavery references—what he calls a "rootedness within the center of African American cultural sensibilities and ancestral connections" (Harris 2003:245)—contributes to this logic, as well as his thinking that black representation is inescapably tied to white attitudes.

Berkhofer's conclusion to *The White Man's Indian* poses a question that seems to have significant relevance here. Given the inescapability of white cultural premises, "to what extent can new meaning be infused into the old term to cancel old prejudices and invent a new evaluative image?" (Berkhofer 1979:196–197). His question suggests that, given the constraint of white imaginations exerting control over ethnic self-representation, reappropriation is the only way to achieve a "balance of power among peoples" (197). He does not disdain these representations as rooting people in their own oppressions endlessly, as Harris fears, nor does he champion the eradication of damaging stereotypes as mascot and place-name protestors might. Berkhofer's call to invent new Native images is a direct request to image producers—artists—to engage in reappropriation of damaging stereotypes. This intervention requires that these image producers have the means by which to circulate their alternative paradigms widely.

I suggest that two key issues must be resolved before unencumbered self-representation can be successful. One is for both Native communities and their audiences (museumgoers, art patrons, tourists, and government bureaucrats) to embrace a pan-Indian sensibility as a valid identity construct. These images—whether negative, neutral, or positive—serve a useful function in mobilizing group ideology and resolving internal and external communication challenges. The mobilization of pan-Indian ideologies should concurrently recognize that multiple identities also exist, that images alter through time and circumstance, and that eradication may also be necessary to confront blatant and dangerous hateful speech and acts. The other, as Harris indicates, is to cultivate indigenous knowledge as an alternative strategy. An embrace of indigenous knowledge (or in Harris's [2003:245] terminology, "African American cultural sensibilities and ancestral connections") indicates that it is possible to escape the totalitarianism of white ideology. Alternative knowledge systems as purveyors of newly invented images possess the ability to dismantle the purely mentalist and realist categories that so often plague visual culture discourses. The advancement of holistic conceptualizations of visual, verbal, and cognitive ideologies is dependent on non-Western frameworks to both structure and carry these debates. Existing institutional frameworks will find themselves challenged to accommodate these alternative constructs, given the weight of monopolized representations over time.

Both the deconstruction of pan-Indian biases and the advancement of alternative indigenous ideologies require Native American spokespeople. It is advocated that these leaders in image politics debates be recognized as contemporaneous professionals who are also authentic Natives. Contemporary artist Jaune Quick-to-See Smith summarizes thus:

> Native American scholars will have to interpret Contemporary American Indian Art for the mainstream, which is the path to recognition and credibility.
>
> The African American community has cultural critics such as Henry Louis Gates, bell hooks, Cornel West, and Lowery Sims, to name a few, who have been interpreting the art of Black America for two decades or more. Latinos have Amalia Mesa-Baines, Alejandro Anreus, Coco Fusco, and others interpreting contemporary Latino art. These writers are as noted as the artists they are writing about.
>
> The writing must come from within our own communities, and the ripples will extend outward to the mainstream writers who will advance the dialogue. [Personal communication with author, March 3, 2007]

It is at this personal and applied level of intervention that the power of representational identity will likely find its greatest challenge. I target this difficulty not to suggest that there are no trained, polished, and articulate Native leaders, but to indicate that reappropriated image representations and truly unique indigenous worldviews as substitutes for disdained stereotypes will likely result in exposure of enormous conceptual differences. The bridging of these ideological gaps may be said to be dependent upon the ability of non-Natives to accept Native Americans as contemporaneous thinkers pursuing distinctive intellectual paradigms.

Notes

1. Quotations from Laura Fragua Cota in this chapter are from the author's interview with her, February 5, 1991.

2. Shelley Niro, interview by author, June 15, 2003.

3. Quotations from Charlene Teters in this chapter are from the author's interview with her, February 15, 1994.

CONCLUSION

"I Know What's Going On"

Equality in image politics requires not only the self-articulation of Native American identity but also the distribution and general acceptance of these images by the dominant public. Clearly, access to training, the mandates of the market, gender bias, and restricted notions of selfhood inhibit self-representation, yet the dissemination of these ideologies represents an even greater challenge.

The opening of the Smithsonian National Museum of the American Indian (NMAI) signaled a new engagement in these debates. Previous efforts to achieve Native self-representation in tribal museums or individual exhibits had generally received either neutral or positive appraisals, but the NMAI's premiere represented indigenous imaging on a grander scale. The museum-going audience was challenged to respond not only to the existence of Native Americans as contemporary people (the flip-phone-using Natives described by Stuever in chapter 1) but also to the curation of exhibits that addressed the genocide and survival of indigenous peoples in all of North and South America. From the perspective of the average visitor who was still struggling to comprehend that Indians do exist, NMAI could be seen to present an overwhelming amount of information to process. From the perspective of Native American artists and consultants knowledgeable about both the level of ignorance to which they were responding and the cultural sensitivity involved in self-disclosure of their communities, exhibit planning was an exercise in diplomacy and balance. Imagine the collective dismay, then, in response to comments like those of Edward Rothstein of the *New York Times*, whose review of NMAI surmised, "The notion that tribal voices should 'be heard' becomes a problem when the selected voices have so little to say" (2004:B5).

I want to look closely at Rothstein's article for indications that the premises I have shown to be problems in Native image politics (the disavowal of homogenous referents and the nonrecognition of indigenous knowledge) are present. Rothstein claims that the

> ambition of creating a "museum different" [quoting NMAI director W. Richard West Jr.]—the goal of making that museum answer to the needs, tastes and traditions of perhaps 600 diverse tribes, ranging from the Tapirape of the Brazilian jungles to the Yupik of Alaska — results in so many constituencies that the museum often ends up filtering away detail rather than displaying it, and minimizing the difference even while it claims to be discovering it. [Rothstein 2004:B5]

The result, according to Rothstein, is "the studious avoidance of scholarship"; an emphasis on "a kind of warm, earthy mysticism with comforting homilies behind every façade, reviving an old pastoral romance about the Indian"; and a "self-celebratory romance" (B5). His conclusions that "the museum almost seems afraid of distinctions" and that "a great opportunity was missed in this museum. Individual tribes could have been explored in more depth" (B5) indicate that a collectivist orientation is not permitted. The rationales behind this rejection of a pan-Indian sensibility include the idea that this positioning is not scholarly and that a collective identity serves only a "sociological function" (B5).

An essential consideration for deconstructing Rothstein's review is his rejection of subject communities' self-representation. He states, "It is not a matter of whose voice is heard. It is a matter of detail, qualification, nuance and context. It is a matter of scholarship" (Rothstein 2004:B5). It is essential to note in this statement the very real (realist), enduring embrace of Robert Berkhofer's attack on pan-Indian sensibilities. To speak of pan-Indianism is to engage in nonscholarly appraisals that serve only a so-called sociological function. This rejection of the collective manifestations of colonialism perpetuates a willful ignorance of the American government's systematic attack on Native nations as an undifferentiated group. Pan-Indian constructs are the result of government policy. A denial of this responsibility prohibits Native American museum professionals from constructing exhibits that speak to their experience of racism in America. To use the strategy of inversion as an illustration, can one imagine a reviewer insisting that the US Holocaust Memorial Museum speak only to the experience of certain regional or ethnic subsets of those inflicted (Jews only—not Gypsies, Poles, or homosexuals) rather than the collective experience of extermination?

Rothstein's analysis fails to recognize that the NMAI is enacting unique indigenous curatorial practices by incorporating regional consultants in the process of design rather than an individualistic Western curation model.

In addition to these more general critiques, Rothstein's piece also fails to demonstrate the very scholarship he champions on more specific items. While he finds fault in the display of collective identity, he appears to consider Indian arts as generic and unworthy of detailed description. None of the four images of Native American art that illustrate the article ("Museum with an American Indian Voice") lists the name of the artist, the title of the piece, the materials of the work, or the dimensions. It is difficult to imagine any other *New York Times* art review that would fail to identify the artwork or artist. Three of the four photos feature the work of Allan Houser, known as the father of American Indian sculpture. One caption notes simply, "Works at the new Museum of the American Indian in Washington." Even the name of the museum is wrong! Another shows Roxanne Swentzell's bronze masterpiece *For Life in All Directions* with the caption "A sculpture at the National Museum of the American Indian" but with no identifying descriptives, such as the artist's name or the title of the piece.

Rothstein's refusal to grant personhood or dignity to the image producers exposes several operative belief systems that continue to inhibit Native self-representation. The rejection of a pan-Indian sensibility indicates that Natives are not able to conceptualize and appropriate the homogeneous identity that has been exercised against them since contact. The denial of the subjective voice shows that only a Western science paradigm is valid: the objective—in Rothstein's words, "scholarly"—approach that privileges secondary sources written in a detached manner and based on established academic fields. Failure to indicate the artists or the artwork in the accompanying photographs exposes a belief that Natives are not contemporaneous human beings or professionals deserving of recognition. These three levels of analysis—ideological, institutional, and individual—are essential considerations in understanding how Native American image politics function in terms of external audience expectations.

An internal analysis is demonstrated by Tessie Naranjo's description of the NMAI curatorial process from the perspective of her identity as a Santa Clara Pueblo community member. Speaking about how she sees herself, including her training as a sociologist, in relationship to her peers in the community, Naranjo muses:

> The way that I move and interact with them, the way that we interact is…almost in a familial way: "How's your mother?" You know…what I love about other people is knowing, appreciating, their humanity, so I

move among my peers with the consideration of our, all of our humanity.

For example...there were four of us that had the opportunity...to go to the Smithsonian to consult with the NMAI people about the Santa Clara exhibit that they're planning. So here we were all sitting there for about two and a half days in consultation, and there was no regard to credentials or noncredentials. We all got paid the same rate when it was all said and done. We had an opportunity to laugh and be together and using the knowledge that we have and our own personal experiences to be able to try to give input to...our philosophical world and which of those philosophies we could share in that exhibit that we were planning for. So it was...an experience of...I guess, what could be collegiality, where there was not highs or low[s] of any one individual. So, at a personal level, I focus on the humanity of us all, acknowledging that we have as human...we are flawed. And it's at that level that I operate. And it works. It works when the other person wants to make it work too.

But there is this other Western notion that comes in—these notions about competition, these notions of individualism. That's when I have problems with other people who have sort of allowed the Western notions to seep in and then there comes that exclusive. But if you have it, if you have those people as I did...my peers went to Washington, DC, with me at the NMAI thing. If we all come with this other notion of—these community notions of acceptance and embracement, then we're all okay. We're all okay.[1]

I want to contrast this processual viewpoint with the analysis of the Santa Clara exhibit from Rothstein's review. Rothstein highlights the Santa Clara component of the NMAI opening as an example of how the exhibits are flawed:

> The exhibits are where the problems begin in earnest. The display for the Santa Clara Pueblo of New Mexico, for example, explains: "We are made up of two major clans, Summer and Winter people." But, the pueblo curator writes: "There is no dividing line. There is just a sense." The exhibit's commentary is limited to comments like "Respect and sharing of yourself is very important." One does not learn what daily life is like or even what the tribe's religious ceremonies consist of. [Rothstein 2004:B5]

Evident in these two narratives is a divergence of aims, expectations, and, as Naranjo poetically phrases it, "philosophies." Rothstein's insistence on scholarship evidences a belief that valid knowledge can be expressed only by those with the proper credentials, who speak in the third person, and who adhere to the mandate of scientific freedom. Naranjo's stance is that indigenous knowledge is not restricted to the academy, that wisdom is related to experience, and that certain forms of knowledge are not to be shared publicly. The values placed on cultural sensitivity—not revealing all aspects of one's culture—were not evident to the general public.

Rothstein's expectation that he would learn "what daily life is like or even what the tribe's religious ceremonies consist of" exposes the audience's lack of cultural sensitivity and awareness that Native people may exercise their right to protect some knowledge, especially religious knowledge, from public display and interpretation. Rothstein describes this lack in the following manner: "Such detail, apparently, was not what the tribal curators thought important. In fact, there is an astonishing uniformity in the exhibits' accounts of religious beliefs, which may have been homogenized by subtle forces within the museum itself" (Rothstein 2004:B5). Note the concepts he refers to—homogenization, uniformity, lack of detail. One can only speculate that the suspicious "subtle forces within the museum itself" are likely the urban, pan-Indian museum professionals who lack the tribally specific authenticity Rothstein deems necessary for a legitimate curatorial statement to be made.

I have examined this curatorial relationship at length to ascertain whether the essentialism of stereotypes researched in this text—as possibly useful and proactive—is an enduring debate. The NMAI example appears to demonstrate that key themes in Native American self-representation persist. I recognize that my call for simultaneous recognition of contemporaneous existence and utilization of homogeneous identities may be seen as a contradiction in terms. Can one both use stereotypes and avoid being one? I present this same quandary in my introduction in a slightly different manner—can one appropriate stereotypes without reifying them? I see the heart of this conceptual divide as the exercise of Native agency to adopt, reject, or remain neutral to stereotypes. I realize that this is a privileged position to take and that modes of reception have historically remained constrained by the perceived one-dimensionality of Native identity.

"The Entire World of the Modern Belongs to Indian People"

Philip Deloria's *Indians in Unexpected Places* (2004) demonstrates how Native Americans have historically been denied the capacity to be simultaneously

Native and part of the contemporary world. He argues that people of color in America, particularly Indian people, were active participants in the production of modernity rather than passive outsiders or victims of modernist discourses. In a fascinating account of the Buffalo Bill Cody Wild West shows, Deloria demonstrates how audiences sustained a belief that the Indian reenactors in these circuslike performances were not acting: "The belief that Indians were historical reenactors foreclosed other stories, including the possibility that Indian people occupied the same space and time as their white audiences" (Deloria 2004:67). Fatimah Tobing Rony makes a similar argument in *The Third Eye: Race, Cinema, and Ethnographic Spectacle*, stating, "The Native Man in ethnographic cinema is not even perceived as being an actor: his performance is always 'real'" (Rony 1996:178).

Should this denial of agency in the visual arts be interpreted as indicative of broader attitudes and biases that translate into other areas of Native life, such as curation of a national museum? Deloria maintains that a significant group of early-twentieth-century Indian people (he terms them "image makers") understood completely the power of representation and cultural production. He cites the efforts of Jim Thorpe and William Hazlett, who in 1936 formed the seventy-five-member Indian Actors Association. This organization tried (unsuccessfully) to join the Screen Actors Guild and petitioned the federal government for a film code requiring that Indian roles be played by Indian people. Deloria argues that Indian performers

> recognized...that political and legal struggles are tightly linked to the ideologies and images—the expectations—that non-Indians have built around native people. In making Indian images, native actors sought to participate in a struggle waged on the cultural front, particularly through the developing forms of mass media, which promised to reach larger audiences. [Deloria 2004:104]

Deloria's analysis supports the claims by Berkhofer and others that image making—in particular, the contestation of flawed images by new image making—is a valid course of action in achieving equal power and status. Mentalist and realist divides seemingly do not apply to the performances in which historic image makers ("Indian Codys") reappropriated white expectations for self-gain, "grabbing media attention, and reflecting white expectations back to the white writers and readers of the mass market dailies while working quietly to challenge those expectations" (105).

Similarly, Anne Ruggles Gere (2004) uses the term *survivance* (citing author Gerald Vizenor) in her characterization of the way in which Native American leaders in the early part of the twentieth century would often engage in stereotypes in order to dismiss or manipulate them. Gere describes this strategy in reference to Winnebago artist and educator Angel DeCora, who often lectured to sympathetic white reformists on the inherent talents of Native artists (an idea frequently articulated by whites) while simultaneously promoting a more radical vision of Indian art as deserving recognition as a part of an American art legacy.

Although the views cited appear openly partisan in favor of Indian agency, Deloria's conclusion adopts a decidedly different stance, documenting what he terms the failure of Indian representational politics. He surmises that the efforts of these early-twentieth-century Indian actors, artists, and athletes did not result in the social change they desired. He provides several viable explanations for this failure: the lack of access to the mechanics of cultural productions; the tendency to reinforce familiar expectations while contesting them; and the shift in economic structures, trends, and interests of the American public—leading one to speculate whether these same constrictions apply today. The larger issue he raises, however, is the tension between the concepts of sovereignty and inclusion in twentieth-century US history.

Historically, African, Latino, and Asian Americans demanded inclusion and incorporation as the means to achieve social justice, but "the tools available to Indian people were very different" (Deloria 2004:236). Deloria concludes that "for many Native people, the most productive avenues to justice seemed to point to sovereignty, treaties, and nation-to-nation political relations rather than to inclusion and the demand for civil rights within American society" (236). The status of Native Americans as domestic dependent nations necessarily situates Native American strategies as distinct from other ethnic groups with different histories. Deloria explains that struggles against exclusion, in the form of legal and political restrictions such as Jim Crow segregation, have largely informed the structure of American culture's inclusive, multicultural rhetoric.

The unique indigenous sensibility of sovereignty, paired with a historic reticence for inclusive political strategies, inescapably places Native American representational politics in a different light from other marginalized groups. Native efforts to engage in existing institutional and conceptual frameworks of mainstream America may easily be misinterpreted as an explicit desire for inclusion in the same manner as similarly oppressed groups. However, Deloria (2004:237) describes American Indian cultural representations in mainstream America as "a very particular kind of inclusion, one based on unique political status."

Deloria's text suggests that the experiences of contemporary Native women as image producers may productively be seen as a part of this larger legacy of participation in nationalistic dialogues, modernist or global. Just as twentieth-century Native American cultural leaders were not confined to the cognitive or physical spaces of reservations, neither are twenty-first-century artists restricted to self-identification as tribal representatives who, according to Rothstein's review, are obliged to explain their religious beliefs to the general public. According to Deloria (2004:232), "the entire world of the modern… belongs…to Indian people."

As members of separate and distinct political entities, Native image makers can feasibly exercise both reappropriation of existing stereotypical discourses and advancement of the types of alternative indigenous ideologies that Michael Harris advocates (see chapter 5). The movement between these competing ideologies should not be seen in simplistic terms—one as constrained affect within a victimizing context and the other as an idealized escape from the realist confines of existing power structures. Likewise, the adoption of these varied strategies does not inherently indicate shallow opportunism. Rather, the recognition of strategic choice in representational politics can be interpreted as a form of self-knowledge and communal identity.

Cayuga beadworker Tammy Rahr offers the following testimonial for how this exercise of identity may function in an indigenous setting:

> I remember a man—he's not with us anymore—he's gone. But he was a medicine man. And he said, "That man was going to kill me. He comes to my house very often, and he gets medicine from [me], and I know that he is using that medicine to try to kill me. But it is my responsibility as a medicine person to give him the medicine he is asking for and to stay one step ahead of him—to just be strong enough to ward it off somehow." He says, "It can't hurt me because of that." He said, "He will never be able to do it, because I know what's going on."[2]

This narrative illustrates an indigenous reading of how subjectivity is exercised even when mediated by hostile outside forces. In this Native consciousness, a responsibility to one's community takes precedence over individual gain or security. There is a confidence, a secure sense of self and ability in understanding "what's going on" that defies victimhood. For Rahr, the story is a metaphor for right living in the highly competitive and individualistic world of Native arts, where she must stay "one step ahead." The beauty of this self-structuring identity is its confident appraisal of external ill intent and internal strength. She, like the other artists I have profiled, knows "what's going on."

Native American self-representation may be mediated by ideological and material constraints but is ultimately defined by the communal standards inherent in the self-definition of what is Native. Exposure of diverse image-making strategies, whether recycled or indigenous, conveys the contemporaneous qualities of indigenous identity constructs. The narratives of Native women in the arts are an essential part of this process.

Notes

1. Tessie Naranjo, interview by author, September 18, 2000.
2. Tammy Rahr, interview by author, June 5, 1991.

APPENDIX ONE

The Five Muses
The Theoretical Aims of "Our Indian Princess": Subverting the Stereotype

Thesis One: Stereotypes

1. Images are central to understanding Native Americans. Altougth visual representations may be said to form identity, proving causality is an overly ambitious project. A more productive route is to consider how images are mobilized to different aims—how images "work."

2. Images of Native Americans tend to "cluster" with related meanings about sexuality, intelligence, complexity, and modernity. These traits are resilient and inseparable.

3. White images of Native Americans in popular culture are often inaccurate and demeaning, depicting Indians as sexually active, of less intelligence, simple, and existing only in the past. Native American artists as image makers are experts on the meaning of these images and are adept at reappropriating these images for generative ends, including critiques of white culture.

4. Contemporary Native American artists are often restricted in their ability to engage in critical dialogues because conventional representations "work" in narrowly prescribed ways.

Thesis Two: Creativity

1. Another way to understand stereotypes is to consider the clusters of meanings as inert conventional representations. Conventional representations have meaning beyond the purely negative aspect of stereotyping.

2. Cultural difference is negotiated through imagery. Even flawed imagery, incomplete and inaccurate, may serve productively as a platform for constructive dialogue about perceived racial differences.

3. Native Americans are not passive victims of negative stereotyping, but active agents of critiquing and employing conventional representations.

4. Native Americans employ conventional representations (stereotypes) to talk about cultural difference. These counternarratives are often employed when the social parameters are defined by outside, traditionally Western forces and are negotiated by contrast principles.

5. Indian stereotypes of non-Indians (whites) help Native Americans articulate proper behavior and core communal values.

6. Total eradication of stereotypes prevents the creative manipulation of these "hateful images" and denies the creative potency of counter-representations.

Thesis Three: Pan-Indianism

1. The conception of Native Americans as monolithic and one-dimensional is often based on a denial of tribal differences and uniqueness.

2. Movements to ban or curtail negative representations commonly object to this generic pan-Indian portrayal while advocating tribally specific referents.

3. Historicism recognizes that the legacy of racial oppression of Native Americans has resulted in a generic group ideology.

4. Employment of the pantribal designations "American Indian," "Native American," and "Indian" allows for a critique of historic racial bias.

5. Designations of Native Americans as a common group are inescapable.
6. Total eradication of stereotypes as multitribal referents prevents the political mobilization of counternarratives based on common histories of oppression.

Thesis Four: Realism

1. Conventional representations may be seen as alternately harmful or inert.
2. Perceptions of conventional representations as harmful are premised on the ability of images to have real social and material consequences. Images cause harm.
3. Perceptions of conventional representations as inert are premised on the inability of images to have real social consequences. Images do not cause oppression; oppression exists, and imagery reflects this bias.
4. A mentalist orientation argues that images are independent of material or political realities. Mentalists frequently advocate for tribally specific imagery based on historical accuracy. Native American craft production and consumption work well with the mentalist ideology.
5. Realism recognizes that bias exists and that images reflect this racial bias. Realists often recognize the potency of pantribal referents and the embrace of modernism in Native communities. Contemporary Native American fine arts production and consumption work well with the realist ideology.
6. Status-based prejudice is more active in realist, contemporary Native arts production and consumption than in mentalist, historic crafts realms. Native American artists producing in the individualist sector of fine arts are in direct competition with non-Natives, triggering a denial of either their status as Native Americans or their status as artists.

Thesis Five: Binaries and Alterity

1. The employment of imagery is often premised on a comparative analysis. Native American imagery typically appears as a contrast between civilized and primitive, communal and individualist, traditional and modern. These conventional frames of reference in binary form are the language from which signification speaks.

2. Active contrast (mobilization of alterity) addresses both internal self-resolutions and external social tensions.

3. Inversion (based on contrast) is one strategy among many (eradication, reclamation) utilized in response to harmful imagery.

4. Theoretically, alterity is often cast only in negative terms as associated with structuralism and positivism. Alterity can be ethically neutral and serve as a "device of meaning-production" (van Alphen 1991:3).

5. Essentialized identities, especially those mobilized in the arts and visual culture, do have theoretical value and can be "reclaimed" for politically progressive ends.

APPENDIX TWO

American Indian Fine Arts—The Reception Equation

Mentalist
- Crafts
- Traditional
- Rural
- Poor
- No formal education
- Authentic
- Tribally specific
- Segregated
- Philanthropic urge
- No competition for resources
- Secondary status
- No change
- Sovereign

Realist
- Fine arts
- Modern
- Urban
- Upwardly mobile
- University trained
- Authenticity questioned
- Pan-Indian
- Inclusivity desired
- Active capitalism
- Competition for resources
- Status-linked prejudice
- Change
- Sovereign

References

Albers, Patricia
1983   Introduction: New Perspectives on Plains Indian Women. *In* The Hidden Half: Studies of Plains Indian Women. Patricia Albers and Beatrice Medicine, eds. Pp. 1–26. New York and Lanham, MD: University Press of America.

Albers, Patricia, and Beatrice Medicine
1983   The Role of Sioux Women in the Production of Ceremonial Objects: The Case of the Star Quilt. *In* The Hidden Half: Studies of Plains Indian Women. Patricia Albers and Beatrice Medicine, eds. Pp. 123–137. New York and Lanham, MD: University Press of America.

Alcoff, Linda Martin
2000   Who's Afraid of Identity Politics? *In* Reclaiming Identity: Realist Theory and the Predicament of Postmodernism. Paula M. L. Moya and Michael R. Hames-García, eds. Pp. 322–323. Berkeley: University of California Press.

American Psychological Association
2005   American Psychological Association Public Interest Directorate: American Indian Mascot Resolution. www.apa.org/pi/pi/indian_mascots.html, accessed January 14, 2009.

Anderson, Benedict
[1983] Imagined Communities: Reflections on the Origin and Spread of Nationalism. New 2006   York: Verso Press.

answers.com
         Anselm Kiefer. www.answers.com/topic/anselm-kiefer.

Babcock, Barbara A.
1978   Introduction. *In* The Reversible World: Symbolic Inversion in Art and Society. Barbara A. Babcock, ed. Pp. 13–36. Ithaca, NY: Cornell University Press.

Barth, Fredrik
1969   Ethnic Groups and Boundaries. Boston: Little, Brown.

Basso, Keith
1979   Portraits of "The Whiteman": Linguistic Play and Cultural Symbols among the Western Apache. New York: Cambridge University Press.

Bataille, Gretchen M., ed.
2001   Native American Representations: First Encounters, Distorted Images, and Literary Appropriations. Lincoln: University of Nebraska Press.

Baumann, Gerd
2004   Grammars of Identity/Alterity: A Structural Approach. *In* Grammars of Identity/Alterity: A Structural Approach. Gerd Baumann and Andre Gingrich, eds. Pp. 18–50. New York: Berghahn Books.

Baumann, Gerd, and Andre Gingrich
2004   Foreword. *In* Grammars of Identity/Alterity: A Structural Approach. Gerd Baumann and Andre Gingrich, eds. Pp. ix–xiv. New York: Berghahn Books.

Bay, Mia
2000   The White Image in the Black Mind: African-American Ideas about White People, 1830–1925. New York: Oxford University Press.

Becker, Carol, ed.
1994   The Subversive Imagination: Artists, Society, and Social Responsibility. New York: Routledge.

Becker, Howard
1982   Art Worlds. Berkeley: University of California Press.

Berkhofer, Robert F., Jr.
1979   The White Man's Indian: Images of the American Indian from Columbus to the Present. New York: Vintage Books.

Berlo, Janet Catherine, and Ruth B. Phillips
1998   Native North American Art. Oxford: Oxford University Press.

Biebuyck, Daniel P., ed.
1969   Tradition and Creativity in Tribal Art. Berkeley: University of California Press.

Bieder, Robert
1981   Anthropology and History of the American Indian. American Quarterly 33(3):309–326.

Bird, S. Elizabeth, ed.
1996   Dressing in Feathers: The Construction of the Indian in American Popular Culture. Boulder, CO: Westview.

Bonami, Francesco, ed.
2003   Dreams and Conflicts: The Dictatorship of the Viewer—The 50th International Art Exhibition—La Biennale di Venezia. New York: Rizzoli Books.

Bonilla-Silva, Eduardo
2004   From Bi-racial to Tri-racial: Towards a New System of Racial Stratification in the USA. Ethnic and Racial Studies 27(6):931–950.

Briggs, Martha
2002   Inventory of the Bureau of Indian Affairs Indian Relocation Records, 1936–1975, Bulk 1956–1958. Chicago: The Newberry Library. www.newberry.org/collections/FindingAids/relocation/Relocation.html, accessed January 14, 2009.

Brody, J. J.
1971   Indian Painters and White Patrons. Albuquerque: University of New Mexico Press.

Bunzl, Matti
2004   Boas, Foucault, and the "Native Anthropologist": Notes toward a Neo-Boasian Anthropology. American Anthropologist 106(3):435–442.

Carpenter, Edmund
1969   Comments. In Tradition and Creativity in Tribal Art. Daniel P. Biebuyck, ed. Pp. 203–213. Berkeley: University of California Press.

Champagne, Duane, and Jay Stauss
2002   Defining Indian Studies through Stories and Nation Building. In Native American Studies in Higher Education: Models for Collaboration between Universities and Indigenous Nations. Duane Champagne and Jay Stauss, eds. Pp. 1–15. Walnut Creek, CA: AltaMira.

Chris Rock Enterprises Inc.
1996   Bring the Pain. DVD. Keith Truesdell, dir. Beverly Hills, CA: DreamWorks Records Home Video. Distributed by Universal Music and Video Distribution.

Clifford, James
1997   Spatial Practices: Fieldwork, Travel, and the Disciplining of Anthropology. In Anthropological Locations: Boundaries and Grounds of a Field Science. Akhil Gupta and James Ferguson, eds. Pp. 185–222. Berkeley: University of California Press.

Coombe, Rosemary J.
1996   Embodied Trademarks: Mimesis and Alterity on American Commercial Frontiers. Cultural Anthropology 11(2):202–224.

Corbey, Raymond, and Joep Leerssen
1991   Studying Alterity: Backgrounds and Perspectives. In Alterity, Identity, Image: Selves and Others in Society and Scholarship. Raymond Corbey and Joep Leerssen, eds. Pp. vi–xviii. Amsterdam: Rodopi.

Cotter, Holland
2001   Art/Architecture; Beyond Multiculturalism, Freedom? New York Times, July 29: Arts and Leisure 1. http://query.nytimes.com/gst/fullpage.html?res=9906E0DE1F3AF93 AA15754C0A9679C8B63&scp=2&sq=Beyond+ Multiculturalism, accessed January 14, 2008.

Crenshaw, Kimberle
1991   Mapping the Margins: Intersectionality, Identity Politics, and Violence against Women of Color. Stanford Law Review 43(6):1241–1299.

Cruikshank, Julie
1990   Life Lived like a Story: Life Stories of Three Yukon Native Elders. Lincoln: University of Nebraska Press.
2007   Melting Glaciers and Emerging Histories in the Saint Elias Mountains. In Indigenous Experience Today. Marisol de la Cadena and Orin Starn, eds. Pp. 355–378. Oxford and New York: Berg.

de Alba, Alicia Gaspar
2004 There's No Place like Aztlán. New Centennial Review 4(2):103–140.

Dei, George J. Sefa, Budd L. Hall, and Dorothy Goldin Rosenberg
2000 Introduction. *In* Indigenous Knowledges in Global Contexts: Multiple Readings of Our World. George J. Sefa Dei, Budd L. Hall, and Dorothy Goldin Rosenberg, eds. Pp. 3–17. Toronto: University of Toronto Press.

Deloria, Philip J.
1998 Playing Indian. New Haven, CT: Yale University Press.
2004 Indians in Unexpected Places. Lawrence: University of Kansas Press.

Des Garennes, Christine
2007 Chief Is Out. Champaign-Urbana News-Gazette, February 16.

Dilworth, Leah
1996 Imagining Indians in the Southwest: Persistent Visions of a Primitive Past. Washington, DC: Smithsonian Institution Press.

Dissanayake, Ellen
1988 What Is Art For? Seattle: University of Washington Press.

Dubin, Margaret
2001 Native America Collected: The Culture of an Art World. Albuquerque: University of New Mexico Press.

Duncan, Kate
2001 1001 Curious Things: Ye Olde Curiosity Shop and Native American Art. Seattle: University of Washington Press.

Eriksen, Thomas Hylland
1993 The Epistemological Status of the Concept of Ethnicity. http://folk.uio.no/geirthe/Status_of_ethnicity.html, accessed March 3, 2007.

Etzkorn, K. Peter
1973 On the Sphere of Social Validity in African Art: Sociological Reflections on Ethnographic Data. *In* The Traditional Artist in African Societies. Warren L. d'Azevedo, ed. Pp. 343–378. Bloomington: Indiana University Press.

Fagg, William
1969 The African Artist. *In* Tradition and Creativity in Tribal Art. Daniel P. Biebuyck, ed. Pp. 42–57. Berkeley: University of California Press.

Fauntleroy, Gussie
1992 No Word for Art in Tewa Language—Only Meaning. Santa Fe New Mexican Pasatiempo, October 9–15: 7.

Fenelon, James
2003 Race, Research, and Tenure: Institutional Credibility and the Incorporation of African, Latino, and American Indian Faculty. Journal of Black Studies 34(1):87.

Fenstermaker, Sarah, and Candace West, eds.
2002 Doing Gender, Doing Difference: Inequality, Power, and Institutional Change. New York: Routledge.

Ferris State University
    The Jim Crow Museum of Racist Memorabilia. www.ferris.edu/news/jimcrow.

Fisher, Jean
1987   Guidelines. *In* We the People. Pp. 8–9. New York: Artists Space.

Fixico, Donald L.
2000   The Urban Indian Experience in America. Albuquerque: University of New Mexico Press.

Geertz, Armin W.
1991   Native American Art and the Problem of the Other: An Introduction to the Issues. European Review of Native American Studies 5(2):1–5.

Gere, Anne Ruggles
2004   An Art of Survivance: Angel DeCora at Carlisle. American Indian Quarterly 28(3/4):649–684.

Gingrich, Andre
2004   Conceptualizing Identities: Anthropological Alternatives to Essentializing Difference and Moralizing about Othering. *In* Grammars of Identity/Alterity: A Structural Approach. Gerd Baumann and Andre Gingrich eds. Pp. 3–17. New York: Berghahn Books.

Ginsburg, Faye, Lila Abu-Lughod, and Brian Larkin, eds.
2002   Media Worlds: Anthropology on New Terrain. Berkeley: University of California Press.

Graburn, Nelson H.
1976   Introduction: Arts of the Fourth World. *In* Ethnic and Tourist Arts: Cultural Expressions from the Fourth World. Nelson H. Graburn, ed. Pp. 1–32. Berkeley: University of California Press.

Green, Rayna
[1975] The Pocahontas Perplex. *In* Unequal Sisters: A Multicultural Reader in US
 1990   Women's History. Vicki L. Ruiz and Ellen Carol DuBois, eds. Pp. 15–21. New York: Routledge.
1983   Native American Women: A Contextual Bibliography. Bloomington: Indiana University Press.

Gupta, Akhil, and James Ferguson
1997   "The Field" as Site, Method, and Location in Anthropology. *In* Anthropological Locations: Boundaries and Grounds of a Field Science. Akhil Gupta and James Ferguson, eds. Pp. 1–46. Berkeley: University of California Press.

Handler, Richard
1994   Is "Identity" a Useful Concept? *In* Commemorations: The Politics of National Identity. John R. Gillis, ed. Pp. 27–40. Princeton, NJ: Princeton University Press.

Hanson, Jeffrey R., and Linda P. Rouse
1987   Dimensions of Native American Stereotyping. American Indian Culture and Research Journal 11(4):33–58.
1991   American Indian Stereotyping, Resource Competition, and Status-Based Prejudice. American Indian Culture and Research Journal 15(3):1–17.

Haozous, Bob
2005   Indigenous Dialogue. Santa Fe, NM: Institute of American Indian Arts Museum.

Harris, Michael D.
2003   Colored Pictures: Race and Visual Representation. Chapel Hill, NC: University of North Carolina Press.

Hatcher, Evelyn Payne
1985   Art as Culture: An Introduction to the Anthropology of Art. New York: University Press of America.

Hernández-Avila, Inés, ed.
2005   Reading Native American Women: Critical/Creative Representations. Lanham, MD: AltaMira.

Hertzberg, Hazel W.
1971   The Search for an American Indian Identity: Modern Pan-Indian Movements. Syracuse, NY: Syracuse University Press.

Heyer, Sally
1990   One House, One Voice, One Heart: Native American Education at the Santa Fe Indian School. Santa Fe, NM: Museum of New Mexico Press.

Highwater, Jamake
1980   The Sweetgrass Lives On: Fifty Contemporary North American Indian Artists. New York: Lippincott & Crowell.

Hill, Richard W., Sr.
1990   The Rise of Neo-Native Expressionism. *In* Our Land/Ourselves: American Indian Contemporary Artists. Deborah Ward, ed. Pp.1–5. Albany: University Art Gallery, University at Albany, State University of New York.

Himmelman, Michael
1989   Indian Art vs. Artifact: A Problem of Ambiguity. New York Times, May 1. http://query.nytimes.com/gst/fullpage.html?res=950DEFD7163DF932A35756C0A96 F948260&scp=1&sq=Ames%2C+Michael, accessed January 14, 2007.

Hoffman, Gerhard
1986   Frames of Reference: Native American Art in the Context of Modern and Postmodern Art. *In* The Arts of the North American Indian: Native Traditions in Evolution. Edwin L. Wade, ed. Pp. 257–282. New York: Hudson Hills.

Holmes, Leilani
2000   Heart Knowledge, Blood Memory, and the Voice of the Land: Implications of Research among Hawaiian Elders. *In* Indigenous Knowledges in Global Contexts: Multiple Readings of Our World. George J. Sefa Dei, Budd L. Hall, and Dorothy Goldin Rosenberg, eds. Pp. 37–53. Toronto: University of Toronto Press.

Huhndorf, Shari M.
2001   Going Native: Indians in the American Cultural Imagination. Ithaca, NY: Cornell University Press.

Hutnyk, John
2000   Critique of Exotica: Music, Politics, and the Culture Industry. London: Pluto.

Huyssen, Andres
1989   Anselm Kiefer: The Terror of History, the Temptation of Myth. October 48(Spring):25–45.

Indian Country Today
2004   Natives Must Educate America, or Perish. Editorial, November 16. www.msnbc.msn.com/id/6505026/print/1/displaymode/1098/, accessed November 22, 2004.
2006   A Note to American Journalists: More Balance, Please! Editorial, February 24. www.indiancountrytoday.com/archive/28168269.html, accessed September 10, 2008.

Jaimes, M. Annette
1987   American Indian Studies: Toward an Indigenous Model. American Indian Culture and Research Journal 11(3):1–16.

Johansen, Bruce E.
2003   Putting the Moccasin on the Other Foot: A Media History of the "Fighting Whities." SIMILE: Studies in Media & Information Literacy Education 3(1). www.utpress.utoronto.ca/journal/ejournals/simile, accessed November 26, 2005.

Jolivétte, Andrew, ed.
2006   Cultural Representation in Native America. Lanham, MD: AltaMira.

Katz, Jane
1995   In My Family, the Women Ran Everything: Emmi Whitehorse. *In* Messengers of the Wind: Native American Women Tell Their Life Stories. Jane Katz, ed. Pp. 55–65. New York: One World/Ballantine Books.

Kidwell, Clara Sue
1992   Indian Women as Cultural Mediators. Ethnohistory 39(2):97–107.

King, C. Richard
2003   De/Scribing Squ*w: Indigenous Women and Imperial Idioms in the United States. American Indian Culture and Research Journal 27(2):1–16.

Kleeblatt, Norman L.
1998   Master Narratives/Minority Artists. Art Journal 57(3):29–35.

Lail, Thomas
1991   Exhibit Takes Very Few Risks. Albany Times Union, March 14:11.

Layton, Robert
1991   The Anthropology of Art. 2nd edition. Cambridge: Cambridge University Press.

LeRoy, John
1985   Fabricated World: An Interpretation of Kewa Tales. Vancouver: University of British Columbia Press.

Leuthold, Steven
1998   Indigenous Aesthetics: Native Art, Media and Identity. Austin: University of Texas Press.

Lévi-Strauss, Claude
1963   Structural Anthropology. New York: Basic Books.

Liddle, Nancy
1990 Our Land/Ourselves: American Indian Contemporary Artists. Albany: University Art Gallery, University at Albany, State University of New York.

Lippard, Lucy
1990a The Color of the Wind. *In* Our Land/Ourselves: American Indian Contemporary Artists. Deborah Ward, ed. Pp. 7–15. Albany: University Art Gallery, University at Albany, State University of New York.
1990b Mixed Blessings: New Art in a Multicultural America. New York: Pantheon Books.
1991 Shimá: The Paintings of Emmi Whitehorse. *In* Neeznàà: Emmi Whitehorse, Ten Years. Santa Fe, NM: Wheelwright Museum of the American Indian.

Lobo, Susan
1992 Interview with Jean LaMarr: Supporting Native Pride: A Native American Artist Talks about Her Community Art Project for Reservation and Urban Indian Youth. Cultural Survival Quarterly 16(3). www.cs.org/publications/ csq/csq-article.cfm?id=941, accessed January 14, 2008.
2001 American Indians and the Urban Experience. Walnut Creek, CA: AltaMira.

Lomawaima, K. Tsianina
1994 They Called It Prairie Light: The Story of the Chilocco Indian School. Lincoln: University of Nebraska Press.

Lorde, Audre
1984 Sister Outsider. Trumansburg, NY: Crossing.

Mankekar, Purnima
1999 Screening Culture, Viewing Politics: An Ethnography of Television, Womanhood, and Nation. Durham, NC: Duke University Press.

Mankiller, Wilma
1998 Editor's Note. *In* The Reader's Companion to US Women's History. Wilma Mankiller, Gwendolyn Mink, Marysa Navarro, Barbara Smith, and Gloria Steinem, eds. P. xvii. New York: Houghton Mifflin.
2004 Every Day Is a Good Day. CO: Fulcrum.

McEvilley, Thomas
1992 Art and Otherness: Crisis in Cultural Identity. Kingston, NY: McPherson.

McMaster, Gerald
1998 Living on Reservation X. *In* Reservation X. Gerald McMaster, ed. Pp. 19–30. Seattle: University of Washington Press.

Mihesuah, Devon Abbott
1993 Cultivating the Rosebuds: The Education of Women at the Cherokee Female Seminary, 1851–1909. Urbana: University of Illinois Press.
1996 American Indians: Stereotypes and Realities. Atlanta, GA: Clarity.
2003 Indigenous American Women: Decolonization, Empowerment, Activism. Lincoln: University of Nebraska Press.

Mikkelsen, Leatrice
1992 Decolonizing the Mind: End of a 500 Year Era. Seattle, WA: Center on Contemporary Art.

Mitchell, Nancy Marie [Nancy Marie Mithlo]
1993   The Negotiated Role of Contemporary American Indian Artists: A Study in Marginality. PhD dissertation, Department of Anthropology, Stanford University.

Mithlo, Nancy Marie
1994   Demonstrations of Culture, Charlene Teters: The Rosa Parks of Campus Racism. Crosswinds 6(4).
1995   Is There Really No Word for Art in Our Language? Paper presented at the biannual Native American Art Studies Association meeting, Tulsa, OK, October 20.
2004   "Red Man's Burden": The Politics of Inclusion in Museum Settings. American Indian Quarterly 28(3/4):743–763.
2005   Re-appropriating Redskins—Pellerossasogna (Red Skin Dream): Shelley Niro at the 50th La Biennale di Venezia. Visual Anthropology Review 20(2):22–35.

Monthan, Doris
1990   R. C. Gorman: A Retrospective. Flagstaff, AZ: Northland.

Moya, Paula M. L.
2000   Introduction: Reclaiming Identity. *In* Reclaiming Identity: Realist Theory and the Predicament of Postmodernism. Paula M. L. Moya and Michael R. Hames-García, eds. Pp. 1–26. Berkeley: University of California Press.

Mutua, Kagendo, and Beth Blue Swadener
2004   Introduction. *In* Decolonizing Research in Cross-cultural Contexts: Critical Personal Narratives. Kagendo Mutua and Beth Blue Swadener, eds. Pp. 1–23. Albany: State University of New York Press.

Myers, Fred
2004   Ontologies of the Image and Economies of Exchange. American Ethnologist 31(1):5–20.

Naranjo, Tessie
2000   Pueblo Pottery Remains Down to Earth: Old Beliefs Wrestle with New Influences. Santa Fe New Mexican Pasatiempo, January 1–6: 8.

New, Lloyd
1975   Charter, Administration and Curriculum, Institute of American Indian Arts. Santa Fe, NM: Institute of American Indian Arts Archive Collection.

Newsom, Barbara Y., and Adele Z. Silver, eds.
1978   The Art Museum as Educator. Berkeley: University of California Press.

Niro, Shelley
2003   The Shirt. Videotape. Toronto: V Tape.

Ortiz, Alfonso
1972   Ritual Drama and the Pueblo World View. *In* New Perspectives on the Pueblos. Alfonso Ortiz, ed. Pp. 135–161. Albuquerque: University of New Mexico Press.

Ostrowitz, Judith
1999   Privileging the Past: Reconstructing History in Northwest Coast Art. Seattle: University of Washington Press.

Otten, Charlotte M., ed.
1971   Anthropology and Art. Austin: University of Texas Press.

Owens, Louis
2001   As If an Indian Were Really an Indian. *In* Native American Representations: First Encounters, Distorted Images, and Literary Appropriations. Gretchen M. Bataille, ed. Pp. 11–24. Lincoln: University of Nebraska Press.

Papadopoulos, Nikoleta
2005   Curator Speaks on Lessons Learned. Sophian, October 6: 1.

Parkin, David
2001   Escaping Cultures: The Paradox of Cultural Creativity. *In* Locating Cultural Creativity. John Liep, ed. Pp. 133–143. London: Pluto.

Pearce, Roy Harvey
[1953] The Savages of America: A Study of the Indian and the Idea of Civilization.
 1965   Baltimore, MD: Johns Hopkins University Press.

Pfister, Joel
2004   Individuality Incorporated: Indians and the Multicultural Modern. Durham, NC: Duke University Press.

Pilgrim, David
2005   "Jim Crow" in the 21st Century. African and African American Studies Winter 2005 Lecture Series, Stanford University, January 21.

Plumwood, Val
2002   Feminism and the Logic of Alterity. *In* Representing Reason: Feminist Theory and Formal Logic. Rachel Joffe Falmagne and Marjorie Hass, eds. Pp. 45–70. New York: Rowman & Littlefield.

Pratt, Mary Louise
1982   Conventions of Representation: Where Discourse and Ideology Meet. *In* Contemporary Perceptions of Language: Interdisciplinary Dimensions. Heidi Byrnes, ed. Pp. 139–155. Washington, DC: Georgetown University Press.

Reed-Danahay, Deborah, ed.
1997   Auto/Ethnography: Rewriting the Self and the Social. New York: Berg.

Rich, B. Ruby
1994   Dissed and Disconnected: Notes on Present Ills and Future Dreams. *In* The Subversive Imagination: Artists, Society, and Social Responsibility. Carol Becker, ed. Pp. 223–248. New York: Routledge.

Rodriguez, Richard
1994   Victim of Two Cultures: Richard Rodriguez. DVD. Betsy McCarthy, prod. and dir. The Moyers Collection: A World of Ideas. Princeton, NJ: Films for the Humanities & Sciences/Public Affairs Television, Inc.
2002   Brown: The Last Discovery of America. New York: Penguin.

Rony, Fatimah Tobing
1996   The Third Eye: Race, Cinema, and Ethnographic Spectacle. Durham, NC: Duke University Press.

Rosaldo, Renato, Jr.
1978   The Rhetoric of Control: Ilongots Viewed as Natural Bandits and Wild Indians. *In* The Reversible World: Symbolic Inversion in Art and Society. Barbara A. Babcock, ed. Pp. 240–257. Ithaca, NY: Cornell University Press.

Rosenstein, Jay
1997   In Whose Honor? Videotape and DVD. Harriman, NY: New Day Films.

Rothstein, Edward
2004   Museum with an American Indian Voice. New York Times, September 21: B1, B5.

Said, Edward W.
1978   Orientalism. New York: Vintage Books.

Saltz, Jerry
1996   Kara Walker: Ill-Will and Desire. Flash Art 29(191):82–86.

Saper, Bernard
1993   Since When Is Jewish Humor Not Anti-Semitic? *In* Semites and Stereotypes: Characteristics of Jewish Humor. Avner Ziv and Anat Zajdman, eds. Pp. 71–86. Westport, CT: Greenwood.

Sheffield, Gail K.
1997   The Arbitrary Indian: The Indian Arts and Crafts Act of 1990. Norman: University of Oklahoma Press.

Shoemaker, Nancy
1988   Urban Indian Choices: American Indian Organizations in Minneapolis, 1920–1950. Western Historical Quarterly 19(4):431–447.

Shulman, Ken
2000   The Buckskin Ceiling and Its Discontents. New York Times, December 24. http://query.nytimes.com/gst/fullpage.html?res=9C06E7DD1039F937A15751C1A96 69C8B63&scp=1&sq=The+Buckskin+Ceiling+and+Its+Discontents.+, accessed January 14, 2008.

Silver, Harry
1979   Ethnoart. Annual Review of Anthropology 8:267–307.

Simpson, Audra
2006   On Ethnographic Refusal: Citizenship and Nationhood in Contemporary Kanhawake. Paper presented at the American Anthropological Association invited session "Critical and Dangerous Issues in Ethnographic Research in Native North America," San Jose, CA, November 18.

Smith, Andrea
2005   Conquest: Sexual Violence and American Indian Genocide. Cambridge, MA: South End.

Smith, Linda Tuhiwai
1999   Decolonizing Methodologies: Research and Indigenous Peoples. London: Zed Books.

Smith, Sidonie, and Julia Watson, eds.
1998   Women, Autobiography, Theory: A Reader. Madison: University of Wisconsin Press.

Smithsonian Institution National Museum of Natural History Anthropology Outreach Office
1996   Erasing Native American Stereotypes. www.nmnh.si.edu/anthro/outreach/Indbibl/sterotyp.html, accessed January 14, 2009.

Snipp, C. Matthew
1986   Who Are American Indians? Some Observations about the Perils and Pitfalls of Data for Race and Ethnicity. Population Research and Policy Review 5:247–252.

Spicer, Edward H.
1971   Persistent Cultural Systems. Science 174(4011):795–800.
1972   Plural Society in the Southwest. In Plural Society in the Southwest. Edward H. Spicer and Raymond H. Thompson, eds. Pp. 21–76. New York: Interbook.

Steiner, Christopher B.
1994   African Art in Transit. Cambridge: Cambridge University Press.

Straus, Terry, and Debra Valentino
2001   Retribalization in Urban Indian Communities. In American Indians and the Urban Experience. Susan Lobo and Hurt Peters, eds. Pp. 85–94. Walnut Creek, CA: AltaMira.

Stuever, Hank
2004   A Family Reunion. Washington Post, September 22: C1, C8.

Szasz, Margaret
1974   Education and the American Indian: The Road to Self-Determination, 1928–1973. Albuquerque: University of New Mexico Press.

Taussig, Michael
1993   Mimesis and Alterity: A Particular History of the Senses. New York: Routledge.

Thornton, Russell
1987   American Indian Holocaust and Survival: A Population History since 1492. Norman: University of Oklahoma Press.

Trask, Haunani-Kay
1993   From a Native Daughter: Colonialism and Sovereignty in Hawai'i. Monroe, ME: Common Courage.

Traugott, Joe
1992   Native American Artists and the Postmodern Cultural Divide. Art Journal 51(3):36–43.

University of Illinois
2007   Chief Illiniwek Will No Longer Perform: NCAA to Lift Sanctions on Illini Athletics. Press release, February 16.

van Alphen, Ernst
1991   The Other Within. In Alterity, Identity, Image: Selves and Others in Society and Scholarship. Raymond Corbey and Joep Leerssen, eds. Pp. 1–16. Amsterdam: Rodopi.

Venne, Sharon
2004   She Must Be Civilized: She Paints Her Toe Nails. *In* A Will to Survive: Indigenous Essays on the Politics of Culture, Language, and Identity. Stephen Greymorning, ed. Pp. 126–139. New York: McGraw-Hill.

Vickers, Scott B.
1998   Native American Identities: From Stereotype to Archetype in Art and Literature. Albuquerque: University of New Mexico Press.

Villani, John
1993   Teters, Munoz Open at CCA with Powerful Statements. Crosswinds, August 27–September 2.

Visweswaran, Kamala
1994   Fictions of Feminist Ethnography. Minneapolis: University of Minnesota Press.

Vizenor, Gerald
1993   The Ruins of Representation: Shadow Survivance and the Literature of Dominance. American Indian Quarterly 17(1):7–30.

Wade, Edwin L., with Rennard Strickland
1981   Magic Images: Contemporary Native American Art. Tulsa, OK: Philbrook Art Center.

Warren, Kay
1997   Narrating Cultural Resurgence: Genre and Self-Representation for Pan-Mayan Writers. *In* Auto/Ethnography: Rewriting the Self and the Social. Deborah E. Reed-Danahay, ed. Pp. 21–45. New York: Berg.

Wax, Rosalie H., and Robert K. Thomas
1961   American Indians and White People. Phylon: Atlanta University Review of Race and Culture 22(4):305–317.

West, Candace, and Don H. Zimmerman
2002   Doing Gender. *In* Doing Gender, Doing Difference: Inequality, Power, and Institutional Change. Sarah Fenstermaker and Candace West, eds. Pp. 3–23. New York: Routledge.

West, W. Richard, Jr.
1998   The Centrality of Place. *In* Reservation X. Gerald McMaster, ed. P. 11. Seattle: University of Washington Press.

West, W. Richard, Jr., ed.
2000   The Changing Presentation of the American Indian: Museums and Native Cultures. Seattle: University of Washington Press.

Whitehorse, Emmi
2007   Unlimited Boundaries. Published in conjunction with the art exhibition shown at the Albuquerque Museum of Art & History in Albuquerque, NM.

Whitely, Peter
1997   The End of Anthropology (at Hopi)? *In* Indians and Anthropologists: Vine Deloria, Jr., and the Critique of Anthropology. Thomas Biolsi and Larry J. Zimmerman, eds. Pp. 177–207. Tucson: University of Arizona Press.

Witherspoon, Gary
1977 Language and Art in the Navajo Universe. Ann Arbor: University of Michigan Press.

Wolff, Janet
1981 The Social Production of Art. London: Macmillan Education.

Wong, Hertha Dawn
1992 Sending My Heart Back across the Years: Tradition and Innovation in Native American Autobiography. New York: Oxford University Press.

Woodward, Denni Dianne
2001 When the "Indian" Was Mascot. ComingVoice XXX(1):9.

Worth, Sol, and John Adair
1977 Through Navajo Eyes. Albuquerque: University of New Mexico Press.

Wylie, Alison
2003 Why Standpoint Matters. In Science and Other Cultures: Issues in Philosophies of Science and Technology. Robert Figueroa and Sandra Harding, eds. Pp. 26–48. New York: Routledge.

Young Man, Alfred
1991 Token and Taboo: Academia vs. Native Art: Problems in Teaching North American Indian Art at the Post-secondary Level. European Review of Native American Studies 5(2):11–14.

Zeller, Tom, Jr.
2007 Ending a Tradition That Some Find Racist, Others Noble. New York Times, February 16. http://thelede.blogs.nytimes.com/2007/02/16/ending-a-racist-noble-tradition/?scp=1&sq=Ending+a+Tradition+That+Some+Find+Racist%2C+Others+Noble+Zeller%2C+Tom%2C+Jr., accessed January14, 2008.

Index

acculturation, 48–49
aestheticization, defuses social concern (Whitely), 122, **plate 14**
aesthetics (indigenous): absence of artistic vocabulary, 56; autonomy with participation, 53; born an artist, 75–77, 80–84; communal aspects, 5; contextual "ethnoaesthetics" (Hatcher), 56–57; essentialist/biological, ahistorical/ideological, 75–78; hózhó (Witherspoon), 54; inclusion dismisses uniqueness, 57; "intentionally paint beauty" (Whitehorse), 41–42; modernist, 124; Navajo, 54; place-based (de Alba), 95–97; separation of conceptual categories, 124–25; separatism, nationalism, sovereignty, 56, 72; Western and indigenous compared, 47–48, 56; women's perspective, 8. See also art, roles and purposes of; political nature of art
agency, 48, 50, 71; active in community/politics, 84–86; adjust strategies (Swentzell), 39–40; appropriations for essentialized identities, 79, 134; how exercised with Western norms, 27; and othering, 116; reappropriation of stereotypes, 104–5, **plate 11**; and victim binary, 31, 103–4
aims of book, 154–57; dismantle essentialized images as culprit, 128–29; embrace indigenous knowledge, 7; examine identity in art production, 93–94; review, reappropriate, 26; subvert hateful images, 7, 16. See also methodology/context of book
Albany Times Union (Lail 1991), 89
Albers, Patricia, and Beatrice Medicine, family, community in Sioux, 28
Albers, Patricia, restricted material/research, 8
Alcoff, Linda Martin, essentialism, 20
alterity: counternarratives approach, 19; inversion in ritual (Babcock), 113–14; Native women as alter (Taussig), 2; as neutral, 116; and oppositional terms, 101; to resolve internal/external, 126; social tool, symbolic, 112. See also alterity, patterns of
Alterity, Identity, Image (Corbey & Leerssen 1991), 116
alterity, patterns of: boarding schools create identity, 107–8; concept of in three ethnographies, 105–10; content/form of narratives convey value, 109; gendered, 106, 109–10; oppositionality, 109; "Whiteman," 105–7
American Indian Religious Freedom Act (1978), 66
American Psychological Association (APA), 20
Amerman, Marcus, 83
Anderson, Benedict, 94
Anthropological Locations (Gupta & Ferguson 1997), 92–93
"Anthropology and History of the American Indian" (Bieder 1981), 37–39
Appendix One: Five Muses, theoretical aims of book: Binaries and Alterity, 157; Creativity, 155; Pan-Indianism, 155; Realism, 156; Stereotypes, 154
Appendix Two: Fine Arts Reception, Mentalist/Realist clusters, 158
art, roles and purposes of: assimilation/acculturation, 44; cultural values of gender and race, 17; cultural/ethnic community, 44–46, 55; economic, 44–46; fine arts or cultural, 47; healing, 44–46; political, 46, 81–84; process before commodity or exhibit value, 55; remembrance, documentation, 85; rewriting history, 91; telling the story of the reservation, 84–91; as totality of life, 75–76. See also aesthetics (indigenous); political nature of art

173

"art stars/honorary whites," 100–120; gender, 100–101; pursuing notoriety, 101–2, **plate 11**; stereotypes, 103–4
art training/institutions. *See* institutions, art (indigenous)
Artist Resource Files, IAIA Museum (Dailey), 23
artistic paradigms. *See* paradigms
artist's role. *See* Native women artists, roles
arts, women, essentialism: three variables, 24–32; constructs of discourse, misconceptions, 25–27; false assumptions, 25. *See also* essentialism; image construction
assimilation, 44; boarding school experience, 64; passivity and agency, 48–50; pluralism, 57; and roles of formalism, materialism, 48

Babcock, Barbara A., 113–14, 130
Barth, Fredrik, dichotomies, boundaries, 94, 113
Basso, Keith, 105–7, 109–10
Baumann, Gerd, and Andre Gingrich: identity definition fluid, 117–18; structural approach flexible, 117–18; ternary structure, grammars, 117–18
Bay, Mia, 111
Becker, Howard, 50
Berkhofer, Robert F. Jr., 127, 129; generalizing pantribal identities, 65–66; image in white minds, 33; invent new images, 142–43; later identity scholarship, 101–3; paradigm of polarity, 30; white premises, 140, 142–43
BIA, 44, 64
Bieder, Robert, mentalist/realist theories, 37, 38, 39, 128
binary constructs of identity: agent/victim, 31; critiques of, two arguments, 114–15; dichotomies, boundaries (Barth), 113–14; domestic/public, 28; and economic necessity, 29, 31; gender, "honorary whites," 100–101; individual/collective, 28; oppositional terms, paradigms, 101; oppositionality (Clifford), 93; pantribal, pan-Indian, 24, 30; place-based or fluid, 98; reject or embrace culture, 89; serve to classify, maintain group, 113; symbolic inversions/reversals, 113–14; tension of, 30–31. *See also* dualities for artists; paradigms
Bitsui, Sherwin, 136
boarding school experience: strengthens identity (Lomawaima), 107–8; tool for assimilation, 64
born an artist, 75–99; "born into doing," 75–77; natural attribute, 75–77, 83–84
Bradley, David, 83
Briggs, Martha, 44
Brody, J. J.: acculturation, separatism, 48–49; constraint of white reception, 51; no Native voice, 49–50
Brown: The Last Discovery of America (Rodriguez 2002), 94
buckskin ceiling, 34
Bunzl, Matti: genealogy of secondary explanation, 78; historization, 90
Bureau of Indian Affairs (BIA), 44, 64

causality: identity constructs, mascots, 38; images and representation (Pratt), 37–39
censorship: by art shows (Whitehorse), 51; cultural spokesperson, 72; refusal (Simpson), 72; self-imposed (Cota), 69–70
Champagne, Duane, and Jay Stauss, 13
Chilocco Indian School, 107–8
Clifford, James, 93
colonialism, 10, 12, 90, 95; effects on ethnicity, 54; extending, control land, 92, 94
Colored Pictures: Race and Visual Representation (Harris 2003), 140
comedy. *See* humor and media
commercial values. *See* economic values
commonality of indigenous experience, 62–63. *See also* pan-Indian debate
communal ethnicity: communal aspects of aesthetics, 5; communal standards in image politics, 152–53; community support of artist, 50; cultural context of art (Lippard), 55; effects of colonialism on, 54; fluid, global vs. land-based societies, 92–93, 98; hybridity, multiculturalism, 18, 89; identity and anticommunal expressions, 125; indigenous values over commercial, 45; Native women as icons, 5; salvage material culture (Traugott), 59. *See also* pan-Indian debate
communal identity vs. individual or tribal: artist part of, not at odds with, community, 29; domestic and public art (Sioux), 28; in pan-Indian debate, 64, 67–68
contemporary world: agency in modernity, 150–52; communal standards define strategies, 153; image politics of Deloria, 149–52; modern belongs to Indian, 149–53; NMAI opening and review, 145–49; reappropriation, alternative ideologies, 152
contextual "ethnoaesthetics" (Hatcher), 56–57
Corbey, Raymond, and Joep Leerssen, alterity, 116
cosmopolitanism and prestige, factors of, 25–26
Cota, Laura Fragua, interview: allegiance to community, agency, 71; father, 70; Hopi maiden cheapened, 121–22; *Just Because You Put Feathers*, **plates 12a, 12b**; motivation, 123–24, **plate 15**; on painting what sells, 29; poster of mask burning, 70; teachers at IAIA, stereotypes, 80; "they've got it all wrong," 121–22
counternarratives, 19
Crenshaw, Kimberle, 17

Critique of Exotica (Hutnyk 2000), 39
Crown Point boarding school, 62–63
Cruikshank, Julie: as female ethnographer, 105–6; interpretation of storytelling, 108–9; women's autobiography genre, 108
cultural field, homogenization (Parkin), 61

Daily, Charles, museum, 23, 82
de Alba, Alicia Gaspar, 96, 98
Decolonizing Methodologies (Smith, L. 1999), 12
De Cora, Angel, artist, 151
Deloria, Philip, 48, 86, 149–52; active agency in image making, 150–51; difference from other marginalized groups, 151; early Native actors, media, 150; failure of image politics, 151; inclusion and sovereignty, 151
"De/Scribing Squ*w" (King 2003), 130–31, 133–34
Dilworth, Leah, 44
"Dimensions of Native American Stereotyping" (Hanson & Rouse 1987), 126–29
domains of image discourse. *See* binary constructs of identity; image construction; paradigms
dualities for artists, 95–99; place-based vs. fluid identities, 98; Rahr: family first, going back, 95–97; "jumping creek," 96–97. *See also* binary constructs of identity; Native women artists

economic values, 52, 77, 79; emphasis on art product, economic determinism, 54; land-based vs. global capital, 95; and legal system (Rahr), 31–32; materiality, contradictory meanings of, 45; on painting what sells (Cota), 29; "Van Gogh syndrome," 29
Emerson, Gloria, interview: community of clan, family, 13; matriarchy, assimilation, 11; painting not traditional, elitist, 84–85, 91; remembrance of agony, 85, **plate 8**; *Rock Desert*, 73, **plate 7**; sand painting tradition, 74; School for Advanced Research (SAR), 74; story of what happened, 84–88, 90–91; "tensions" in aesthetics, 73
essentialism, 120; "exteriority" (Said), 76; false binary (Berkhofer), 30; insider/outsider tension, 30; of liminality, 114–15; othering, 116; prisonhouse, 93; stereotypes, maneuvering images (Alcoff), 20; strategic, 16, 20
essentialized images: dismantle as culprit, 128–29; reclamation of, 79, 134. *See also* stereotypes
Ethnic and Tourist Arts (Graburn 1976), 48
Ethnic Groups and Boundaries (Barth 1969), 94, 113
ethnicity. *See* communal ethnicity
"ethnoaesthetics," contextual (Hatcher), 56–57
ethnography: accidental, "salvage," 4; not a construct for Native arts, 25
Etzkorn, K. Peter, 56
exclusion: of artists, 43–48; urban relocation program, 44

Fabricated World (LeRoy 1985), 112
"A Family Reunion" (Stuever 2004), 32–33, **plate 3**
Fenstermaker, Sarah, and Candace West, eds., "doing gender," 8
Fighting Whites, U. of Northern Colorado, 131
fine arts, 36, 47, 57, 74; criteria, ethnic, crafts, 75–76, 78; disavowal of term *art*, 78–79; elitism, "master's tools," 84–85; individual above collective, 85; mentalist/realist reception, 158
First Americans Festival, 32–33
Fisher, Jean, 89
Fixico, Donald L., 132–33
Fourth World/indigenous identity, 63. *See also* identity; pan-Indian debate
Freestyle exhibit (Golden), 89
From a Native Daughter (Trask 1993), 12

Geertz, Armin W., 71–72
gender: alterity, form of, 106; "doing gender" (Fenstermaker and West), 8; patterns of alterity, 109–10
Gere, Anne Ruggles, 150–51
Goins, Jimmy, 32–33, **plate 3**
Gold, Pat Courtney, 117, **plate 13**
Golden, Thelma, 89
Gorman, R. C., 101, 115–18
Graburn, Nelson, 48
Green, Rayna, 7
Gupta, Akhil, and James Ferguson, 92–93

Handler, Richard, 123
Hanson, Jeffrey R., and Linda P. Rouse: competition for resources, 127–28, 129; demeaning pan-Indian stereotypes, 127; emerging pluralistic paradigm, 126–27
Harris, Michael D.: analysis of artist Walker, 141–42; black/white identities a fiction, 140–41; concern with white audience, 142; identities depend on opposition, 141; rootedness, 89–90; "signifyin" or "shining," 90; stereotypes maintain powers, 141; strategies rooted in oppression, 140–42
Hatcher, Evelyn Payne, 56–57
Hazlett, William, 150
Hertzberg, Hazel W., 30, 68
Hill, Richard W. Sr., 23, 87
historicism, 90–91, 95
Hoffman, Gerhard, 57–58
Holmes, Leilani, 95

homogenization, cultural field (Parkin), 61
Houser, Allan, sculptor, 147
hózhó (Witherspoon), 54
humor and media, 134–40; different aims/causes, 137–38; engagement with, 134
Hutnyk, John, 39
hybridity, 18, 89

IAIA. *See* Institute of American Indian Arts
identity: art training at institute, 86–87; beyond squaw/princess images, 11–14; border/engagement articulates, 110; communal identity vs. individual, 28, 64, 67–68, 85–87, 89; constrictions in art market, 23; and cultural differences, 94; defining indigenous and control, 94; family, community in Sioux (Albers & Medicine), 28; fluid, multidimensional, 117–18; formation through art, 19, 123–24; historically determined (Straus and Valentino), 65; indigenous as political, sovereignty (Venne), 98; indigenous knowledge systems, 11; insider/outside, essentialism, 30; means of self-perception, 108; mobile, contemporary, tribal, 26–27, **plate 2**; multiple, 18, 41; Rahr, 15–16; self-actualization, cultural identity, 82; "sites of identity" and place, 96; stereotypes strengthen, 103–5, 112–13; stereotypes, usefulness of myths, 118; T. Naranjo, 17–18; "trying to convince the world you exist" (Stuever), 15–19, 32–33. *See also* binary constructs of identity; images; Native women artists, roles; pantribal identity; political nature of art
ideologies. *See* binary constructs of identity; paradigms; strategies
Illiniwek, Chief, sports mascots, 20, 38; Teters's eradication strategy, 138–39
image construction in arts, 79; constructs of discourse, misconceptions, 25–27; domains of image discourse (*See* binary constructs; paradigms); how constructed (*See* strategies). *See also* institutions, art; political nature of art
image politics. *See* political nature of art: image politics
image producers. *See* image construction in arts; Native American artists; political nature of art
images and representation: appearance, power of, 2; "buckskin ceiling," 34; causality, mascots, 37–39; cultural/political, institutional training, 80–84; deconstruction of stereotypes, 16; "doing gender," alternatives, 8–9; image production, media, 34; Indian princess (Swentzell), 1–2; insider/outside, essentialism, 30; institutional resources, 36–37; meaningless, 36; Native women as "alter" (Taussig), 2; Native women as cultural icons, 5; restricted material, research (Albers), 8; squaw/princess stereotypes, 7–8; "trying to convince the world you exist," 15–19, 32–33; use and manipulation of, intent, 39; visibility (Hutnyk), 39. *See also* identity; representation, uses and abuses; stereotypes
images, debating the power of: deny or assert power, 36; mentalist/realist clusters, 158; mentalist/realist theories (Bieder), 37–39; modern/traditional categories, 32–34; museum showings, 35; One Nation, casino kingpins, 35; positive stereotype, as caretaker, 35–36. *See also* sports mascots
inclusion: "artist first, Indian second," 57–58, 78, 89; fine arts standing, 57; pluralism, 57–58; and unique sensibility, 57
Indian Actors Association, 150
Indian art organizations. *See* institutions, art (indigenous)
Indian Arts & Crafts Act of 1990, 83
Indian Child Welfare Act (1978), 66
Indian Painters and White Patrons (Brody 1971), 48–49
Indian Reorganization Act (1934), 9
Indian women. *See* Native women; Native women artists
Indians in Unexpected Places (Deloria 2004), 149–52
indigenous: define, control, 94; as political identity, 98
indigenous knowledge, 20, 41, 95; cultivate as strategy, 143; protocols as communal people, 12–14. *See also* Native women artists
individuality, individualism, 25, 49, 78–79; "artist first, Indian second," 57–58, 78; and communal norms, 67–68; and community, 70, 84–87, 89; historical, culturally contrived (Pfister), 68; individual vs. tribal, 27–28
Institute of American Indian Arts (IAIA), ix, 23, 49, 57, 69, 86; art training, institutional factors, 80–84; self-actualization, cultural identity, 82; "stuck in own stereotypes," 80–84
institutions, art (indigenous), 86; art gallery as trading post, 53; collective production of art, 80–84; image production for Indian audience, 87; institutional factors, at IAIA, 80–84; patriarchal, mentorship, 87–88; political nature of, 81–83; unique ethnicity, 57. *See also* NMAI and IAIA
intersectionality (Crenshaw), 17
intervention, feminist, 11
interviews/conversations with artists, 50. *See also* Amerman; Bradley; Cota; Emerson; LaMarr; Naranjo, T.; Naranjo-Morse; Niro; Rahr; Swentzell; Teters; Whitehorse
inversion: asserting self-representation, 123;

renaming (as squaw), 130–31; stereotyping of whites, 112–14; symbolic inversions (Babcock), 130; U. of N. Colorado Fighting Whites, 131

Jaimes, M. Annette, 63
Jim Crow Museum of Racist Memorabilia, 134–35

Kiefer, Anselm, 116–17
King, Richard C.: comedy and censure, 134; inversion, erasure, reclamation, 7, 130–31, 133–34, 139; tools of "remembrance," 137
Kleeblatt, Norman L., resistant critique, 40
Koons, Jeff, self-promotion, 111–12

Lail, Thomas, 89
LaMarr, Jean, interview: art program at Berkeley, 43–45, 49–50; community values over commercial, 45; educational work, 46–47; holistic, indigenous philosophy, 45; instructor at IAIA, 53; money/reputation, 115; mural project, 45–46; printmaking, 46; reappropriation, 71; urban relocation, 44, 64
LaMarr, Jean, Jack Malotte, and youth, *Our Ancestors, Our Future* murals, **plates 5a, 5b**
land-based tribal sensibility, 91–99; "deterritorialized world," 93; diminishing collective mobilization, 94; global displacement, 93; "place-based aesthetics" (de Alba), 96; vs. fluid, global, 92, 95, 98
Language and Art in the Navajo Universe (Witherspoon 1977), 55
Layton, Robert: art object, 50; false assumptions about culture, 25; internal constraints, 51
LeRoy, John, Kewa tales: conflicts, 112; moral/ethical, 112
Leuthold, Steven, indigenous aesthetic, 47–48, 53
Lévi-Strauss, Claude, 110
Life Lived like a Story (Cruikshank 1990), 105–6, 108–10
Lippard, Lucy, 15; hybrid cultural identity, 18; process, cultural context, 33
Locating Cultural Creativity (Parkin 2001), 61
Lomawaima, Tsianina, 107–8
Lorde, Audre, 85

Malotte, Jack, Jean LaMarr, and youth, *Our Ancestors, Our Future* murals, **plates 5a, 5b**
Mankekar, Purnima, 11, 27
Mankiller, Wilma, 7, 28
McEvilley, Thomas, 90–91
McMaster, Gerald, 98
media, 150; humor, 134–40; and image production, 34–36, 136; as racist culprit (Mihesuah), 36
medicine man (Rahr), 152
mentalist/realist clusters of analysis, 38, 128–29, 158
methodology/context of book: accidental, "salvage ethnography," 4; choice of artists, 3–4, 24; counternarratives genre, images, 19; fieldwork conversations, gender, 106; first-person narrative, 51; focus of research Native women, 3, 7; "intervention," multiple disciplines, methods, 4; interviews, 23; mentors, friends, 22; multiple perspectives, variables, topics, 16–17; museum work, 81–82; narrated self-reflection, 107; narratives as intellectual data, 21–22; not included, 21–24; political nature of art/institutions, IAIA, 81–83; reappropriating terminology, 26; testimonials, authority of, 5–7; theoretical intervention, interdisciplinary, 20; three dialogues in image representation, 125. *See also* aims of book; testimonials
Mihesuah, Devon Abbott, 36
Mikkelsen, Leatrice, 56
Mithlo, Nancy, vii, viii; Chiricahua Apache, viii; growing up, Jackson, MS, vii; passing, viii; research, personal not separate from academic, x
Mixed Blessings (Lippard 1990), 15
modernism, 26, 124
Moya, Paula: identity constructs contradict, 124; liberation/oppression of identity, 132
Myers, Fred: Aboriginal art copyright, 31; the Dreaming in Australia, 45; social dramas, 53

Naranjo, Tessie, interview, 23; artist's role in community, 28–29; communal values over individualism, 107; identity as sociologist, academic, 17–18; NMAI curatorial process with peers, 147–48
Naranjo-Morse, Nora, interview: art as anticolonial, 10–11; art enacts indigenous knowledge, 10; independent thought threatening, 9–10; *Our Symbols*, **plate 1**
narratives as storytelling: content and form convey value, 109; as function of other, 114, **plates 12a & 12b**; symbols of right living (Cruikshank), 114. *See also* testimonials
National Museum of the American Indian (NMAI), 57, 81–82, 97, ix; belief systems, audience expectations, 147; opening of at Smithsonian (2004), 145; problems of image politics, 145–47; Rothstein review, *NY Times*, 145–47, 149; T. Naranjo's curatorial process, 147–48; tribal curators' right to protect knowledge, 149
"Native American Art and the Problem of the

Index   177

Other" (Geertz 1991), 71–72
Native American artists: choice of individuality or ethnicity, 70; choices complex, 73; separatisst minimize ethnicity, 49; situational choice of strategies, 65
Native American women: as "alter" (Taussig), 2; assert leadership for family, land, 12; as cultural icons, 5, 12; "doing gender," 8
Native women artists, ix; cosmopolitanism, prestige factors, 25–26; indigenous knowledge of, 20; negotiations in Western art market, 64. *See also* Native American artists; political nature of art
Native women artists, roles and identity of: "artist first, Indian second," 57–58, 78, 89; artist, woman, Native, 6; Athapaskan, 9; born an artist, 75–77, 80–84; communication, self-perception, 108; in community, 13, 28–29; cultural expression, economic gain, 6, 52; as culture bearers, 9; difference of men (Teters), 29–30; domestic/public and squaw/princess stereotypes, 28; embody culture, tribal identity, 2; explore inner world, 86–87; grammatical/ structural approach, 118–20; home is with family, 91–92; identity in opposition to Western ideal, 118–19; as image producers, 7, 16; inseparable roles, 15– 17; men, patriarchal leadership, 9–10; mobile, contemporary, tribal, 26–27; negative comparison, 107; physical appearance/authenticity, 1–2, 126; political, 81–84; protocols as communal people, 12; self-actualization, 82; telling the story, 84–86; totality of life, 75–76; usefulness of myth of stereotypes, 118–20; "Van Gogh syndrome," 29; what sells, 29. *See also* identity; images
"Navajo Film Themselves Project, The," (Worth and Adair 1966), 54
New, Lloyd, 82
"Niggas vs. Black People" (Rock 1996), 135
Niro, Shelley, interview: film *The Shirt,* 137, **plate 16**; parents' oppression, 137; Red Skin exhibition, 136–37
NMAI. *See* National Museum of the American Indian
noninterference (Wax and Thomas), 72–73
Northwest Coast art (Ostrowitz), 78

oppositional terms, 101, 109, 112–13. *See also* binary constructs of identity; paradigms; strategies, oppositional
Ortiz, Alfonso, 106
Ostrowitz, Judith, 78
other: colonial subjects as, 114; exotic other, 7, 28; Ilongots (Rosaldo), 114; mask of Indian Other, 79; seeing self as, 60, 71; stereotypes signify, 104. *See also* alterity
othering, politics of new stereotype: avoidance of limiting, 120; engagement not erasure, 104; as ethically neutral, 116; grammatical/structural approach, 118–20; negative characterizing as tool, 115–20; in opposition to Western ideal, 118–19; parallels oppositions, binaries, 116; "positively-other-than," 119–20; replaces stereotyping as term, 116; star vs. communal artist, 119; useful to communicate identity, myths, 118
Our Land/Ourselves exhibit (J. Smith), 89
Owens, Louis, 79, 84–86, 87

pan-Indian debate, 61–69; common experience, unique identity, 62–66; communal identity vs. individual or tribal, 30, 64; criticism of multitribal referents, 4; identities historically determined, 65; intertribal Indian artificial, 64; retribalization, 65. *See also* communal ethnicity
pantribal identity: choices restricted, 69; binaries, 30; boarding schools strengthen, 107–8; challenged if no tribe, 68–69; homogeneity, 67–68; hybridity, 18; objections to, 64–66; tribalism, organic, 18. *See also* pan-Indian debate
paradigms: artistic freedom/lone genius vs. cultural artist, 51, 81; autonomy vs. ethnicity, 70; individualism vs. communalism, 70; separatist vs. inclusive, 70; "third eye," 70; variables, tension, 74. *See also* binary constructs of identity; essentialism; strategies; structuralism
Parkin, David, 61
passing, viii
passivity of artist: acculturation, 48–49; assimilation, 48–50
Pearce, Roy Harvey, 102
Pfister, Joel, 68
Pilgrim, David, 134–35
place. *See* land-based tribal sensibility
Plumwood, Val, 119–20; "positively-other-than," 119–20
pluralism: cultural (Berkhofer), 30; inclusive, 57–58
political nature of art: art training/institutions, 81–83; cultural identity as political (Bradley), 83; Indian Arts & Crafts Act of 1990, 83; inversion, eradication, reclamation, 129–34; museum training, 82; role as warrior for people, 83; unique legal status, 83
political nature of art: image politics, 122–25; antimascot activism, 136, 138–39; characterize distinct communities, 129; competing for economic resources, 127–28; contrast to

resolve internal/external, 126; distribution, acceptance of, 145; diverse strategies, 138–40; essentialized images vital to groups, 128; group characterizations, 126–29; identity, anticommunal expressions, 125; Indian writers/scholars as leaders, 143–44; reactionary stance constricts, 133; reclamation of essentialized stereotypes, 130–32, 133, 134; reinforce squaw/princess, 126; stereotypes seen as cause of oppression, 132. *See also* strategies

politics of othering. *See* othering, politics of new stereotype

Portraits of "The Whiteman" (Basso 1979), 105–7, 109–10

poststructuralist theories, 4

Pratt, Mary Louise, 37–38

princess, Indian. *See* squaw/princess images

process of artistic work, 53, 54–55

race, racism, 22–23, 85, 89–90, 124, ix; *Colored Pictures: Race and Visual Representation,* 140; Jim Crow Museum of Racist Memorabilia, 134–35; prohibitions inhibit positive effects, 136

Rahr, Tammy, interview: beaded moccasin commission, 31–32; distance from family, 97; home/family first, 95–97; identity, 15–16; medicine man, 152; *Portrait with David,* 97, **plate 10**; *Wedding Moccasins,* **plate 2**; woman's role as educator, 13

realist ideologies, 16; postpositivist, 20

reappropriation, 58–61; agency, for essentialized identities, 79; allegiance to community (Cota), 71; and alternative ideologies, 152; focus of book, 60; "genealogy of secondary explanation" (Bunzl), 78–79; image production, institutions, 36–37; noninterference (Wax and Thomas), 72–73; salvaging (Traugott), 59; "third eye" perspective, 60; traverses ideological patterns, 74; when art restricted (LaMarr), 71; of white expectations, 150

reclamation of stereotypes, 130–34; engagement vs. reactionary constrictions, 132

reform "Americanization," 44

relocation government program, 44

representation (Indian), uses and abuses, 121–44; aesthetics defuse social concern, 122; cathartic (Cota), 123, **plate 15**; conventional, 16; multiple means to understand, 123; reappropriate non-Indian images, 122, 150, 152; separate conceptual categories, 124–25; three dialogues in, 125. *See also* images and representation; pantribal identity; political nature of art: image politics

Reservation X (McMaster 1998), 98

restrictions in art, 69–74; and agency, reappropriation, 71; at Berkeley (LaMarr), 71; censorship, 69–72; refusal (Simpson), 72

retribalization (Straus and Valentino), 65

reversal. *See* inversion

Reversible World, The: Symbolic Inversion (Babcock 1978), 113–14

"Rhetoric of Control, The," (Rosaldo 1978), 114

Rich, B. Ruby, 72

Rock, Chris, 135

Rodriguez, Richard, 94

roles/identity of Native women as artists. *See* Native women artists, roles and identity

Rony, Fatimah Tobing: Indians in cinema seen as real, 150; "third eye," 60; viewing self as object, 60, 70–71

Rosaldo, Renato, 114

Rothstein, Edward, review: does not identify art, 147; exhibits flawed, 148–49; *NY Times* review of NMAI, 145–47; pan-Indian view as unscholarly, 146–47

Said, Edward, "exteriority" of tradition, 76

salvaging material culture (Traugott), 59

Santa Clara Pueblo display, NMAI, 148–49

Santa Fe, New Mexico: as base of art commerce, 26; IAIA, ix, 53; market environment, 52, 70, 126

Saper, Bernard, 135–36

Savages of America, The (Pearce 1953, 1965), 102

Scholder, Fritz: individuality, 58; white man's artistic goal (LaMarr), 115

School for Advanced Research (SAR), 74

Search for an American Indian Identity, The (Hertzberg 1971), 30, 68

self-representation. *See* image construction, images and representation, identity

separatism, 75; contextual/comparative aesthetics (Hatcher), 56–57; "no word for art," 55–56

Shoemaker, Nancy, 69

Simpson, Audra, 72

"Since When Is Jewish Humor Not Anti-Semitic?" (Saper 1993), 135–36

Smith, Jaune Quick-to-See: Indian writers/scholars as leaders, 143–44; terminology in arts, 26

Smith, Linda Tuhiwai, 12

Social Production of Art (Wolff 1981), 77

sovereignty, 12, 56, 72, 93; and inclusion (Deloria), 151; political in arts, 82–83, 98; relation to place and ideologies, 98; self-actualization, cultural identity at IAIA, 82

Spicer, Edward H.: discrimination, 63–64; identity by opposition, 113

sports mascots, 19–20, 35, 38, 94; engagement not erasure, 104; eradication, 138–39

Index   179

squaw/princess images: beyond the image, 1–14; group characteristics, 126–29; impact of negative stereotypes, 7–9; misconceptions of squaw (Rahr), 15; "pretty Indian princess" (Swentzell), 2; tradition (squaw), exotic other (princess), 28

stereotypes: agency in reappropriation of, 104–5, **plate 11**; border/engagement articulates identity, 110; buckskin ceiling, 34; deconstruction of, 16; in defense of language/terms, 115; demeaning pan-Indian, 127; demeaning sports symbols, 19–20; and economic competition, 127–28; engage to manipulate, 150–51; eradication of, 104, 130–31, 138–39; healthy and harmful (Fixico), 133; historically determined identities, 65; maneuvering essentialized images, 20; new self-identity, 19–21, 101–20; NMAI debates demonstrate themes, 145–49; not negative or positive, 104; prohibiting inhibits positive effects, 135; signifying other, 104; strengthen tribal identity, 103; "stuck in own stereotypes" at IAIA, 80. *See also* images; Native women artists, roles; squaw/princess images

stereotypes, as modern myths: binaries, 112–15; engagement vs. erasure, 104; essentialized construct as grammar of proper behavior, 105, 110–11; moral/ethical oppositions, 112; symbolic inversions, 112–14; usefulness for identity, 118; "Whiteman," 112

stereotypes, othering as new stereotype, 115–18; negative characterizing as tool, 119–20; othering misread, 117, **plate 13**; "Whiteman," 115

strategic essentialism, 16, 20

strategies, 79; artists make situational choices of, 65; characterize distinct communities, 129; diverse, 138–40; in humor and media, 134–40; inclusion, pluralism, 55, 57–58; interact, 60; inversion, eradication, reclamation, 129–34, 136; reactionary stance constricts, 133, 142; reappropriation, 55, 58–61, 140–44; reclamation of essentialized stereotypes, 130–32, 133, 134; between resistance and assimilation, 40; to resolve community vs. autonomy, 55; separatism, 55–56. *See also* binary constructs of identity; image construction; paradigms; political nature of art: image politics

strategies, oppositional: cultivate indigenous knowledge, 143; embrace pan-Indian identity, 143; Indian writers/scholars as leaders, 143–44; when suitable, 140–44

Straus, Terry, and Debra Valentino: historically determined identities, 65; pan-Indian artificial foil, 64–65; retribalization, 65

structuralism, 101, 109, 117–18

Stuever, Hank, "trying to convince world you exist," 15, 32–33, **plate 3**

Subversive Imagination, The (Rich 1994), 72

Susanville, Pit River Tribe, 46

Swentzell, Roxanne, interview: barefoot image at Indian market, 1, 126; as cultural carrier, 6; home is with family, 91–92; labels as a box, 39–40; *For Life in All Directions*, NMAI, 147; men, women, becoming somebody, 100–101, **plate 11**; profession communal, for family, 5–6; *Woman in Stone*, **plate 9**

Taussig, Michael: artifice, 79; Native women as "alter," 2

telling the story: agency, political, 86–87; documentation, remembrance, 84–85; Emerson, story of what happened, 84–88, 90–91; individual in community, 85–87, 89

terminology, categories in arts: misleading, 26; muddled meanings (J. Q. Smith), 26; resistance, compliance (Mankekar), 27. *See also* binary constructs of identity; paradigms

testimonials: and alternative knowledges, 39–42; authority of, 5–7; multiple identities, 41; narrated self-reflection, negative comparison, 107; narratives as secondary readings, 78; *testimonio* genre (Warren), 41. *See also* narratives as storytelling

Teters, Charlene, interview: children and conditioning, 138–39; difference of male artist, 29–30; eradication of stereotypes, 136, 138–39; exhibit Into Indian Country, 139

The Anthropology of Art (Layton 1991), 25, 50, 51

The Third Eye (Rony 1996), 60

They Called It Prairie Light (Lomawaima 1994), 107–8

"third eye" perspective (Rony), 60, 70–71

Thorpe, Jim, 150

Traditional Artist in African Societies, The (Etzkorn 1973), 56

Trask, Haunani-Kay, 12

tribal art/artist: community support for, 50; constraints, 51. *See also* Native women artists

tribal college, ix. *See also* Institute of American Indian Arts

tribe, concept of, retribalization (Straus and Valentino), 65

tribes of artists interviewed: Cayuga, 13; Jemez Pueblo, 72; Mohawk, 136; Navajo, 11, 27, 73; Pit River/Paiute, 43; Santa Clara Pueblo, 2, 28

uniqueness in Native arts: and consumer demands, 61; "cultural field," 61; deemphasizing individuality, 61; discrimination, dis-

tinctive experience (Spicer), 63–64; ethnicity of organizations, 57; Fourth World/indigenous identity, 63
Urban Indian Experience in America (Fixico 2000), 132–33
US Indian Claims Commission, 66

van Alphen, Ernst, other/alterity, 116
Venne, Sharon, colonialism, 92, 94
Vickers, Scott B., 132; homogeneity from colonizing, 67–68, 131
Visweswaran, Kamala, 123
Vizenor, Gerald, 67

Walker, Kara: black exoticism reinforced, 142; mythic in history, 116–17; "trivializes slavery" (Harris), 141–42
Warren, Kay, 41
Wax, Rosalie H., and Robert K. Thomas, 72–73
West, Candace, and Don H. Zimmerman, 8
West, W. Richard Jr., 97
White Image in the Black Mind, The (Bay 2000), 111
White Man's Indian, The (Berkhofer 1979), 33
Whitehorse, Emmi, interview: born into doing, art as totality, 75–78; censorship by art shows, 51–52; conflict of selling vs. values, 111–12; "dark ones" not liked by dealers, 51–52; feel like foreigner, 60; F.O.N., 52, **plate 6**; harmony, 59–60; identity, woman/Indian artist, 27; "intentionally paint beauty," 41–42; *Nahasdzáán*, 41–42, **plate 4**; Navajo metaphysical view, 55; process; grandmother, 53; reservation to boarding school/dual world, 62–63, 64; stubborn, picky, 52
Whitely, Peter: diversion of social concern, 122, **plate 14**; image politics, 125
"Whiteman" (Basso), 105–7; absent relationship, 106–7; binary opposition of male humor, 105; genre, 105; symbol enables definition, 115. *See also* stereotypes
Witherspoon, Gary, 55
Wolff, Janet, 77
women artists, Native. *See* Native women artists
Wong, Hertha Dawn, tribal identity, 67
Worth, Sol, and John Adair, 54
Wylie, Alison, "standpoint," 26

Young Man, Alfred, ix

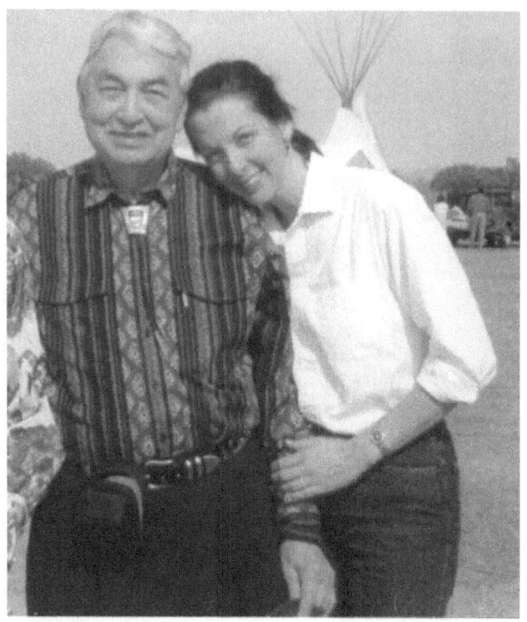

The author and her father, Roy D. Mitchell. 1999, Bill Watson Mithlo Memorial Feast, Apache, Oklahoma. Photographer unknown.

Nancy Marie Mithlo, an assistant professor of art history and American Indian studies at the University of Wisconsin-Madison, received her PhD from Stanford University in 1993, writing her dissertation on the career strategies of contemporary Native American artists working in Santa Fe, New Mexico. For more than twenty years, her research has been associated with the Institute of American Indian Arts (IAIA), a congressionally chartered tribal college. She has taught courses in museum studies, repatriation, American Indian film, visual anthropology, Native American aesthetics, and cultural anthropology at the IAIA, the University of New Mexico, Santa Fe Community College, and Smith College. Utilizing indigenous curatorial methodologies, Mithlo directs historic American Indian photography research in New Mexico and Oklahoma and organizes contemporary art exhibits at the Venice Biennale.

www.ingramcontent.com/pod-product-compliance
Lightning Source LLC
Chambersburg PA
CBHW031621210526
45464CB00004B/1685